CRASH, BANG, WALLOP

Also by Iain Martin

Making it Happen: Fred Goodwin, RBS
and the Men who Blew Up the British Economy

CRASH, BANG, WALLOP

The Inside Story of London's Big Bang and
a Financial Revolution that Changed the World

IAIN MARTIN

SCEPTRE

First published in Great Britain in 2016 by Sceptre: an imprint of Hodder & Stoughton
An Hachette UK company

1

Picture Credits

© Getty Images: 12/Heritage Images, 29/Universal History Archive,
61/Icon Communications, 76/Stan Meagher, 88/Steve Burton,
133/New York Daily News Archive, 222/Maria R. Bastone/AFP,
249/Evening Standard, 277/Shomos Uddin. © Copyright Guardian
News & Media Ltd 2016: 268/photo Sean Smith. © PA/Press
Association Images: 149. © REX/Shutterstock/Clive Limpkin/Daily
Mail: 188. © Telegraph Media Group Limited 1973: 79/photo
Kenneth Mason.
Excerpt from *Serious Money* on p. 187 reproduced
by kind permission of Caryl Churchill.

A CIP catalogue record for this title is available from the British Library

Hardback ISBN 9781473625068
Trade Paperback ISBN 9781473625075
Ebook ISBN 9781473625082

Typeset in Dante by Hewer Text UK Ltd, Edinburgh
Printed and bound by Clays Ltd, St Ives plc

Hodder & Stoughton policy is to use papers that are natural, renewable
and recyclable products and made from wood grown in sustainable
forests. The logging and manufacturing processes are expected to conform
to the environmental regulations of the country of origin.

Hodder & Stoughton Ltd
Carmelite House
50 Victoria Embankment
London EC4Y 0DZ

www.sceptrebooks.co.uk

For William Martin

'*The future is only the past again, entered through another gate.*'

The Second Mrs Tanqueray, by Sir Arthur Wing Pinero (1893)

CONTENTS

CONTENTS

INTRODUCTION

'We had a good day, we made money. That's what it's all about.'
Martin Pope, Hoare Govett & Co., 27 October 1986

In the beginning was Big Bang, but was it good? Thirty years on from that moment of creation in the City of London in the autumn of 1986, when a switch was flipped and the Stock Exchange was opened up, liberalised and computerised, there is no consensus about what it meant or on whether its impact was benign or malign. Was the Thatcher government's Big Bang in the City inevitable, almost an accident of historical circumstances, or a knowing innovation by ideologues? Did the changes to how the City worked license an explosion of greed, selfishness and bonus-driven excess in the Square Mile and beyond that contributed to the causes of the crisis of the late 2000s and ongoing problems with the financial system? Or was the financial revolution a creditworthy development essential to maintaining London as a leading financial centre?

That these questions do not have simple, pat answers suggests that the real story of the City revolution in the 1980s is much more interesting than the crude caricature of shouty men in red braces guzzling 'shampoo' (champagne) by the gallon and waving their wads (and worse) at the rest of us. But then, in Big Bang – when foreign banks were allowed into the Stock Exchange, with old British demarcations governing the City swept away – and in the wider revolution of which that day was a key part, we too often see what we want to see. It can be made to fit any version of history you want, from Left to Right and all points of view in between.

For critics of finance, it is clear that it was a profoundly harmful development. Big Bang was emblematic of the wider liberation of markets and of international capitalism reasserting itself. Hubris abounded. Almost exactly a year afterwards came the international crash of October 1987. The new global architecture of open financial markets survived the shock and rebounded surprisingly quickly, making some people a lot of money for almost two decades, until the edifice came falling down in the crisis of 2008, at great cost to the rest of us. That's one version, in which the City is a demon. Indeed, the imagery associated with the City at points of crisis has become one of the defining motifs of the age. Whenever there is a tremor or full earthquake in the markets, when prices dip or a bank has done something it should not have, television crews are sent to film traders looking stressed about the trouble they have landed themselves and us in. Standing at desks shouting at their colleagues used to be standard procedure on these occasions. Now they are encouraged to look less agitated in front of the cameras and just sit there looking at their screens. It is the media cliché – of the trader as ruthless, overpaid arbiter – repeated like a pseudo-religious ritual when we want an explanation for why the economy is not doing what we want it to.

In that reading, Margaret Thatcher in the 1980s deliberately instigated this financial revolution and unleashed greed on a gargantuan scale. In attempting to outdo New York and Wall Street in terms of excess and selfishness, the Square Mile made itself a city-state cut off from the concerns of Britain's less affluent citizens. The two cities, New York and London, collaborated and competed frenetically until their combined efforts almost blew up the global financial system in 2008. That explanation can be heard on the Left and sometimes among traditional Conservatives too.

There is an alternative view, which holds that the reforms introduced were among the most positive of Thatcher's eleven years in office, and her defining international achievement outside the Cold War. Not only was the domestic City subjected to a welcome blast of meritocracy, in which the old school tie mattered a lot less than it used to, it was also reopened to the world, restoring it to the once dominant financial position it had enjoyed for the century leading up to the beginning of the First World War. This new 1980s openness was the modern equivalent of the bold British switch to free trade in the mid-nineteenth century. Just as happened then, British reforms inspired policy makers and financiers in other countries and the Thatcher approach to open markets and privatisation became the international norm. And anyway, most of what goes on in finance is nothing like the media caricature of screaming traders and massive bonuses. Pay for most City workers is not in the stratosphere. Post-Big Bang the place is an engine room of social mobility and opportunity. It is a British success story just as Wall Street is the humming motor of American capitalism. That is roughly how free market advocates see it.

For others, Big Bang represents the melancholy passing of a particularly English approach to capitalism, in which a gentleman's word was supposedly his bond and a decent lunch kicking off with gin and tonic followed by white burgundy, claret and port was a seemingly ancient birthright. Out went British ownership and dominance in the City; in came ever more of the hardworking Americans, ensuring that something intangible and peculiarly English was lost.

It certainly had another impact too, one that is entirely positive and often overlooked by men. Before the 1980s some women had begun to be employed in the Square Mile, but it was not until the Thatcher government's reforms that serious numbers of women started to make inroads. As recently as the 1960s it had been an almost exclusively male environment in which the employment of one woman on the floor of the Stock Exchange in Dublin could cause such a shock that the authorities in London took legal advice to protect themselves against anything of that kind happening in the City.

That glimpse of the financial universe pre-Big Bang illustrates that the changes of 1986 did not happen in a historical vacuum. While Monday 27 October was an emblematic exciting moment that encapsulated Thatcherism and the resurgent power of markets and those who work in them, there was plenty of life before it. Big Bang was just one development among many that marked London's re-emergence as a global financial centre over the course of several decades from the 1960s. That is a story with deep historical roots, which is why Part One of this book, 'Ignition', charts the origins and development of the ancient City of London from Elizabethan times, through centuries of war, fire and reconstruction, right up to the emergence of another equally ruthless leader in the late 1970s, Margaret Thatcher. In terms of how finance is regarded in the popular imagination, the transformation of the Square Mile has a claim to be the BC and AD moment. But a lot that matters happened long before. The modern City and finance make a good deal more sense if you understand where they came from, and also understand the interplay between London and other great global financial centres.

Part Two, 'Friction', tells the inside story of Big Bang and the people in politics and the City who engineered it. It deals not only with the City and high politics. The architecture, theatre, music, fashion, satire and media of the 1980s also feature. Indeed, London itself changed markedly in that decade, when a small group of property developers, public officials and financiers established a rival to the traditional City on the dockland wasteland in the East End. The City itself had to respond, by wiping away the grime and building higher in glass and steel. Part Two also includes an early appearance by a young journalist called Boris Johnson.

Part Three, 'Combustion', then deals with the crash of 1987, the serial scandals of the era, the dramatic growth of the City in large part thanks to the euro, the battle for supremacy with New York, and the disaster of 2008 and subsequent recovery. I close by assessing the City revolution – thirty years on – with the help of some of the most interesting players of the period. And I offer my own assessment. But what of the future? The Afterword assesses the challenges facing the City as it tries to come to terms with the UK's vote to leave the European Union, against the backdrop of the next financial revolution already underway. Politics, disruptive technology, and new digital currencies are about to reshape the City once again. That Afterword is entitled 'The Fate of the City and the Future of Money' – something we should all be concerned about.

Writing my last book about the collapse of RBS in 2008 and the wider financial crisis, it became obvious to me that a good deal of what I thought I knew previously about finance, politics and people had been wrong. I must confess that as a political commentator working on a leading national newspaper, I wrote about the financial crisis of 2007-2009 with only a limited understanding of many of the underlying concepts. That is why, a few years later, I sought as a baffled and furious taxpayer to understand the RBS failure, and to write about it.

Similarly, underpinning this book is an attempt to explain how and why the story of the West since the Second World War is to a large extent about an 'explosion of money'. This process has been driven by increasing debt, financial innovation, cross-border trade and the development of new technology making it easier to move that money ever faster around the globe. London is critical – and Big Bang was a decisive moment in the evolution of money – because a small patch of the British capital was used as a test site for a global experiment. We have all, in our different ways, been affected by the fallout and continue to be.

Crash, Bang, Wallop is not meant to be a dry, technical tale, however. It is told with the help of a remarkable cast of personalities, some of whom got into all manner of farcical scrapes and chicanery along the way. What became apparent, interviewing some of the key participants from the 1970s and 80s, and examining archive material, is that the architects of the financial reforms had no clear idea where it would all lead, or of the bonus bonanza and cultural conflict it would entail. 'I think the truth is that they didn't know what they were unleashing,' says a Thatcherite former cabinet minister. Sceptics will smirk at that. Didn't many of those involved go on to do very nicely in City boardrooms afterwards? That is true, of course, but there was, no matter what anyone might try to tell you, no one clear and dastardly plan for a financial revolution. Events proceeded at times chaotically, with the participants attempting to adapt to what we now think of as globalisation.

The bigger picture that emerges from the history of the City over almost five centuries is of invigorating innovation, openness to the outside world, frequent crashes followed by growth taking place in a peculiar environment, where generations of traders have usually resisted attempts at central planning or mapping the future. Indeed, the City's rise is the story of visionaries and rascals, and of the combined efforts of millions of souls trying to make themselves a living, constantly repeating the cycle of wealth generation, excessive excitement, panic, bust and renewal.

What is perhaps most striking about the City's development through those upheavals, in recent decades and over the centuries, is the strong retained sense of place, even though it has been burnt down several times and bombed to bits. Elsewhere, industries tend to rise on one spot and then, when trading patterns change, within a century or less they can be gone, leaving scrubland or a heritage site. One thinks of coalmining, or docks, or fishing, or ships, or car manufacture. In contrast, with varying degrees of success, what the City is doing it has essentially been doing for many centuries on one patch of ground. Trading in goods gradually developed from the sixteenth century into expertise learnt abroad in the art of trade financing, then into making money from money, always ring-fenced from the rest of us to an extent because of the City's secretive self-government that stretches back almost a millennium and was recognised by William the Conqueror. In that respect, the place has more in common with hallowed religious sites that draw their power from the physical connection to the past, reminding worshippers that there were people here before us and there will be others after we are gone. The City, with its evocative street-names, gothic rituals, baffling codes of behaviour, and temporal temples to mammon, looks to this visitor like the international financial equivalent of Harry Potter's Hogwarts.

To take a leisurely walk along modern Bishopsgate at the eastern end of the City, dodging the crowds of impatient workers rushing by on their way to a sandwich shop or a meeting, is to walk through history. Bishopsgate is named after a long-demolished three-towered medieval gate at the City Wall, which was paid for by foreign merchants from the Hanseatic League in the fifteenth century in return for their continental trading privileges. The heads of traitors were displayed on spikes on top of the gate. Later, the area was home to coaching inns serving visiting merchants, residents and 'stock men' driving animals to one of the many nearby stock markets. Walk past the church, St Helens of Bishopsgate, which was first consecrated in the twelfth century. That is where the merchant Sir Thomas Gresham was buried in 1579. St Helens miraculously survived both the Great Fire of London in 1666 and the attentions of the Luftwaffe in the early 1940s, although Gresham's altar tomb only narrowly avoided destruction when the church was badly damaged by two IRA bombs exploding in the early 1990s. Bishopsgate is also where Gresham, an Elizabethan trader and loyal friend of the Queen, had his London house. From there he travelled from Thames-side wharves to do deals in Antwerp, then the leading market or bourse in Europe. It is with the peripatetic Gresham, and a vital innovation he brought back from his travels, that this story begins.

Iain Martin
London, 2016

PART ONE
IGNITION

I

ON THE MAKE

'A public, or a private robber; a statesman, or a South Sea jobber.'
Jonathan Swift, to Mr Gay (1728)

Thomas Gresham – merchant, foreign adventurer, financial schemer, property developer, Royal advisor prepared to keep a rival of Queen Elizabeth I under house arrest[1] – was born to be one of the great figures in the history of the City of London. His wealthy merchant father became Lord Mayor, and grew the fortune of his well-established Norfolk family from London, where he became a supplier to Henry VIII and a witness to the turmoil of Tudor politics. Thomas – born in 1519 – was sent to Cambridge, but he was destined to follow his father by becoming a merchant, although he would soon eclipse his achievements and become an early archetype of what a smart, scheming trader can achieve with some chutzpah and an eye for the main chance. He also reshaped the City with a vital innovation.

To begin his career Thomas went first to the Square Mile, to become a member of the Mercer's Company, the exalted livery company or trade body that represented merchants. The City was the wellspring of wider London and already the centre of commercial power in England. The square mile or so of land on the north bank of the Thames had been colonised by the Romans, who built Londinium as a port protected by city walls. Abandoned after their departure, then repopulated from the ninth century and connected to a network of villages such as Westminster outside the walls, the City by Gresham's time was the centre of English trade in all its

*Sir Thomas Gresham – merchant, innovator, agent of the Crown – welcomed
Elizabeth I to name his Royal Exchange in the City in 1571.*

forms. On its wharves on the river, goods were loaded and unloaded. The stock markets – stock then meaning stall – were where for centuries butchers, fishmongers and others practised their trade. Through the streets, cattle were driven to market and produce carried to the herb markets. Some of the place-names in the City still reflect that comestible heritage: Poultry, Bread Street, Pudding (meaning offal) Lane, Milk Street and Honey Lane – the last two adjoining Cheapside (a medieval term for market). Since at least the Norman Conquest, the City had enjoyed a degree of self-government and autonomy within London, which remains the case today. As the medieval period gave way to the modern, and London continued to expand outside the boundaries of the Square Mile, the City of London remained distinct with its own customs, atmosphere, local government and legal personality. The City was of London but also apart from it.

But Thomas did not stay long. While he maintained a base in London, initially he went to the Low Countries and to what was then one of Europe's greatest trading centres and ports, Antwerp, where he developed his skills as a trader. It was where moneylenders, financiers and merchants of all varieties from across the continent did business. The Portuguese had begun to use Antwerp as an outlet for the sale of their spices from the East and the unrefined sugar sourced from its empire. German merchants and refiners were drawn like bees to the honey pot and the English had also established a trading house there in the early sixteenth century. The international flavour of Antwerp illustrated the extent to which the countries and city-states of Europe were bound together by money-making. In Antwerp's Bourse, the exchange where the traders gathered, Gresham became well connected.

That meant he was ideally placed to help when in the early 1550s the English monarchy got itself into yet another financial mess and the affairs of Edward VI, son of Henry VIII and half-brother of Elizabeth I, were unravelling. The problem facing the Royal Family in 1551, as so often, was the debts it had run up. As Edward VI's advisors at court squabbled over how to settle the young King's bills, new loans were taken out abroad, which only exacerbated matters. The rates of interest charged in Antwerp were ruinous. This is where Gresham came in most useful as the Crown agent. One of the solutions, Gresham concluded, was an early form of currency market manipulation. If he could, by hoarding currency and making it scarce, artificially drive up the value of the pound as it was traded in Antwerp, then the monarch's debts in other currencies would – proportionately – become smaller and easier to pay off. It took a couple of years, and several of his other schemes came to nothing, but it worked and the burden of royal debts was eased. A figure from a leading City of London family had arranged a bailout of the monarchy, rescued the royal reputation and bolstered his own connections at court.

Even then in finance you were only as good as your last deal. Favour could vanish quickly with a change of monarch. The advisors to Mary, Edward's successor, were suspicious of Gresham's influence. He was briefly excluded and had to work his way back. It took the elevation to the throne of the much cannier Elizabeth in 1558 for him to enjoy full royal favour again. It also helped there that Gresham's close friend was Sir William Cecil, who on the death of Mary became Secretary of State, principal advisor to the monarch. Gresham agreed to keep Lady Mary Grey, who had a potential claim to the Crown, under house arrest at his properties, and he was at Hatfield House in November 1558 for Elizabeth's first council as Queen. Even then, that day, he made the case that English merchants and moneymen deserved better protection from the Crown and complained that foreign traders had it too easy in London.

While the Elizabethan elite was in favour of trade, this should not be confused with free trade or open markets, concepts that would only gain credence two centuries later. Gresham and his fellow merchants operated in an era of mercantilism, a system in which the Crown guided economic policy and attempted to create trading monopolies protected by military force. The aim was for the country never to buy more from other countries than it sold because that way England might accumulate reserves of bullion and protect itself in war. Gresham was interested in innovation, however. And when he undertook an ambitious project designed to boost English finance and trade – first floated by his father[2] – the interests of a mercantilist monarchy and an ambitious merchant with a house on Bishopsgate were perfectly aligned.

Gresham's great innovation was the addition of what became the Royal Exchange, a bourse modelled on the institution in Antwerp and designed by a foreign architect with the City's livery companies paying for the land. In establishing this enterprise and overseeing its construction, Gresham was, in modern parlance, seeking to 'give something back'. His only son had died young and the opening of a bourse gifted to the City was an act of philanthropy, although, ever the man of business, he retained the leases on the shops overlooking the courtyard. The rents would enable him to recoup some of his outlay.

The spot he chose for that building – at what today is the busy junction at Bank – remains the financial City's polestar. Nearby Gresham Street runs into Lothbury Street, behind the Bank of England building. The Victorian iteration of the Royal Exchange stands on the original site of Gresham's Exchange, with a weathervane on the roof that is a golden grasshopper, representing the Gresham family crest. In the mid-sixteenth century, that early piece of City property development by Sir Thomas Gresham changed the face of the City. Previously, merchants and dealmakers transacted trade in a haphazard fashion on the street and in inns. This was the first time they would have a dedicated spot with proper protection from the elements, creating the potential for a multiplying effect by which traders on the make would know where to find their allies and rivals if they wanted to do a deal.

This innovation was deemed such an advance that the Queen was prepared to give it her royal imprimatur. On 23 January 1571, Elizabeth I left her residence at Somerset House on the Strand, accompanied by a guard with trumpeters heralding the monarch, and headed for a dinner in the City. Her short journey took her through Temple Bar, along Fleet Street, on to what is now Cheapside and Threadneedle Street, before she arrived in Austin Friars, near Bishopsgate, at the mansion of Sir Thomas. According to the account of Monsieur La Motte Fenelon, the French Ambassador who was at the table, there was playful discussion of the Queen's marriage prospects before, in the early evening, with dinner finished, a torchlit procession set off to open the first Royal Exchange. The historian John Stow, in his *Survey of London*, published in 1598, described what happened next: 'Her majesty returning through Cornehill, entered the burse on the south side; and after that she had viewed every part thereof above the ground . . . she caused the same burse by an herald and trumpet to be proclaimed the Royal Exchange, and so to be called from thenceforth, and not otherwise.'

The rising confidence and increased assertiveness of the Tudor merchant class is illustrated by the other attempts made by Gresham and his contemporaries to reduce the domestic influence of far stronger European rivals. It rankled with English merchants that London did not even have unhindered control of its own trade. On the site of what is today Cannon Street Station, the Hanseatic League (established in the fourteenth century) ran the Stillyard, a network of wharves by the Thames handling imports and goods for export to other parts of Europe. The power of the League, originating in Lubeck, Germany, stemmed from its mastery of cross-border commerce and control of trading routes. In Gresham's lifetime, the Stillyard or Steelyard still enjoyed privileges from the Crown in return for guarantees to help guard the City in the event of an uprising. The Liberal MP, author, playwright, soldier and spy, A.E.W. Mason, wrote in 1920 that 'the Stillyard was to the modern understanding, one of the strangest institutions which the world has ever seen. It took its origin from the debts of the early English kings and the money with which the German traders from the Baltic, the Easterlings as they were called, were able to provide them.'[3]

Gresham wrote to Queen Elizabeth deploring the existence of the Hanseatic League's trading house in the City: 'The Stillyard hath been the chiefest point in the undoing of this your Realm and the Merchants of the same.' A spasmodic crackdown had begun in Edward VI's reign, when the liberties of the foreigners with their trading empire by the Thames were removed. Queen Elizabeth banished them entirely in 1598 after Gresham's death, although under James I they were readmitted. The land was finally sold, by German owners, to a railway company in the 1850s. In those sixteenth-century squabbles involving Gresham and his friends, some of the major themes of the City's subsequent development – including notions of monopoly, skulduggery, foreign competition and the role of government – were already apparent. To what extent did London's trade have to be open to the outside world? Who did the City's senior figures truly serve other than themselves? How should London adapt to thrive?

There was a shady postscript to Gresham's career, however, that will sound familiar to those used to hearing about the misbehaviour of some modern financiers. An inquiry by the Crown into his dealings on its behalf found a number of apparent irregularities. Gresham could explain it all, he said. The lavish entertaining on expenses of foreign merchants was essential for the transaction of deals, and the high profits he had made in working on royal business were deserved, he claimed. Everything was accounted for, he assured the Queen. She was persuaded and Gresham was paid the last of what he was owed by the Crown. One of Tudor England's richest men, he died suddenly on 21 November 1579 on his way from a meeting at the Royal Exchange.[4]

Gresham may have given the City a commercial centre, to complement the ancient Guildhall from where the Corporation governed the City, but at the start of the seventeenth century in England the business of trading money, of making money from money, was underdeveloped. What was traded were principally real goods, such as cloth, timber, food, spices and jewels. At that point the notion of buying shares in companies and selling them to others was alien and the City of London was far behind where the Venetians had been centuries earlier, when by the early 1300s Venice had already begun to develop a commercial system capable of coping with the complexities and risks of long-distance trade. They had limited-liability joint-stock companies, with pools of shareholders; sophisticated markets for the trading of debt; mortgages; some education in business; bankruptcy laws; double-entry accounting; and a proper currency, Venice's ducat. The traders in Antwerp and other trading hubs had adopted and evolved these ideas, which had then been transmitted back out across Europe by merchants eager to diffuse risk and make more money. In the seventeenth century it was the Dutch, and only later the English, who exploited such innovations and became particularly good at the business of money.

It helped that London's Royal Exchange had an early boost following the sacking of Antwerp by the Spanish in 1576, an event that also caused the Low Countries to unite against Spain. The waning power of Spain then created a vacuum which the Dutch provinces filled in the late sixteenth and early seventeenth century. In the Dutch golden age that followed, Amsterdam became for a while the wealthiest and most innovative financial centre on earth. In war, at that point, the Dutch tended to best the English too, most embarrassingly in 1667 when the Dutch fleet sailed into the Thames estuary and at Chatham set a large part of the English fleet on fire before towing away two prized ships. Samuel Pepys, then Secretary to the Navy Board in Whitehall, wrote in his diary: 'Most sad to be sure. And, the truth is, I do fear so much that the whole kingdom is undone, that I do this night resolve to study with my father and wife what to do with the little that I have in money by me.'

It was a combustible period in the City. For Londoners the Dutch incursion looked like another God-given sign that the end of days was approaching, or at least that yet more tumult was on the way. In the Civil War, much of the City had backed Parliament, ostensibly out of resentment over the Stuarts' taxes and financial impositions. After all, the newly assertive merchant class of London was also used to a degree of self-government in the Square Mile. Even after that upheaval, there was no respite. On top of war and regicide came plague and then fire, against which the tightly packed pitch-covered timber houses were like dry tinder. In September 1666, when the Great Fire took hold, much of the City was burnt to the ground, including the first St Paul's Cathedral and the Royal Exchange. Pepys noted in his diary on 5 September 1666: 'The Exchange, a sad sight. Nothing standing there of all the statues or pillars.' Only the statue of Gresham remained, said Pepys and others who visited the scene.

Every disaster presents an opportunity, however. And in the rebuilding that followed and with the development of insurance, a new generation of men on the make took their chance. Those dwelling or working in the City lived permanently with such risks disrupting their activities and killing their customers. That being the case, sensible property owners and merchants needed ways to offset risk and to protect themselves against the possibility of further disaster after the Great Fire. One man in particular, Sir Nicholas Barbon, made it his business to exploit these opportunities to the full.

Barbon was the son of the puritanical Praise-God Barebone (his real name) and a physician trained in medicine in the Netherlands, an economist, a rapacious property developer, a Member of Parliament and a financial innovator. He was the archetypal financial adventurer in the late seventeenth-century style who not only began rebuilding the City from the ashes, buying up land at fire-sale prices and constructing rows of terraced houses made of brick. He also offered property insurance.

The idea of a contract, in which the businessman paid a premium for protection and payment if disaster struck, was not in itself new. Insurance contracts had existed in Genoa in the fourteenth century. But in the aftermath of the Great Fire, Barbon's mass-market application of the technique to houses was swiftly copied when its potential profitability became understood. His Insurance Office for Houses (later renamed Phoenix) operated from a building close to the site of the destroyed Royal Exchange and as many as five thousand homes in the rebuilt City were covered by his policies. Fire services were also launched by the individual insurance providers, although the resulting attempts at extinguishing blazes could be chaotic. The insurance companies would only put out the fires of their own customers, an approach not conducive to public safety.[5]

As well as leading the way on insurance, Barbon was also a pioneering writer on free market economics, and in *A Discourse of Trade* he dealt with interest rates, prices, currencies and the encouragement of commerce, describing the City of London as 'the Largest, Richest, and Chiefest City in the World, for Trade'. He died in 1698 or early 1699[6] at his country property, Osterley House in Middlesex. It was a house that had been owned by a previous City pioneer, Sir Thomas Gresham, more than a century before. Despite his success in building and insurance and in the development of economics, Barbon ultimately had less success in the other rapidly developing field of business that dominated the efforts of adventurous types in the City in the 1690s, namely banking. The developing English economy needed banks.

Once again, the requirements of the Crown played a key role in reshaping finance, when another monarch found himself short of money. England's new Dutch and Protestant monarch William III wanted to rebuild the navy and had to be able to borrow to pay for it. The emergence of the Bank of Amsterdam, and the founding of the first central bank by Sweden in 1688, suggested that the establishment of a Bank of England would provide a way to enable the government to borrow. A scheme proposed by a roguish speculator, the Scotsman William Paterson, was suddenly deemed attractive.[7]

The Bank of England was established in 1694, and offices on Walbrook were opened less than two hundred metres away from the Royal Exchange. From there it became the government's banker, the model central bank on which other nations based their own institutions. Privately owned, it was licensed by the government with a monopoly in England to issue notes. It eventually controlled the national debt and, in time, as they developed, the straightforward commercial banks would eventually be overseen by the Bank.

Other, smaller banks had developed out of the goldsmiths trade that thrived along the City's Cheapside. Goldsmiths had secure vaults, knew how to safeguard wealth and look after deposits, and some started to develop a sideline in banking and loans. In 1672, the goldsmith Richard Hoare founded the bank which later became C. Hoare & Co. He moved it to Fleet Street in 1690 and the bank is still owned by the Hoare family, trading on the same site. Barclays was on Lombard Street, where two Quakers – members of the radical, dissenting Protestant movement – set themselves up in business in 1690. John Freame and Thomas Gould financed Quakers launching new trading enterprises in the Caribbean and America, and backed the Welsh Copper Company and the London Lead Company. In Edinburgh, the Scots were also moving into banking, but in England banking was largely restricted to London at this stage, only spreading outwards across the country in the eighteenth century as commerce grew.

Then there were the joint-stock companies. The idea of companies with many shareholders owning a firm is common now and widely understood. It is how all manner of business household names and banks are structured, with financial institutions and individual investors buying tradable shares entitling them to a chunk of the profits, in the form of a dividend, in return. The model, though, has its roots in the mercantilist push for empire by England and then Britain from the sixteenth century on to the domination of India in the eighteen and nineteenth centuries, with a small group of investors putting up funds for adventure and exploration that might lead to trade.

The Muscovy Company of the 1550s had originated as the Mystery and Company of Merchant Adventurers for the Discovery of Regions, Dominions, Islands, and Places unknown, founded by three adventurers. A mission to Moscow was, mercifully, well received by Ivan the Terrible, and the building the Company used in the Russian capital still stands near Red Square. Other companies plied different trading routes, including the Levant Company, founded in 1581, which later merged with the Venice Company. These early adventurers and the Crown had struck a bargain. British explorers, in competition with foreign rivals, would claim new territory from which the Crown would gain revenue and global reach.

The Companies were not state-owned, although they operated with the encouragement of the Crown. The Elizabethan establishment of an American colony in Virginia, the first successful English colony, was exploited successfully later by the Virginia Company with its Royal Charter.

It was the companies established in Asia that changed the game, and once again the intense rivalry and colonial interplay between the Dutch and the English produced important innovation. England's East India Company was founded in 1600 to take on Dutch traders, who responded with the Dutch East India (1602). The Dutch, though, had a new weapon that spurred growth. Shares had been traded before in piecemeal fashion; now the Dutch East India built a stock exchange where they could be bought and sold alongside the bonds issued to raise debt. It introduced scale and the excitement of large amounts of speculation, meaning that in trying to outflank the English, the Dutch in Amsterdam had invented the modern stock market.

The English were slow to understand what was happening. The market for shares only developed gradually, as new companies such as the Hudson Bay Company and the Royal African were established. Their owners gradually learnt the possibilities and the joint-stock enterprises started to pay large dividends from plundering the New World. However, it was not until the late 1680s that shares were frequently traded in London, and this was driven by the Nine Years' War with France which meant that domestic merchants, their possibilities for overseas trade limited, looked for other outlets for their capital. When trading happened, there was a ready-made venue where business could be done, in the Royal Exchange alongside the merchants buying and selling goods and arranging shipments.

Buying shares was quickly understood to be perilous because the price rested on speculation about future profits, discoveries, lucrative new contracts or the commercial overspill from war and political upheaval. Perhaps for that reason, the stockjobbers and brokers started to develop a reputation as excitable types who thrived on rumour and made profits from hot air. It is perfectly understandable that early activities of the stockjobbers and brokers were seen as morally dubious, although there was a hunger for what they were selling. That contradiction is still apparent today, with clients complaining about the motives of those dealing shares or trading financial instruments while coming back for more in search of personal profit. In it, too, may lie the origins of contemporary complaints that the City does not produce anything solid or real, unlike manufacturers.

It didn't help in a deeply religious age that trading in shares or debt obviously involved selling and buying the inherently intangible, whereas a merchant selling a shipload of spice, grain or cloth could point to it or at least be held accountable if a consignment out in the field failed to materialise at the dockside. Stockjobbing was a seemingly magic trade, based on pieces of paper, promises and profits conjured from thin air, in an era when fears of sorcery and witchcraft still dominated in the popular imagination. Resentment of the stockbrokers and their black magic was already apparent in the aftermath of the joint-stock mania of 1693–5, during which there had been a flurry of trading as all manner of new manufacturing enterprises turned themselves into companies seeking investment. The frenzied activity looked a lot like gambling. In the parliamentary inquiry that followed, the commissioners investigated the 'pernicious art of Stock-jobbing'. Some of the unscrupulous and 'unjust' first subscribers, it was noted, sold the stock on for inflated prices to 'ignorant men' hungry for a quick profit.

Not for the last time, legislation was introduced aimed at regulating their activities. Stockbrokers had to be licensed by the Lord Mayor and take an oath to be true and faithful. They even paid a fee, and accepted a bond that would be forfeited in the event of bad behaviour. Their number was capped at 100, to curb the propensity to over-excitement and panic. In the Royal Exchange the joint-stock mania prompted a change too. Whether they were asked to go, or decided to leave of their own accord, it is unclear, but in 1698 the stockjobbers left the Royal Exchange and migrated to the streets nearby. The Royal Exchange had given them their first home. Next they congregated in Exchange Alley, or Change Alley, where they met in coffee houses such as Garraway's and Jonathan's. There, the new rules introduced by Parliament started to be disregarded and the throng of brokers and jobbers, both licensed and unofficial, grew with the market. The total amount invested in joint-stock companies was rising too. It is estimated that it rose from £4,250,083 in 1695 to £8,447,401 in 1703, at a time when the total industrial wealth of England was only in the region of £33m.

The stockjobbers of the early eighteenth century were operating in a city that had developed many – although not all – of the main constituent parts of a modern financial centre. In the Bank of England it had a national bank that could organise government debt; a busy trade in commodities based around the Royal Exchange; currency trading; gold trading; markets in insurance for property, business transactions and shipping; as well as the stockjobbers themselves. The City in which they worked had also been rebuilt in the decades after the Great Fire to become far more impressive. The new St Paul's Cathedral built to Wren's design was completed by 1710, and around it stone buildings and grand constructions replaced much of the timber-framed London of old. The energy and bustle were captivating for those who saw in the rise of the City the promise of London becoming a global nexus.

The historian Peter Ackroyd has called eighteenth-century London 'voracious London', a vortex sucking in money, along with the needy, the greedy, the aspirational and the wicked. With three-quarters of English trade passing through the City, all roads pointing to the capital, and its citizenry constituting one-tenth of England's population after the arrival of immigrants from Europe, it was as though London sat at the centre of an enormous web, spinning and casting out its thread ever further. The noise, the smell, the crush of crowds, the imprecations of the mob and the pressure always to make money, or just to survive, made it close to being bedlam. The City, where the money was, was the place during the day where the madness was most intense.

At the centre of the maelstrom stood the Exchange. For Joseph Addison, founder of the *Spectator* magazine, the place was a source of wonderment in the early eighteenth century.

> There is no place in the town which I so much love to frequent as the Royal Exchange. It gives me a secret satisfaction, and in some measure gratifies my vanity, as I am an Englishman, to see so rich an assembly of countrymen and foreigners consulting together upon the private business of mankind, and making this metropolis a kind of emporium for the whole earth.[8]

That same year, in 1711, as Addison marvelled at the growing power of the City, a new joint-stock company was being formed that would soon create the greatest excitement of all among investors across England.

Debt was at the root of it, of course. The South Sea Company began with an argument about the size of the national debt when a new Chancellor of the Exchequer, Robert Harley, came to office. The cost of war and the over-reliance of the government on the Bank of England as a source of borrowing meant that a new source of funds was mooted. A state lottery was launched before Harley's brother Edward and his associates came up with what sounded at the time like a better idea. The £9m national debt would be consolidated and those who held it would get tradable shares in a new company, the South Sea. It would also have exclusive rights to planned trade in South America. Investors would be attracted to this public–private partnership and great riches would flow. There would be a human cargo too. The Company was one of those involved in shipping thousands of slaves from Africa to Jamaica.

That first incarnation of the Company was a flop when it became embroiled in political squabbles. It was in the second phase, with the Prince of Wales – the future George II – as titular head, and the political Establishment heavily invested in the venture, that a wild fashion for the South Sea Company in particular and investing in general took hold. Events in France fuelled the excitement, certainly.

The Scottish adventurer John Law, who escaped from prison in London after killing a rival in a duel, appeared to be working miracles with France's finances. He not only controlled the banking system; he had merged it with the Mississippi Company, which owned vast tracts of land in America. The speculation seemed to be renewing French national wealth. John Blunt and the other directors of the South Sea bought more of the national debt, almost £31m of it, and issued new shares.

In the City, in Change Alley, this was the moment of ultimate opportunity. The lure of speculation, easy profits and sudden wealth brought in crowds of investors. A newspaper described the scene: 'The greatest ladies thither came, and plied in chariots daily, or pawned their jewels for a sum, to venture in the Alley.' Not only the aristocracy put in their money. Anyone who could get their hands on a little money could travel to the City and take part. The immigrants that swelled the London population added to the throng, along with ambitious Scots who had travelled south in greater numbers after the Act of Union of 1707. The streets of the City around Change Alley were crowded with people of all religions seeking profit. The playwright William Chetwood satirised the scene in his play *South-Sea; or the Biters Bit*.

> **Plow:** A Stock-jobber! Pray, Sir, what Religion may he be of?
> **Scrape:** Religion! Why, they don't mind Religion in Change-Alley. But Turks, Jews, Atheists, and Infidels, mingle there as if they were a-kin to one another.

This was unsettling for some, considering the extent to which religion and fear of invasion by Catholic powers dominated thinking about politics. But not for the last time, a boom in the City was remaking the social firmament, breaking down barriers and creating opportunities for rapid advancement. It also obsessed those with capital or an interest. Edward Harley, one of those who had started the business, noted that even the most mundane correspondence in England at the time had to include talk of dividends and share prices. Gossip about stocks was the highly valued new commodity in London and beyond, as anyone with a little money to spare rushed to join in for fear of missing out. Inspired by the South Sea Company, a host of other ventures were launched, with companies embarking on all manner of schemes, from insurance to weird experiments in livestock breeding and waterworks that never transpired.

Not all of the activity was maniacal or ill judged. The amount invested in joint-stock companies rose from £20m in 1717 to £50m three years later, meaning that canny investors who bought and sold at the right moment did well, although such was the level of excitement that those trading with imperfect information, and without accurate data, were taking ever-larger risks as prices increased sharply. In early 1720 there was concern expressed in Parliament about the possibility of a crash. The so-called Bubble Act 'to Restrain the Extravagant and Unwarrantable Practice of Raising Money by Voluntary Subscription for Carrying on Projects Dangerous to the Trade and Subjects of the United Kingdom' became law in June. A crackdown on companies without official charters was attempted.

It was rather late in the day to attempt regulation though, and the speculation resumed in its intensity. In August of that year the price of a share in the South Sea Company peaked. The first great bubble in the City's history had been inflated. But bubbles do burst.

2

IMPERIAL CAPITAL

'Shares. O mighty Shares! . . ."Relieve us of our money, scatter it for us, buy us and sell us, ruin us, only we beseech ye take rank among the powers of the earth, and fatten on us!"'

Charles Dickens, *Our Mutual Friend* (1865)

The City was well used to plague, fire and war, but in the autumn of 1720 came a new type of manmade catastrophe in the form of a proper stock market crash. When the final efforts of the South Sea Companies directors and their corrupt political allies in Parliament to inflate the stock price were exhausted, the gravitational pull of market forces exerted itself on investors, who realised too late they had bought in to a fraud. From a high in the region of 1000, down and down plunged South Sea shares, a dizzying process punctuated by the occasional rally and rumours of salvation, until by September the price stood at 175. Exacerbating the crisis, many of those who had willingly allowed themselves to be duped had paid with borrowed money, or promises written on paper, paying in instalments, meaning that they owed huge amounts for shares they had purchased on the assumption of ever-rising prices. The stock was on the way to being almost worthless but they still had to make the payments or be pursued by bailiffs.

Out in the country, as news of the catastrophe spread among investors, anger turned rapidly to despair. On 27 September, a William Windham wrote to his brother Ashe with an update of his situation. 'There never was such distraction and undoing in any country. You can't suppose too the number of families undone. One

*Bubble trouble: in William Hogarth, England had the perfect satirist
to capture the aftermath of the madness for shares which gripped
the country in the South Sea scheme (engraving, 1721).*

may almost say everybody is ruined who has traded beyond their stock. Many a hundred thousand man not worth a groat, and it grieves me to think of some of them . . . not a penny stirring.'

William was not the only Windham in trouble. Other members of his family had also invested and James was almost wiped out. 'Poor Jimmy's affairs are almost Irretrievable', William wrote later that year. 'Almost all one knows or sees are on the very brink of destruction, and those who were reckoned to have done well yesterday are found stark nought to-day. These devils of Directors have ruined more men's fortunes in this world than I hope old Beelzebub will do souls for the next.'

The new newspapers that had sprung up, alongside invigorated pamphleteers, hounded those in charge with an intensity bordering on the vengeful. Not for the last time, there was also a vicarious pleasure to be had for readers in learning of the misfortune of others who had over-extended themselves in the rush for riches. Artists and satirists joined in too. An engraving from 1720 lists some of the 'bubbles' that had been inflated in the excitement generated by the South Sea Company, with companies established promising profits in all manner of areas, including in the coal trade of Newcastle, stockings, Irish sail cloth, a water engine, the bleaching of hair, sugar, insurance on horses, radish oil and the work of the Pennsylvania Company. Underneath an illustration of a ruined gentleman holding up a money bag, now empty, is a description of a previously wealthy investor cursing the 'pack of knaves' he had trusted with his fortune.

> Behold a canting miser who of late, For twice the value sold a
> fair estate,
> To purchase South Sea Stock, in hope to grow as rich as
> Croesus.

He was ruined 'among the rest', but had no one else to blame but himself, wrote the unknown author, because he had put his faith in the equivalent of 'games' and 'dice'. In this way trading in stock was presented as nothing more than gambling by the greedy, an image still invoked by critics of the City today.

William Hogarth, the greatest satirist of the period, also found his *métier* with his *South Sea Bubble*. Underneath the print, an inscription declared:

> See here ye Causes why in London,
> So many Men are made, & undone,
> That Arts, & honest Trading drop,
> To Swarm about Ye Devils shop.

In the 'Devil's Shop', in Change Alley itself in late 1720, as the denizens of the coffee houses digested the disaster, panic was followed by eerie calm when the crowds of profit-hungry investors disappeared. A ballad of the time[1] recorded the transformed scene: 'Change Alley's so thin, that man may now walk, and if he'll now listen may hear himself talk.' The action soon switched to Parliament, where in the Commons and Lords the government's enemies hoped to discredit the Whig Establishment. Members of the government had taken enormous bribes and free shares in the South Sea Company and there were calls for the directors, who included MPs, to be arrested and punished for their role. The financial destruction wrought on parts of the English, Scottish and Irish aristocracy by the bursting of the City of London's first proper bubble was certainly an insurrectionist's dream. The Duke of Montrose was exposed, Lord Londonderry was down £50,000 and the Duke of Portland was brought close to ruin. The Duke of Chandos, patron of the composer Handel, was one of the hardest hit. He had invested heavily and was left saddled with enormous debts. Only the financial acumen of his second wife, Cassandra, ensured that their position was not even worse.[2] She had also invested in the South Sea Company but had wisely diversified in time, putting at least some of her own money into assurance. After the Duke's death, the house he had built, Cannons, was demolished by his successor and the fixtures and fittings auctioned off, scattering artworks, along with the house's golden gates and its chapel, to other great houses. In Ireland, where the aristocracy had been keen investors, the Bubble produced a bank run in October 1720 and a decade of Irish economic stagnation.

For those further down the financial scale, those who lacked the connections and large amounts of land as collateral that would guarantee continued access to credit, the impact was often life changing. One anonymous investor, hitherto comfortably off, wrote a pitiful letter to his Member of Parliament explaining how his friend – a Mr S – had come to stay the night in the country and persuaded him and his wife to put all they had into South Sea stock, promising them riches. Now, three months later, they and their children were destitute and living in fear of the bailiffs. He beseeched

Parliament to help and pleaded for answers, without acknowledging that no one had forced him to mortgage his family's future in such a reckless manner.

Who, such correspondents wanted to know, had really caused this disaster? The directors and managers of the South Sea Company who had swaggered around the City and Parliament, hailed as alchemists, were certainly guilty. But they had not acted alone. The Westminster Establishment was complicit and an estimated four hundred and fifty MPs[3] had bought or been gifted South Sea stock at one point or another, along with more than half of the 200 peers in the House of Lords. The monarchy and its ministers had connived as though they ran a 'banana republic' at a time when everything was for sale for the right price, whether it was honours, government jobs, favours, insider information or justice. For that reason, with blame so widespread in the Establishment, the parliamentary investigations resulted in a great deal of noise and then a cover-up. The shameless scheming of the leading government minister, Robert Walpole, ensured that it was so. Yes, the most socially ambitious chancer from the Company, John Blunt, was stripped of almost all his wealth and banished to Bath. But his corrupt co-conspirator and assistant, Robert Knight, who fled to France with company papers (later 'lost' by the government) detailing the fraud and shady dealings, escaped with government help.

The bursting of the bubble was not a disaster for everyone who bought stock, of course. Such crashes rarely are. Those who had been smart enough to sell at the peak of the market did well. C. Hoare & Co, the private bank, records its partners making substantial profits for themselves and customers from speculation in the South Sea Company. Thomas Guy, a bookseller, who had begun with a shop near to the Royal Exchange, had made almost £250,000, and his fortune endowed a London hospital that carries his name still. But for understandable reasons, those who had been bankrupted or impoverished made more noise than those who had sold up in time. Their anger prompted action of a kind. On the same day that the House of Commons report into the South Sea Bubble was published in 1721, Parliament passed legislation to curtail stockjobbing.

The historian Stuart Banner describes the enduring legacy of the 1720s crystallising public opinion about stock markets. It defined attitudes about finance that crossed the Atlantic to the US in the eighteenth and nineteenth century, he says, and shaped much later arguments about regulation on Wall Street. 'Where one laid the blame for the bubble was important,' wrote Banner,

> because it dictated the kind of reform that would be necessary for the future. If a small number of dishonest stockjobbers was at fault, then they could be punished, and perhaps the market should be regulated so as to make it more difficult for similar dishonesty to prevail in future. But if the market itself was to blame – if securities trading was inherently bad, regardless of who the particular traders were at any given time – then a more drastic solution was necessary.[4]

That argument, about how much or how little markets should be regulated, rages still, and the same question – is it the City and Wall Street in general or just a few bad apples to blame? – is posed every time a bubble bursts.

There was another reason the British got over it relatively quickly after a period of fury and recrimination. Cheeringly, it was apparent that France had suffered a simultaneous disaster that overshadowed Britain's reverse. The collapse of John Law's schemes, and the exotic innovations that had helped inspire Blunt and his associates, produced an economic emergency in France in the autumn of 1720 that was even worse than that taking place in London. The Mississippi Company, based on inflated claims of the riches that would flow from Louisiana, had been merged with Law's bank and he was made finance minister of the tottering edifice. At the point of collapse Law managed to escape but France did not.

This humiliating national failure even helped create the conditions for the French Revolution that took place almost seven decades later. Post-Law, many of the French were left with a fear of paper money and shares and a suspicion of investment that hampered the development of banking, commerce and industry. Without adequate access to capital, innovations could not get sufficient funding and wealth remained excessively concentrated. The economy was tightly controlled by the bloated government and a vast royal household, pursuing a mercantilist policy that inhibited innovation and industry. The tax burden landed on the lower orders, who inevitably did not like it or the economic mismanagement. Eventually, revolution was the result in 1789.

The British experience in the eighteenth century was very different. After the South Sea experiment, old-fashioned land and solid property certainly came back into vogue because it seemed to have been proved much more reliable than the new-fangled paper money and share certificates, but attempts at restricting speculation and stockjobbing were largely unsuccessful. They presented too good an opportunity to make money. By the 1760s, the coffee houses of Change Alley such as Jonathan's were deemed insufficient for a growing trade, and the brokers leased a building of their own in Sweeting's Alley. The words 'The Stock Exchange' were inscribed above the door. In the aftermath of the South Sea disaster, the City had rebounded, not for the last time, as a result of ambition, determination and the tendency of the next generation of traders to push on and forget their predecessors' mistakes.

Empire also provided a vital impetus to the next period of expansion, as the East India Company plundered its way across Bengal. The word 'loot', for ill-gotten gain, was borrowed from Hindustani slang and entered the English language at this time. In the City, the East India Company's stock was a favourite investment. Trade obviously meant an increased flow of physical goods from the colonies passing through London's docks, goods which then flowed back out to Europe, producing profits for the merchants that they could then invest. The expanding commercial fleet needed insurance, and deals if they are to be done properly require lawyers and clerks to keep records.

How much of this came down to slavery? A considerable part of the trade that drove this growth was in people, in the slaves that were bought and kidnapped in Africa and then shipped to the Caribbean and to North America. Between 1750 and 1807 it is estimated that 2,307,986 slaves were exported by the English trade across the Atlantic[5], but in London, too, as many as 15,000 African slaves were bought and forcibly employed as domestic servants, often being treated appallingly. In Britain more widely, the building of new stately homes, the development of estates, spending on the art market, exploration, industrial development and the widening availability of sugar, tea and coffee came, in part, at the cost of epic African misery. The City was up to its neck in slavery. Men such as William Beckford (1707–70),[6] one of England's richest individuals, enjoyed fortunes built on the back of their plantations in Jamaica and elsewhere. Beckford was Lord Mayor of London twice and his monument stands in the Guildhall, the administrative centre of the City.

After the bursting of the Bubble, the South Sea Company continued to do business in a reduced form and from South Sea House on Bishopsgate its managers sent slave ships to Africa until the mid-1730s. Indeed, the Square Mile was peppered with other offices in which the slave trade was planned and conducted. The Royal African Company was based in Leadenhall Street, although it lost its monopoly when new rivals emerged to challenge it. The East India Company – part corrupt company, part political behemoth – was also based on Leadenhall Street and traded slaves via Madagascar in the Indian Ocean. Lloyd's insurance market in the Royal Exchange was where the slave traders and investors insured their ships and cargo. The City was also largely deaf to appeals of the campaign for abolition, apart from the Barclays who were Quakers and anti-slavery. David Barclay was exceptional in paying £3000 to free slaves and ship them to freedom in Philadelphia when he became the owner of a slave plantation in settlement of debts.

While the City's complicity in an abhorrent trade is not in doubt, it was not uniquely at fault. Many slaves were processed through other British port cities, notably Bristol and Liverpool. And neither were the British the only nation involved. The Belgians in Africa and the Dutch in their colonies had a deplorable record. What is disputed is the extent to which slavery was a defining factor that explains the City's rise, as is sometimes claimed by its most vehement critics. A study by the historian Nicholas Draper suggests that over a third of London's dock investors at the end of the eighteenth century, just before a long campaign for abolition was successful, were involved in the slave trade. Until they were moved eastwards, the docks were still in the Square Mile itself and the trade was enmeshed in the commercial life of London. As Draper says, while slavery was neither marginal nor dominant, it contributed materially to the foundation of the modern City.

Other powerful forces – financial innovation, the increasing economic weakness of rivals such as France, and hunger for profit – also drove its development. Even the reverse in the Americas, when British colonial arrogance caused a rebellion that led to independence, did not impede London's progress for long. Neither did the disruption of the French revolutionary and Napoleonic period. Britain had too many advantages, thanks to the beginnings of the Industrial Revolution in the north of England and the increasing sophistication of the financial system in the City. For all those reasons, Britain was becoming the world's most dynamic economy.

The Bank of England – which had been a prime mover in that transformation – was strengthening its position too as a model for the development of a strong central bank, which gave the state a usually reliable source of funding and monetary stability. After moving in 1734 to new premises on Threadneedle Street, next to the Royal Exchange, it expanded its footprint steadily and developed as the UK's central bank, attempting to satisfy the government's demand for money and managing a growing national debt that was increasing with every war that was fought. That debt was a trading opportunity, of course, because it could be bought and sold. Traders gathered in the Bank's new building – in the rotunda

– for that purpose, making such a racket that they were eventually expelled.

The City of London did not seed the Industrial Revolution that powered Britain's rise, however. Those funding the steam-driven inventions and industrial innovations in the West Midlands and the north of England often had to rely on more local sources of capital, and the limited interest that the City showed in funding domestic investment coloured the country's view of the City again. The City was certainly in Britain, but to its critics it seemed to stand apart, more interested in pursuing its own particular interests than in funding British enterprise. *The Economist* later observed drily that the City was more concerned during the Industrial Revolution with 'the course of events in Mexico' than with what happened in the West Midlands. That deep and enduring suspicion of the City, traceable to the South Sea Bubble, had continued to manifest itself in popular culture. In his bestseller *Every Man His Own Broker*, published in 1761, Thomas Mortimer explained the activities of those selling shares and castigated them for greed. The book was reprinted many times in subsequent decades.

Not everyone was put off, however. The City was becoming a fizzing entrepôt for the ambitious as the banks and financial businesses started to exert a magnetic pull, sucking in the aspirational in pursuit of employment. Recruitment for the Bank of England was still by recommendation of the existing directors and employees, although the report by a Bank Committee of Inquiry appointed in 1783 to investigate working practices reveals that applicants were from a surprisingly broad range of social backgrounds and experience, by the standards of the time, although they were all men and all Protestants.[7] The Bank preferred to recruit from the ranks of those who had left school at fourteen or fifteen, rather than looking for the university educated. These were the early stirrings of the City as the southeast of England's engine of social mobility, providing opportunities for advancement to clerks and managers prepared to tolerate painstaking and repetitive work. The clerks worked nine to five, although often longer, with the bosses getting away earlier when it was quiet. Mr Bentley told the Inquiry that he was 'seldom out of the office before 8 at night, if the business is heavy much later, & on a Saturday generally 'till 10 or 11 o'clock'.

The City was also a place that needed and welcomed hardworking immigrants from abroad. The Huguenot refugees fleeing persecution of Protestants in France in the sixteenth and seventeenth century had sought sanctuary in London and their churches peppered the City. Of the 45,000 or so Huguenots that moved to England, it is estimated around half settled in London, where in Spitalfields they manufactured silk. With the proceeds their anglicised descendants diversified and moved into finance and other City businesses. The French revolutionary period also drew other Europeans to London when continental bourses closed and the mainland succumbed to the chaos of war. The French occupation of Amsterdam in 1795 meant that brokers including Samuel de Zoete landed in London. Unrest in Germany also prompted Nathan Rothschild to leave Frankfurt and establish himself as a banker in the City. After the Battle of Waterloo in 1815, he is said to have made millions by cleverly learning and trading on the news of Wellington's victory over Napoleon ahead of the British government. Although a messenger overlooking the battlefield delivered the news back to London, the sums made that day as a result of it have certainly been exaggerated. Still, Rothschild and his fellow immigrants and their heirs brought a renewed continental perspective to the City.

When the economy recovered from the shocks of the Napoleonic period, and the debts incurred had been dealt with, London was the pre-eminent financial centre. The physical character of the City was changing too. The old wharves on the river within the City were inadequate and the water was too shallow for the new, larger ships. The first new docks were built further down the river and throughout the century trade pushed further eastwards until the docks dominated what became the East End, with its miles of wharves and warehouses. The City itself still had its markets serving London: food at Leadenhall, the wholesale meat market at Smithfield founded in the tenth century and the ramshackle fish market at Billingsgate. But increasingly financial affairs dominated the life of the City. When those food markets began to be served by the new railways, and the produce arrived at the City's stations near the markets, the old practice of livestock having to be herded and shepherded in from the countryside for slaughter diminished.

The streets of the City's financial heart were becoming cleaner as a result. The new buildings were growing grander, their motifs more imperial. The destruction by fire of the Royal Exchange, again, in 1838, meant that the architect Sir William Tite designed the imposing neo-classical building that is still there today, with a statue of the Duke of Wellington at its steps. Insurance companies, and Lloyd's the insurance market, occupied a large part of the space. Tite also designed numerous train stations in the capital and across Britain.[8]

The railway revolution in which Tite participated had another important impact on the architecture and atmosphere of the City. Not only did it mean large-scale demolition, to accommodate the new lines and stations; it also forced out the residential population as the land became more valuable for offices, now that the City was developing proper transport links that began to allow the clerks, bankers, stockbrokers and other workers to make their homes further away in the developing suburbs. The first rail terminus in the Square Mile opened in the City in 1841, at Fenchurch Street. The vast stations built south of the river – on cheaper land – such as Waterloo and London Bridge, with their lines stretching out across what was countryside to the southwest of London and towards Greenwich, made commuting increasingly feasible and popular for workers, who flooded into the City each morning. Not many of them worked in the Stock Exchange, however, which was very much a closed shop to which it was difficult to gain entry. In 1801 the brokers had moved to a new building in Capel Court, near the Bank of England, and from then on became much more efficiently organised, with an official list of prices.

Those involved still had a reputation for being interested merely in quick profits. The economist David Ricardo in 1814 described stockbrokers as attentive to their business, and hot on detail. They were not much interested in finance 'as a subject of science', preferring to 'consider more, the immediate effects of passing events, rather than their distant consequences'. There are regulators and contemporary chief executives of banks today, struggling to control more rapacious investment bankers and traders, who would say something similar about those chasing bonuses.

The members of the Stock Exchange in Capel Court in the nineteenth century were like their modern equivalents in another respect, in that they knew how to have fun, and booze-fuelled pranks were commonplace. Coat-tails were set on fire and the managers in charge had to issue warnings in an attempt to prevent the brokers on the Stock Exchange floor playing football or letting off fireworks. High-spirited City behaviour was not restricted to downtime between trades. In a succession of booms, new generations showed that the appetite for risk – essential in financial enterprises – could get out of control, but then, from the rubble of a correction or a crash, the market would restart and fresh, profitable innovations would be attempted. This is what happened in the railway investment booms of the mid-1820s and the 1840s, when there was a mania for steam and new possibilities. A hucksterish railway promoter such as George Hudson, who earned the sobriquet of 'Railway King' in the 1840s, could become exceptionally rich and then lose his fortune and the money of investors. But when the smoke cleared, and Hudson and others were penniless, the railway lines and a valuable national network that powered trade existed.

This also applied in the case of the so-called Foreign Funds, meaning the Foreign Exchange, which initially operated from the Royal Exchange and whose members were moved to the Stock Exchange in 1828. New states in Latin America wanted to borrow and there was a push to invest. In the most celebrated case, investors were duped by outright fraud, when General Gregor MacGregor (a Scot, who fought on the Republican side in the Venezuelan war for independence) claimed to be leader of the state of Poyais in Central America. It did not exist and the government bonds he sold were fake. He eventually returned to Venezuela and was given a state funeral in 1845.

The Latin American panic led to defaults and losses, of course. Reputations were ruined and fortunes lost, but London had extended its international reach yet again in a way that proved it was not insular, even if greed could on occasion cloud common sense. After all, openness to the outside world was the British way by the mid-nineteenth century when the country's leaders abandoned mercantilism and tariffs on goods and embraced the philosophy of free trade in a manner that split the Conservative Party. That extraordinarily bold decision, condemned by Conservative critics as contrary to the national interest, turned out to be one of the most important decisions of the century. The idea that free trade would increase prosperity in all territories, rather than disadvantaging native producers, was the origin of what in the late twentieth century came to be called globalisation. The Victorians got there first, and the City at the centre of this free trading imperial capital could only benefit when London's appeal as an open market increased.

The world was shrinking, offering even more opportunities for investment abroad. Technology surmounted distance and allowed prices or news that would once have taken a week to cross the Atlantic to reach London in minutes. The telegraph, invented in 1837, had already hooked up the London Stock Exchange to the regional stock exchanges that operated in Britain's major cities. Banks too now had access to much more information delivered speedily.

These improvements came at an obvious price. It was easier for shocks and bad news as well as good to be transmitted internationally from and to London. The panic of 1857 that began in the United States was the first such global crisis, and the effects were felt in Britain almost immediately. The slowdown in a booming US hit American railroad stocks and induced runs on the country's banks. British banks and financial institutions that had lent rail barons money were vulnerable and the British government had to relax banking rules to provide extra liquidity and prevent collapse.

The emergency also had an ideological impact. In that panic of 1857, Karl Marx detected the beginnings of the collapse of the capitalist model, although it turned out that he was wrong. Still, his analysis that capitalism and financial markets seem prone to surges of optimism and over-confidence – with excessive financial speculation creating a cycle of crisis after crisis – is hard to dispute. What his ideology blinded him to was the way in which for all the periodic setbacks and individual examples of venality and poor practice, over the course of the nineteenth century, banks, the Stock Exchange and the insurance industry grew and prospered, providing employment and the fuel for periods of further growth.

There were some attempts to introduce safeguards against recklessness. Business in the City in the mid-nineteenth century became professionalised as it increased in scale. Theoretically, this should have encouraged sobriety when successive governments sought to codify and construct a framework of law that might encourage economic activity while ensuring better conduct. It did not always work. Either appetites were too strong, or the oversight was too weak, and after the growth of English banking and government policies caused a credit boom, the bust in 1866 was even more spectacular than that of a decade before.

English banking had been way behind that in Scotland, where the Bank of Scotland and the Royal Bank of Scotland had from their formation been joint-stock banks, meaning they had a wide range of shareholders and access to more capital. The Banking Act of 1826 in England was introduced because the innovative Scottish banks were observed to have coped more effectively with the foreign crisis of the previous year. It enabled the creation of joint-stock banks on the Scottish model in England, and with the scrapping of the requirement that royal or parliamentary approval was needed, registering and starting a company became much simpler. The Limited Liability Act of 1855 also protected shareholders, ensuring that they would not be liable for the entire debts of a company if it went bust. This was a further incentive to invest. The new structures needed lawyers to arbitrate, and the need for reliable audits of larger companies spawned the accountancy profession. None of that prevented the crash of 1866, which was another classic financial smash of its kind that then contributed to a downturn in the wider economy.

At the centre of the crisis was Overend, Gurney and Company, a long-established bank and discount house, one of the key intermediaries in the City's financial system. In essence, the discount houses existed to lubricate the market. Banks could park spare money with them, earning a small return but being able to call it back at any time, while the discount house could then lend it out to others at a higher rate of interest. The discount house profited from exploiting the difference. All would be well, and credit would be increased, so long as the discount house was sensible and did not lend out too much. Overend, Gurney was gloriously reckless and the news of its troubles created a panic in London to match even that experienced in 1720 with the South Sea Company.

On Black Friday, at the height of the crisis, the editor of *The Economist*, Walter Bagehot, wrote to the Chancellor, William Gladstone, reporting: 'A complete collapse of credit in Lombard St and a greater amount of anxiety than I have ever seen.' Bagehot also identified why the public, or that part of it with financial interests, tended to be so shocked when an established firm such as Overend, Gurney went down. The British attachment to tradition seemed to have a hypnotic effect on customers. An old name, he wrote, held a 'magical potency over the multitude'. The breaking of the spell resulted in a downturn in the wider economy. But once again the crisis was not purely domestic; it was linked to foreign markets. Another player in the drama of 1866 had been Credit Foncier and Mobilier of England, a rackety outfit that sold dubious investments in companies in France and Italy. The perilous position of Italian financiers exacerbated matters.

What lessons could be learnt from the events of 1866? Inevitably, yet another inquiry was launched, the Stock Exchange was investigated, and attempts were made, and eventually ignored, to limit trading in the shares of bank themselves. A series of commissions of inquiry grappled with the question of how to improve regulation. Many critics thought the simple answer was to send financial miscreants to prison.

Bagehot himself made one of the most important and enduring contributions to the thinking about financial crises, in his classic work of 1873. In *Lombard Street: A Description of the Money Market*, he recommended that the Bank of England should act as the 'lender of last resort' to keep money flowing in an emergency. He was scathing in his criticism of the Bank's capabilities, and noted that training of directors needed to be introduced, especially now that the market was so much bigger and London was increasingly the pivotal centre in trading in foreign funds and international finance. In the City, and financial markets generally, he considered confidence key. Without it, the system would not function, and the Bank of England had a duty to maintain it more effectively. There was another problem, said Bagehot. Those working in the City tended to have short memories: 'Most men of business think – "Anyhow this system will probably last my time. It has gone on a long time and is likely to go on still." But the exact point is, that it has not gone on a long time. The collection of these immense sums in one place and in few hands is perfectly new.'

What was not new was the tendency to over-excitement and recklessness in a boom that offered seemingly easy profits. That questing spirit that had animated investors in the summer of 1720, and in 1866 in Overend, Gurney, was not unique to the City of London either. It was simply that London – as the great financial centre that profited most from the upswing – was particularly liable to suffer contagion in a crisis. No sooner had the lessons of 1866 been digested than an even greater panic was upon the markets. The emergency of 1873 started with the bursting of the stock market bubble in Vienna that May and migrated to New York in September. The international downturn hit London too. When markets fluctuated so regularly and publicly it is hardly a surprise that the greatest writers of the era chose to target the

City and the mores of those who populated it. In *Our Mutual Friend* in 1865, Dickens mocked the fixation with stock market speculation:

> As is well known to the wise in their generation, traffic in Shares is the one thing to have to do with in this world. Have no antecedents, no established character, no cultivation, no ideas, no manners; have Shares . . .Where does he come from? Shares. Where is he going to? Shares. What are his tastes? Shares. Has he any principles? Shares. What squeezes him into Parliament? Shares . . .

Anthony Trollope's masterpiece *The Way We Live Now* (1875) satirised a London in which everything was for sale, including love, family and friendship. He described a city gripped by greed and its wealthier citizens captivated by the chance to buy shares in a charlatan's railway project linking San Francisco and Mexico. In Augustus Melmotte, the novelist created the archetypal City rogue, the richest man in England whose wealth was of dubious provenance. A greedy Establishment desperate for a glimmer of reflected glory clamoured for tickets to his party and even put him in Parliament, before Melmotte's inevitable disgrace. To the Victorians it seemed as though the suspect ways of the City, its elevation of quick profit and its hunger for gossip and tips that could be turned into money, had somehow polluted wider society. Some argued it was the other way round. Perhaps the City of London was just providing a mostly profitable means by which the ever-present and legitimate human desire for financial advancement could be fulfilled, mostly legally.

What happened in the next few decades, particularly with the emergence of the Labour movement, proved particularly problematic for the long-term reputation of the City. The long slump, at the time termed a Great Depression, that ran through the end of the 1870s and through the 1880s following the 1873 panic, showed the British industrial and imperial powerhouse spluttering. How could it be that the wider economy would stagnate for almost two decades and unemployment could rocket while the City would barely feel the effects? How could the stockbrokers prosper while the country did the opposite? Were they only out for themselves? Such questions preoccupied a new, insurgent breed of left-wing politicians who thought the City's ways utterly abhorrent and unfit for the new century.

WEALTH, WAR AND WALL STREET

'Financiers in a fright do not make an heroic picture.'

David Lloyd George

Young aristocrats did not go to work in the City. None ever had until, in 1875, the Duke of Argyll's son announced that he had done something extraordinary. He had got himself a job. This development was thought so outlandish that society chatter centred on whether or not his father would ever permit him to take up the offer of a post with the stockbrokers Helbert, Wagg.[1] Charlotte Rothschild even thought the Duke might object to his son working for a Jew.[2] Not a bit of it. Lord Walter Campbell managed to persuade his father that stockbroking was a worthy career, bought his way in as a partner in the firm and became the first aristocratic member of the Stock Exchange.

Naturally, Helbert, Wagg's hiring was not motivated by charity. The firm wanted to develop its own private clients business and become less reliant on the Rothschilds for a stream of work. Having the son of a duke on the books helped to open the doors of class-fixated potential customers, and as a Christian he was able to transact business on the Jewish Sabbath, Saturday. Campbell's appointment was also an indication that at least a few in the aristocracy were attuning themselves to life in a country in which business and finance were becoming the main route to wealth following the Industrial Revolution. It soon might not be enough to own land and large estates alone, which had long been the principal source of income and status in Britain's upper classes. Opting to work in finance provided additional opportunities to arrange an injection of cash into grand but strapped families, alongside the practice of marrying wealthy Americans. In this period, small numbers of other aristocrats joined City firms, and after one was overheard saying that he felt on the Stock Exchange floor like an orchid in a turnip field, upper-class members were known for a while as turnips.

Even so, the upper reaches of the City remained for the most part the province of the powerful merchant classes. Their colleagues and staff were the aspirational southern middle classes and, in the less elevated roles, the upwardly mobile working-class men who had been lucky enough to have a little education and to know someone who could get them a start as a messenger or junior clerk. Women barely featured in this highly stratified environment in which a great deal of the work, for those not on the floor of the Stock Exchange taking risks, was extremely dull and highly repetitive. The clerks and backroom staff across the City who transcribed the records daily and organised the ever-growing pile of paper were not having a racy time, at least not in the office.

For all that emphasis on procedure and politesse, the City could not shake the popular notion that it was a den of gamblers in which a fraudster could prosper. The scandals of the period saw to that. In the late nineteenth century, assorted rogues launched fake companies that gulled investors, or pilfered from shareholders and fiddled the accounts. Barney Barnato was not a member of the Stock Exchange but he was a leading player in South African mining shares and deeply corrupt. He leapt overboard from the ship bringing him home from South Africa. Horatio Bottomley emerged from an orphanage, got a job as a messenger in a City legal firm, worked hard, learnt how to swindle, made a fortune, lost a fortune, became an MP, went bankrupt, helped to found the *Financial Times*, rabble-roused as a jingoist, went to prison and died broke. Whitaker Wright committed suicide in 1904 after being convicted of fraud over the collapse of his London & Globe Finance Corporation. The bad publicity was troubling for those in the upper reaches of the City, where the emphasis was on protecting the good name of the markets on which they depended. When the illustrious Barings Bank came close to collapse in 1890 as the result of reckless loans made in South America, a fund was organised by the Bank of England, with Rothschild taking part. It was deemed unthinkable that a firm of the standing of Barings could be allowed to go bust. As part of an exclusive network it had to be saved to maintain trust, even if its directors had been wilfully reckless.

Image was starting to matter more, as the democratic impulse spread. Outside the City, the tenor of political debate was changing, and while the socialist critique of the markets as the preserve of wealthy elites and unpatriotic gamblers was not yet widely electorally popular, or not among those men with the votes, the attack was beginning to resonate. The newly formed Labour Party even had a City Socialist Circle, which hosted Labour leader Keir Hardie at a celebratory banquet held in a restaurant on Fleet Street in 1900 after he won a Commons seat for the second time. Even the financial press that lived off satisfying the hunger of readers looking for news of deals, useful information and share issues, professed itself appalled by examples of wrongdoing and rampant cronyism. The *Financial News* was so agitated that under its 'muckraking' editor Harry Marks, who began his newspaper career in the US, the paper delighted in exposing dodgy share issues and presented itself as the investors' friend against an elite it suggested looked after itself. Alas, Marks himself ended up discredited, when it emerged in a series of trials and scandals that he had promoted shares in which he had a personal interest while posing as a crusader against sleaze.[3]

The combination of scandals, speculation and a noisy financial press trading gossip about markets that produced semi-regular crashes led *The Economist* in 1913 to criticise the short-sightedness and corruption of journalists on less elevated publications. There were, it said, degrees of depravity. Some financial journalists indulged in puff pieces about favoured stocks and blackmail, while others favoured abstaining from criticism that might offend advertisers. For all the criticisms, and the examples of wrongdoing, the City's grandees presided over a remarkable inheritance. The best firms had long histories and would go on to dominate the City for a large part of the twentieth century. Cazenove masterminded blue-blood stockbroking. Coutts in the West End, sitting outside the City but connected to it, served the banking needs of many members of the Establishment. Stockbroking names such as Panmure Gordon & Co. and James Capel were well established. Foreign firms had a foothold too. Lazard had been founded by five brothers emigrating from France to the US in the 1840s, and by the 1870s it had a related operation in London, which put it in a good position when later the US finance houses grew in importance in London.

With the growth of the joint-stock banks – such as Barclays and Lloyds Bank, serving more humble customers and businesses, and hundreds of other smaller banking and trading enterprises – and the world's leading insurance market at Lloyd's, London of the early twentieth century was home to the greatest conglomeration of financiers and moneymen on the make ever assembled. Their work was lubricated by a constant flow of gossip and international news, arriving by telegram and wires from abroad, and transmitted again verbally by men swapping inside information on their way to lunch. Most of all, the City immediately before the First World War was the beating heart of the British Empire. The vision of Sir Thomas Gresham more than three hundred years earlier, of his simple exchange trading goods and then financial contracts on a model pioneered on mainland Europe, had been realised a million times over. The City had mushroomed and spread until it was a teeming, seething, cacophonous moneymaking machine. This was the most powerful financial and trading centre in history, a manifestation of British imperial power and international clout.

The Rothschilds arguably had the most clout. They funded the purchase of the Suez Canal for Britain in the 1870s, securing a vital trading link, and later underwrote Cecil Rhodes' work in South Africa. Indeed, the City oiled the wheels of Empire and its architecture embodied the imperial impulse. Opposite the rebuilt Royal Exchange, which had been destroyed again by fire, was the latest incarnation of the Bank of England, designed by the architect John Soane, aping ancient Greece to emphasise the Bank's exalted status. The Mansion House, the residence of the Lord Mayor of London, completed the triptych, and underneath the busy crossroads ran the underground train lines that disgorged tens of thousands of workers every morning and transmitted them back to the suburbs in the evening. The lines skirted their way round the Bank's deep vault, which stored Britain's gold reserves, the largest in the world. In the surrounding Square Mile were the offices of every manner of City enterprise and the suppliers they needed to function, including printers, telegram companies, post offices, stationers, restauranteurs and publicans.

If the Stock Exchange itself had a somewhat rakish, raffish reputation, other City institutions sought to cultivate a sombre, more sober image. Good bankers, then like now, saw the value in pretending to be dull, perhaps because they knew that their inherently risky business rested ultimately on trust and making customers forget that in lending more than they took in they were creating credit and money from thin air. The other tribes in City life – the stockbrokers, the jobbers, the Bank of England staff, members of the insurance market Lloyd's, the lawyers and the accountants – each had their own private codes of behaviour and traditions, which were reinforced by the ancient City guilds and newer associations that met in gilded halls peppering the area. They may have been united by pride in being part of a wider, greater enterprise, with its own distinct government in the City Corporation, but they were discrete and they shunned outsiders. Some were freemasons and many more were members of livery companies. The City more broadly was a club, or a series of related clubs forming a commercial clubland.

The connection with that other male-dominated club Westminster, the seat of political power three miles away along the Thames, was strong, as it had been in the days of the South Sea Company. The smartest grandees of the Victorian City were often MPs and the House of Commons in its irregular hours accommodated the diaries of those who did business in the City in the morning, along with those lawyers who made their money in court. The Commons also started to include financiers who were, perish the thought, not Christians. Lionel de Rothschild was the first practising Jewish Member of Parliament, elected for the City of London Corporation. He only took the oath in 1858, following an eleven-year argument about non-Christians being sworn in as MPs. Those financiers with seats in the Commons served a useful function in Westminster. They could report the thoughts and shifting moods of those in the Square Mile and interpret their demands, fears and requirements. Much like the Commons, the City was steeped in tradition. It was viewed with suspicion for its role in periodic financial calamities but also respected by others for the way it made money from money. The place had a mystique.

Yet even at its Victorian height, at the moment of maximum power and reach, there were the first indications that London's pre-eminent financial position was starting to slip. These came during the Boer War, that unnecessary conflict fought partly over mining rights in South Africa and attacked by Keir Hardie, the father of the Labour Party, and his colleagues. Hardie's main preoccupation was the pay and conditions of industrial workers, but his robust opposition to the Boer War in South Africa was framed as an attack on the market system and on profit itself. 'The war is a capitalist war', he wrote in the *Labour Leader* newspaper. 'The British merchant hopes to secure markets for his goods, the investor an outlet for his capital, the speculator more fools out of whom to make money, and the mining companies cheaper labour and increased dividends.'

Throughout the conflict, in the House, as the members of the Stock Exchange called their building at Capel Court, there were wild declarations of patriotic commitment and community singing when news of key developments in the conflict arrived in London. The jingoistic jobber Charlie Clarke, a veteran of the Exchange, organised and led these noisy displays and the pro-war members celebrated victories and marked setbacks.[4] The Stock Exchange had good cause to be concerned about the Boer War. Investors had loaded up on South African mining stocks in what was known as the

'Kaffir boom', which briefly reached an intensity that would have been familiar to those caught up in the excitement of the South Sea Company's rise. Moreover, the South African mining boom had another unintended and damaging long-lasting consequence, because it drew in fresh interest and a surge of new members keen to profit. In the narrow street outside Capel Court, frenetic trading went on even after the House had closed for business at 3.30pm, in an echo of the early days in Change Alley. The boom in numbers meant that when the Kaffir boom ended, there was a glut of brokers who needed to protect their income.

The Stock Exchange had hardly been unrestricted in its practices. Admission was by election by the existing members and the public was not allowed over the threshold. But following the Kaffir reverse members established new restrictive codes that benefited those working in the City at the expense of customers or clients. Strict rules were devised on stockbrokers and stockjobbers, ensuring that the work of the two could not overlap. Stockbrokers dealt with outside clients – banks and investors – and advised them on the market. When the client needed to buy or sell shares he called in his stockbroker, who then had the firm's representatives on the Stock Exchange floor go physically to talk to the jobbers, with their own firms, to arrange and then make the transaction. The jobbers would become the centrepiece of the market – the so-called 'market makers' – because they took the stock from those seeking to sell it and held it (thus taking a risk) and then matched the orders up with willing buyers. The jobbers' profit came from what was termed the 'spread', the difference they could arrange between the buy and sell price for shares or other financial instruments.

After much consultation and discussion, minimum commissions were also introduced to protect the income of members from the possibility of insurgent rivals undercutting them. In introducing this new rigidity, the Stock Exchange was turning away from the spirit of outward-looking innovation that had defined its rise. Indeed, some of the rules would survive for more than seventy years, until the Thatcher government decided to act in the Big Bang era of the 1980s.

Although the changes of 1909 seemed small at the time, they were dark hints that a period of stagnation and relative decline was on the way, a process which accelerated dramatically in 1914.

As David Kynaston, the historian and author of the definitive four-volume modern history of the City of London, put it: 'The First World War was the worst thing that ever happened to the City.'[5] The impact of the European conflagration was felt even before the first shot was fired. By July 1914 a sell-off was underway as concerns about the international situation deepened. The Stock exchanges on the continental mainland experienced severe difficulties, and when war was declared in August the City was astonished.

In wartime, old enmities were put aside for a while. There was even help available for the government from the City titan Lord Rothschild, who had clashed with Lloyd George over the Liberal government's attempts in the so-called 'People's Budget' of 1909 to increase taxation on the rich in order to pay for increased spending aimed at tackling poverty. 'Really, in all these things we are having too much Lord Rothschild,' the Chancellor complained in a speech at the time, accusing his opponent in the City of trying to block social reform. But in the summer of 1914, Rothschild agreed to a meeting at the Treasury. It soon became apparent that Rothschild grasped the urgency of the situation and saw the need for fresh thinking. 'Lord Rothschild, we have had some political unpleasant-ness—' said the Chancellor, before Rothschild interrupted: 'Mr Lloyd George, this is no time to recall those things. What can I do to help?'[6]

More broadly, the Chancellor was unimpressed by the other City grandees. They were a jittery bunch in a crisis and seemed more worried about their own position than that of the country, Lloyd George concluded. Why did Lloyd George need their help? The government of the day had two financial problems, central to the task of conducting the war. Banks and brokers who had not thought that war would definitely come found themselves owed money from institutions and individuals in countries that were now enemy combatants. It fell to government ministers and the Bank of England to intervene and stall a run on financial firms and banks that would have destroyed public trust and damaged the economy at a difficult moment. The Bank of England and the Stock Exchange arranged for the rules to be suspended, so that bills did not need to be settled immediately, meaning that over-extended firms could survive rather than go under humiliatingly as they might have done pre-war. The government itself had needs too. It needed money to pay for the war, which meant eroding the gold reserves that underpinned the currency and borrowing from investors small and large, in issues administered by City firms and the Bank of England.

With war underway, Rothschild's patriotic advice on how to pay for military spending was straightforward. It is said that he declared: 'Tax the rich and tax them heavily.' For the City and its wealthiest scions, this presented obvious difficulties. It is little wonder that the grandees were worried. As the year came to an end, the atmosphere was one of gloom. A widespread hope that the war would be over by Christmas had turned out to be misplaced and the Stock Exchange did not reopen until the New Year. In the Exchange the mood also turned against outsiders. Understandable patriotism slipped into unattractive jingoism, although the City was hardly alone in that respect, with the popular press and the least attractive politicians of the time capitalising on the slaughter. A campaign was got up against German, Austrian and Turkish members of the Stock Exchange and bans were introduced to ensure that foreigners could not be members, rules that endured in a modified form long after the end of the war. There was a change in the outward-looking international character of the City, developed over centuries of history, sometimes balanced by domestic concerns, but usually expansive and open to profit wherever it could find it. The City was forced by war to withdraw in on itself and a complex system of transcontinental financial capitalism, funding investment, speculation and trade was all but shut down for more than four years.

Into the vacuum stormed New York's Wall Street, the ambitious upstart rival financial centre. Its financiers and investors had taken the model of modern financial capitalism created by the Europeans, and brought to its zenith by London, and were in the process of building something even bigger and more powerful. What had begun on the southern tip of Manhattan Island as a Dutch walled settlement became a slave market in the early eighteenth century and a place for financial dealings. By the late nineteenth century, with slavery gone, Wall Street was a financial market on the verge of making London look elderly and stuffy.

If London was the slow-moving imperial capital, Wall Street was the new, racier model. With the wealthy beginning to migrate to houses further north in Manhattan, Wall Street and the surrounding area were increasingly dominated by banks and financial traders of all types, occupying imposing offices that reflected the scale of American ambition. Vast profits were generated by the rise of US industrialists and hustlers turned magnates, through the railroad booms and busts, the exploitation of natural resources and the creation of epic enterprises in manufacturing that eclipsed anything even late imperial Britain could muster. Those US businesses needed vast capital markets to borrow from and invest in. They needed a large banking system. And their successes, tribulations and failures created a volatile market for shares, along with a popular appetite for profit and rapid advancement.

That era of seemingly boundless gigantism suited big personalities, and in the original J.P. Morgan (John Pierpont) Wall Street had the defining man of the age until his death in 1913. The publicity-shy tycoon was domineering in his business dealings, mesmeric even, and deployed his power to build the first $1bn company, when he bought out the Scottish-born Andrew Carnegie to create US Steel. Morgan was so well connected, with so many industrial and financial interests, that his critics cast him as the enemy of the worker and of democracy itself. When the US government was short of gold in 1895, Morgan was one of those who sold it what it needed, for a good price. In 1907, when share prices on Wall Street plummeted following a bout of reckless speculation by investors, Morgan corralled the other Wall Street banks and arranged the rescue. The family's tentacles extended abroad, where the outlets of the 'House of Morgan' in Europe included Morgan, Grenfell & Co in London. During the First World War, the second J.P. Morgan promoted the Allied cause, for a healthy profit, and in 1915 the bank arranged what was then the largest foreign loan in history, a $500m loan to France. The new plutocrats were owners of railroads, steel and financial interests on a scale that worried some Americans.

Louis Brandeis in *Other People's Money and How the Bankers Use It*, published in 1913, spoke of the American infernal 'curse of bigness', a theme that had been reflected in the agitation against the power of monopolistic big business by the progressive movement and, principally, President Teddy Roosevelt in the early years of the twentieth century. Yet Wall Street easily survived such assaults to become the symbol of thrusting, modern America, a great, glittering casino in New York where rich men multiplied their fortunes, the giant industrial combines bolstered their dominance and, theoretically, millions of Americans could invest, although it took a long time before investing became a mass participation sport. The movement was not all in one direction, and the swings and downturns could be as violent as anything experienced in London for centuries, as 1907 had demonstrated. Such concerns did not worry everyone, however. The trajectory was upwards and something of the audacious spirit of the Wild West permeated New York's financial dealings. Everything was bigger; there was more swagger than in self-satisfied London, and soon there would be more money too.

As power drained away from London, it surged in New York, Washington and Chicago. Not only had the New World come to the rescue of the Old when America entered the war in 1917, but it had cost the US a lot less than it cost Britain and France. Worst of all for London, the war represented the beginning of the end for sterling as the developed world's dominant currency and its replacement by the US dollar. The strict Gold Standard – which stipulated the value of the currency according to a fixed amount of gold, keeping the supply of money and prices stable – had had to be all but abandoned by the Bank of England and the Treasury in Whitehall during the war. There was higher inflation in Europe than in the US, which stuck to the Gold Standard. This made US goods cheaper, relatively speaking, and the Allies were hungry for natural resources to fuel the war effort. Annual American exports to Europe increased from $1bn to $7bn between 1914 and 1917. Simultaneously the Allies were funding their war in part by borrowing in the United States. It meant that while at the beginning of the war the US had been a debtor nation borrowing from Europe, by Armistice Day 1918 the position had been reversed and the US was a creditor nation.

Poor old Britain was close to being skint. Its national debt had soared from £650m to more than £7bn by 1918, or more than 130 per cent of GDP, in only four years. Victory had been extremely expensive for Britain and France, and not just in terms of the lives lost. Despite the British and the French being on the winning side, the financial future looked to be American. In the City immediately after the war the decline was not immediately apparent. This was the age before high-intensity bombing from the air, and while there had been raids by German airships, and a few bombs had fallen on the City, there had been little damage to the physical fabric of the place. The memorials erected to the war dead in the Bank of England, the Stock Exchange and the offices of firms across the City demonstrated that the workforce – messenger boys, members and the sons of partners – had contributed. But with the war over it was possible to imagine that business might resume as normal. A brief boom got underway.

There were portents, though, that the weather was changing. Not only was the surge in London short-lived because debt-ridden Europe succumbed to a post-war hangover; the ideological back-drop was threatening too. In the aftermath of a violent revolution in Russia, the old Liberal Party completed its death march and the socialist analysis grew in popularity, even if most of that creed's adherents in Britain were democrats and patriots opposed to insurrection. The City, the Labour movement's rising stars suggested, was a relic of outmoded Victorian capitalism and a target for attack by those offering a new way of thinking about economics and society. In 1917, the young Herbert Morrison (grandfather of Labour politician Peter Mandelson) was particularly exercised about the self-government of the City and its perks and secretive ways: 'Is it not time London faced up to the pretentious buffoonery of the City of London Corporation and wiped it off the municipal map? The City is now a square mile of entrenched reaction, the home of the devilry of modern finance.'

The 'devils' of the City were facing these threats just as America's growth accelerated. After a brief recession, US gross national product rocketed from $72.99 billion in 1922 to $103.90 billion in 1929[7], wages rose sharply and the modern advertising industry emerged to satisfy the appetites of millions of new consumers. Simultaneously, Wall Street launched into an intoxicating boom of the kind in which London had once specialised. But while London and France had pioneered stock market crashes in 1720 with the bursting of the South Sea Bubble and the unravelling of John Law's schemes in Paris, America in the 1920s would soon prove that it could be equally innovative, and on a much grander scale, in a fashion that would reverberate in Europe. Visiting Europeans were intoxicated by Wall Street's dynamism in the 1920s and the seemingly magical possibilities for making new wealth, or replenishing old wealth, in the New World. Those members of the European elite lucky enough to have access to capital and contacts in North America joined in. Winston Churchill, the son of an American mother, was an enthusiastic investor.

By 1928 the party was in full swing, and even those who had expressed doubts were starting to believe that it was different this time: that most delusional state of mind in any seemingly endless boom. It appeared for a while as though America might be drunk, despite this being the era in which alcohol was banned nationwide by law. Prohibition, in force from 1920, far from encouraging sobriety seemed to induce recklessness and rule breaking. As the historian Thomas Fleming put it:

Prohibition corrupted and tormented Americans from coast to coast. A disrespect, even contempt for law and due process infected the American psyche. Rather than discouraging liquor consumption, Prohibition increased it . . . The 1920s roared with reckless amorality in all directions, including Wall Street. When everything came crashing down in 1929 and the long grey years of the Great Depression began, second thoughts were the order of the day. Large numbers of people pointed to Prohibition as one of the chief reasons for the disaster.[8]

Churchill turned up in New York, on his first trip across the Atlantic in almost three decades, shortly after he had lost his job as Chancellor of the Exchequer in 1929 and just as the boom in Wall Street was past its insane peak. He almost ruined himself, although he was saved from complete disaster by the action of Bernard Baruch, a Wall Street financier and advisor to presidents. Churchill, wrote William Manchester, was a great man. But he was not a great investor: 'He was a disaster.' He bought with alacrity at numerous outlets on Wall Street. When the market collapsed in October 1929 he stood in tears in Baruch's office in New York, convinced that all he had was lost. Chartwell, the house in Kent he loved, would have to be sold. His friend calmed him down and revealed that at least his trading on his account with Baruch's firm had not been calamitous. Baruch had left instructions with his staff for them to buy every time Churchill sold and to sell every time he bought. 'Winston had come out exactly even, he later learned, because Baruch even paid the commissions,' wrote Manchester. This somewhat mitigated Churchill's losses elsewhere.

Very few other investors were so lucky when the faltering boom turned to a spectacular bust on Black Thursday, 24 October, and then Wall Street had its worst day on Tuesday the 29th, during which all the share price increases of the previous year were obliterated. As J.K. Galbraith put it in *The Great Crash*, describing the cycle of despair: 'What looked one day like the end proved on the next day to have been only the beginning. Nothing could have been more ingeniously designed to maximise the suffering, and also to ensure that as few people as possible escape the common misfortune.'

Nothing so terrifying as the sound of crashing paper: a US newspaper reports on the whirlwind that hit Wall Street and the world economy in October 1929.

Endless ink has been spilt since on the question of whether the Great Crash of 1929 directly caused the Great Depression that followed it. How could a stock market crash which was restricted to a small number of investors, relative to the broader population, cause such a severe downturn in the 'real economy'? The debate is pointless and rooted in a misunderstanding of human frailties, the interlinked manner in which investment works and the psychology of an economic emergency. The crash of 1929 demonstrated again that when trust in stock evaporates it can, if the crash is serious enough, evaporate confidence in the wider economy and even weaken political institutions. It creates a justified fear – on the part of investors, manufacturers, employers, employees – that tomorrow will be worse than today, which alters behaviour, with obvious consequences.

In indebted Europe, the 1929 crash certainly created a feedback loop, causing loans from suddenly desperate American banks to be called in, in Germany meaning an intensification of political unrest.

In London the falls on the Stock Exchange were not as severe as in the US, but in the gathering gloom a momentous decision was taken for Britain to come off the Gold Standard to which the government had returned the UK after the First World War. A leading economy such as Britain was a cornerstone of the Gold Standard arrangement, the global exchange rate system in which countries fixed the value of currencies according to an amount of gold. If it prevented governments' bastardising or devaluing their currencies to get themselves out of trouble, it did limit flexibility in a crisis of the kind the global economy was confronting. On Saturday 19 October 1931, with a run on the pound underway, and the Stock Exchange busily trading, it was announced that Britain would come off the standard the following week, which necessitated a temporary closure of the Stock Exchange on the Monday. That month *The Economist* famously described the decision as 'the definite end of an epoch in the world's financial and economic development'. Other countries followed and although it eased the emergency in the UK, the change brought with it an outbreak of economic protectionism as, instead of coordinating policy, nations sought to guard their own industries from currency fluctuations. It was also an important moment because it highlighted so starkly Britain's shift from thinking of itself just a few decades earlier as the dominant global economic power – powered by Empire – to becoming one of a much larger number of economies blown around by the markets.

The impact in Britain of the economic crisis that followed the crash of 1929 and the subsequent recovery after devaluation depended very much on where you lived. The industrial heartlands of the north suffered as heavy industry was clobbered and unemployment rose to 2.5m in 1933. Other parts of Britain had a wholly different experience and by 1935 were booming. The new, modern industries producing chemicals, aeroplanes, washing machines and other household goods and manmade fibres prospered. The suburbs multiplied as 2.8 million houses were built in the decade. Bigger investment firms also prospered and became responsible for a larger and larger chunk of shareholdings and trading. The City was perfectly placed to exploit these brief few years of opportunity and growth as the European security situation deteriorated. There were even accusations of profiteering when Cazenove arranged the private placing of shares in Bristol Aeroplane shortly before the government announced in 1935 that the RAF was about to be increased in size rapidly.

With rearmament and another war on the way, in 1937 the City started to plan for it even if the Prime Minister and the government of the day were making strenuous efforts to avoid conflict. The Stock Exchange formulated a scheme, never implemented, to move to Pinewood studios in Buckinghamshire in order to avoid bombing. In preparation for the feared onslaught, London Stock Exchange firms were also allowed to move their office more than a quarter of a mile from the floor of the Exchange, but it was found that without the old set-up of firms operating within walking distance of each other that intimacy was lost and business could not be transacted with efficiency. It still very much required face-to-face encounters.

There was awareness that the City was an obvious target for German bombers because of its proximity to the Port of London's strategically vital docks, and arrangements were made for fire-watching and emergency plans as the country waited for war. The hope, as it was in the rest of the country, was that conflict with Hitler could be avoided. Indeed, there was celebratory after-hours trading in Throgmorton Street after the Exchange closed at the end of business on 28 September 1938, the day Neville Chamberlain waved his 'piece of paper' proclaiming peace in our time. The optimism did not endure long. Business gradually ran down in the months preceding the declaration of war in September 1939, which helped avoid a repeat of 1914 when so many financiers and traders had been caught out with positions open and money owing.

Staying put when hostilities opened meant that when the bombs fell the workers of the Square Mile found themselves in the front-line, alongside the population living around the docks in the East End. On the worst night of the Blitz, on Sunday 29 December 1940, the City was consumed by a Great Fire almost as intense as the conflagration that wrought such destruction in 1666.[9] A new generation described in letters and diaries the fight to save the City from the Luftwaffe. That night in December at Hoare's Bank on Fleet Street the staff manned the pumps, drawing water from the bank's private well as the bombs fell nearby.

At the Bank of England, senior clerk B.J. Rogers had a lucky escape.[10] After taking the tube from his home in Stanmore on the Sunday evening, to sleep in the office and be sure he was at his desk in the morning, he emerged from the tube station next to the bank and was almost killed by a bomb landing on Lombard Street. After dinner and a drink he went up on to the roof of the Bank of England and in a letter sent to his daughter recorded the scene:

> We were hemmed in by a wall of flame in every direction . . . The building next door to our dining club was alight and of course the churches and Guildhall are only a few yards from us. We could see St Lawrence Jewry already burnt out, glowing like an incandescent coal fire, while the Guildhall was burning furiously. In the distance was St Paul's standing out black in a ring of fire.

The conflagration consumed nineteen City churches and thirty-one of thirty-four guildhalls. A number of publishers went up in flames too, having been centred around St Paul's since the Reformation, when Protestant pamphleteers were encouraged to set up there. In the early hours of the morning a haunting image of Wren's great cathedral was captured by the photographer Herbert Mason and sent around the world. In what the *Daily Mail* described on its front page a few days later as 'war's most famous picture' the dome of St Paul's stood tall, glimpsed through the smoke. The picture was seized on as a symbol of the City and Britain's determination to withstand the onslaught.

But for all the talk of defiance, the cumulative toll of such raids was depressingly high. By 1944, a third of the entire area of the City had been flattened or so badly damaged that it was approved for redevelopment. Many of the oldest, historic buildings in the narrow alleyways had been swept away by bombing and fire, and warehouses, which before the war had taken up almost a quarter of the square footage of the City, had been burnt out along with famous landmarks. The previously unlucky Royal Exchange survived intact, remarkably, and did not need to be rebuilt this time, although it narrowly avoided destruction in January 1941, when a bomb landed on the road intersection at Bank and killed 111 people in the underground ticket station below, and on the stairwells and even the platforms. The Bank of England across the street took assorted hits throughout the war, as did the roof of the Stock Exchange in Capel Court. In nearby streets, bearing the names that told the City's story – Bishopsgate, Poultry and Gresham Street – lay the rubble of hundreds of years of history.

The other problem at the end of the war was that Britain's economy was not in much better shape either. For the second time in three decades, the country emerged victorious but in a perilous financial position. The national debt stood at almost 250 per cent of UK GDP, when little more than thirty years previously on the eve of the First World War it had been at well under 50 per cent. British industry, enterprise and productive capacity had been diverted into producing the instruments of war. Rationing was still in place. The American focus was on reconstructing Germany and Japan. Many financial markets in the City remained closed for several years and restrictions on moving currency out of the country were strictly enforced. Large parts of what had once been the thriving global centre of international capitalism, the fulcrum of an entire system of international trade, were a blackened wasteland.

From the ashes, might the City somehow rise again?

ROAD TO RECONSTRUCTION

'But what are we going to do if it doesn't work out?'

Sir Siegmund Warburg

If the Luftwaffe had failed to break the City of London entirely, despite doing a great deal of damage, it looked as though the new Labour government in 1945 might finish the job. That was certainly the fear in boardrooms and on the floor of the Stock Exchange when Winston Churchill was defeated in the general election held that year in July. Neither the scale of the landslide won by Clement Attlee, producing a Labour majority of 145, nor even the fact of the victory itself, had been expected. Indeed, the *Financial Times* editorial a few days later encapsulated the sense of dread among the denizens of the Square Mile. According to the paper's leader writer, the election result was 'the most serious reverse since the dark days of 1940'.[1]

The City now faced the prospect of a peacetime government committed to extending the collectivist centrally planned approach that had been adopted by the 1940–45 coalition government to build a war-winning machine. The war against poverty and for full employment would be won, Labour ministers said, only by nationalising industry, eliminating the inefficiencies of private ownership and reducing over-reliance on erratic financial markets and tarnished capitalism. To many war-weary Britons the new approach seemed like simple common sense, involving the application of the latest thinking on systems and efficient production to form a plan that avoided profiteering and duplication. It helped Labour that the folk memory of the

1929 crash and the distress and unemployment that followed in the Depression was also still strong. What socialism seemed to offer its adherents was modernity and a fresh start. In this brave new world, a secretive sector of the economy that had a long history of association with periodic bank runs, class-based cosiness and episodes of financial chicanery stretching back more than two centuries was always going to struggle to get a sympathetic hearing. Not only was much of the City in ruins; capitalism more broadly was about to come under attack as the new government got down to work.

The Bank of England was the first citadel to fall in 1946, although under government ownership it retained considerable operational independence and the Labour government needed its City connections to buy and distribute the national debt. It was more straightforward with the coalmines (taken into state ownership in 1947), road haulage and ports (1947), the railways (1948) and iron and steel (1950). The owners of the nationalised companies were compensated, and the Conservative government from 1951 put road transport and steel manufacturing back in private hands, but post-war Britain was collectivist in its outlook no matter which party was in power.

There are always some in the City who can spot an opportunity in times of crisis, and the shares of the soon-to-be-nationalised firms rose on the expectation that compensation would make funds available for investment elsewhere on the Stock Exchange in the shape of companies in newer industries. But the process of state control gummed up the basic workings of capitalism. Distressed companies that might have been bought over by new owners with fresh ideas, or gone out of business, or raised capital in London or on the regional stock exchanges to rebuild after the war, were subsumed into the expanding government sphere. The normal operation of the private sector was constrained, which meant fewer shares and less scope for what the City did, namely trading. The brief period when initial gloom faded and people in the markets were optimistic that the Labour government would not turn out to be as injurious to profits as they feared, came to an end with a devaluation crisis and a fuel crisis as ministers struggled to get the newly nationalised coalmines to function productively amid trade union demands and absenteeism.

State control impacted on the physical character of the City and its environs, too, although this only became apparent more gradually. The unions opposed modernisation and any job losses, which along with the introduction of the dock labour scheme regulating employment condemned the Port of London to a steep decline. Trade unions and government-controlled management were unable to agree on modernisation and automation, which led later to empty docks, as rival ports with waters deep enough took the new, much larger container ships. In this way, London's advantage as a centre for trading goods earned over centuries was surrendered in just a couple of decades. In the City itself, the destruction of the storage warehouses that had made up a quarter of the pre-Blitz Square Mile cleared the way for another transition. Rather than finance and the Stock Exchange being just one part of the area's economy, alongside the food markets, publishing trade and shipping, the balance shifted decisively. Although the rebuilding would take decades, and bombed-out sites were still visible years later, what filled the vast gaps were offices, often constructed cheaply in concrete.

Even there the early attempts at reconstruction brought conflict with the planners and with the modernising spirit of the era. Preparations had begun during the war for reconstruction, and in December 1943 government officials visited the chief engineer of the City of London Corporation – F.J. Forty – to study his plan for rebuilding.[2] The Corporation jealously guarded its autonomy and had declined offers of external help. The officials from Whitehall were appalled by what they found. The proposals were too traditional and lacking a vision, they said, because the Corporation envisaged rebuilding on the former street plan and putting excessive emphasis on office space and the needs of individual developers. 'We are not only disappointed, we are frankly alarmed', wrote a government official. 'Never since 1666 has there been such an opportunity to re-plan parts of the City, and, if the plans we saw are adopted, this opportunity will once again be missed.' The condemnation illustrates the extent to which the Corporation's outlook was at odds with the entire drive of national policy towards central planning by alleged experts, which was not surprising considering that the City was used to self-government and had evolved over centuries according to its own rhythms and tastes. Following a stand-off with Whitehall, the Corporation's plans were denied approval. There was redrafting and the Barbican development, opened in 1969, was one result of the new plan. But the more radical ideas were resisted, rapacious property developers moved in and the footprint of the financial City, around Gresham's Exchange and the Bank of England, and down Bishopsgate, largely retained its shape, although the architecture changed.

The secretive world around that hub appeared to operate much as it had done for decades. There were the stockbroking and jobbing firms, working in the Stock Exchange. The leading merchant banks nearby, such as Barings, Lazards, Kleinwort, Arbuthnot Latham, Schroder and Hambros, were members of the Accepting Houses Committee, the body with never more than 20 members that denoted established status and gave its members access to a pool of capital at the Bank of England on favourable terms. The merchant banks discretely served their clients' needs, advising firms during takeovers, recommending investments and commissioning work from the stockbrokers. The Bank of England oversaw the banking system and managing government debt, gold stocks and interest rates. A range of smaller markets operated with their own traditions, such as the London Metals Exchange. Lloyd's of London was based in Leadenhall Street, having abandoned the Royal Exchange before the war, while large insurance and assurance firms operated outside Lloyd's. All seemed relatively fixed.

In much the same way, it looked as though the traditional career structures would endure post-war. Even under a Labour government, recruitment in the City continued post-1945 for a while much as it had before. Ancestral ties, as well as the old school tie, counted for a lot. Sir Kenneth Kleinwort joined his family's bank after Eton and a French course in Grenoble.[3] His father and his uncle, Cyril, ran the bank, which before that had been run by their father, an astute figure marked out by his long, flowing white beard and habit of leaving the office on the dot and crossing Tower Bridge in his open-topped chauffeur-driven car at 3.30pm every day for an invigorating drive home to Sussex, no matter what the weather. The Kleinwort offices on Fenchurch Street featured a traditional high-ceilinged banking hall and a rabbit warren of wood-panelled rooms and corridors that gave the place a stately and paternal feel. Arriving in 1954, Kenneth was given six months to work out whether being a merchant banker appealed – it did, he loved the look of it – before he underwent a five-year trainee-ship, with spells in the key departments, and began his ascent through the organisation. Lord Rothschild, Jacob, also joined his family bank after Eton, and Oxford where he gained a first in history. But he quickly found the climate too stifling. He would learn more, he concluded, by spending several years in the outside world, first with an accountancy firm, then with Morgan Stanley in the US and a couple of veteran investors who taught him how the markets worked. Thus equipped, he returned to N.M. Rothschild & Sons in the early 1960s and, with his cousins, set about winning new business and replenishing the bank's coffers following decades of gentle decline. In 1960, aged twenty-seven, Bruno Schroder – Eton, Oxford and Harvard Business School, and a good friend of Kenneth Kleinwort – joined the bank started by his great grandfather, and was elevated rapidly following his father's death from a heart attack. Bruno had an accelerated jour-ney to the board, although he was later eclipsed by his brother-in-law. In 1958 Bruno Schroder's sister Charmaine married George Mallinckrodt, an heir to an industrial fortune and a gifted banker. The German-educated George had started work at Schroder's four years earlier, and while Bruno stayed in the background, the arch-networker Mallinckrodt became the dominant force.

In stockbroking and jobbing, too, connections mattered. Nick Durlacher's father was the senior partner in Wedd, Durlacher and Mourdant, one of the largest jobbing firms, and it seemed natural that he would join too.[4] After a traineeship Nick graduated to the floor of the Exchange. It did not seem odd that there were no women, he said, because at school there had been none and at university there were very few either. Durlacher's father was an energetic player, in more than one sense of the word, and business was frequently carved up over drinks in the Angel Court Club, right opposite the Stock Exchange. Most decent-sized outfits also had a 'mess' or dining room providing lunch for the partners, and sometimes guests and managers. There was a degree of social mobility, as there had been throughout the City's history; it would be unfair to suggest there was not, but it took intelligence and considerable good luck to rise beyond what was seen as one's particular station. At Lloyd's of London, the insurance market, in among those wearing old school ties were plenty of members from less affluent backgrounds who had started straight from school and become successful. On the Stock Exchange floor, Brian Winterflood was a self-starter who had been born in East Ham, the son of a bus driver. Joining broking firm Greener Dreyfus as a messenger in the early 1950s he realised that with his humble background he was unlikely to prosper as a broker. He moved to the much less sedate jobbing firm Bisgood Bishop, qualifying as a jobber and becoming a partner in 1974. The Bank of England's Leslie O'Brien had also risen through the ranks and in 1942 was appointed as private secretary to Montagu Norman, the then Governor. O'Brien was a grammar-school boy rather than a product of public school and when he succeeded Lord Cromer as Governor, in 1966, it was an appointment in tune with the egalitarian tenor of the times. It also provided an echo of the recruitment practices in the Bank of England in the nineteenth century, when the managers preferred to recruit bright boys not from grand backgrounds. These were still exceptions, however. While the man – then, always a man – getting on the morning train from the suburbs or the less expensive parts of the Home Counties knew that he might get on through hard work, for the most part the upper echelons remained closed. For all but a few of those working in the City there was very obviously a ceiling on their ambition.

The individual institutions, operating like clubs, still functioned according to a clearly established social hierarchy. The larger broking and jobbing partnerships looked down on the lesser partnerships. The smarter merchant bankers regarded the clearing banks as dull and boring. The clearers were the high-street banks, joint-stock banks owned by a pool of shareholders, although most Britons did not have a bank account until the 1970s. If they were boring, perhaps it was their job to be boring. Building societies, and other mutuals, were thoroughly provincial and existed to provide mortgages. Back in the City, Mullens, as the government's stockbroker, styled itself as the grandest of the grand, although its status rested on handling the government's gilt business (issuing government debt for sale), which involved the ritual of its senior partner walking across from the Bank of England wearing a top hat to announce to the market any changes in the bank rate. If Mullens ever lost its privileges as government broker it wouldn't have much left.

The camaraderie, for those on the inside of any part of this strange world, could be intense. These stockbroking and jobbing firms – large or small – were partnerships, meaning that the partners shared the risks and the profits, giving the senior figures a strong personal interest in paying attention to what risks the staff were taking with their money. Even in the merchant banks such as Hambros that had outside shareholders, the companies were structured in such a way that the family retained effective control. There was a strange logic to the favouritism, the sharing of information and cosy deals, when the primary role of the City then was to manage the money and affairs of perhaps, at most, four or five hundred well-connected British families.

The sense of continuity in the decades immediately after the war was deceptive, however. The City was about to feel the disruptive force of an exceptionally gifted outsider, a German Jewish banker who had arrived as a young man in 1934 when he judged that there would not be a happy ending to the Hitler experiment. He had briefly been enthusiastic, because of the youthful energy he thought was being unleashed in his homeland, but a conversation ('a hint from heaven') with Hitler's first foreign minister, Konstantin von Neurath, convinced him to get out that day with his wife and move to London.[5] Alongside his new partner in business, Henry Grunfeld, another German Jew who had fled the Nazis and lost everything in the process, he formed the New Trading Company, which in 1946 was renamed S.G. Warburg.

Siegmund Warburg was an untypical British merchant banker in other respects. Although he was not the only one of his contemporaries with German lineage and connections, he was avowedly an intellectual on the German model who cared intensely about ideas and literature and corresponded – about politics – with the novelist Stefan Zweig, another German Jewish exile. The flat shared by Siegmund and his wife in Eaton Square, Belgravia, was filled with books and he preferred to avoid reading newspapers, as they were, he said, bad for the brain and not conducive to clear thinking.

Warburg also claimed not to be particularly interested in making a personal fortune, and he did not make much by the standards of what came later. Successful merchant bankers, he said, were not motivated primarily by money. They did it for the 'intellectual sport' and sense of constructive achievement, he claimed in a rare interview in the mid-1960s, with Joseph Wechsberg. Having seen the effects of the 1929 crash on Germany first-hand he stressed the need for wariness and encouraged his team to consider what would happen if their latest clever scheme flopped on contact with economic reality. 'What,' he asked, 'are we going to do if it doesn't work out?'

But Warburg's quixotic attitudes and ordered approach to business, with his pedantic fixation on details and employment of bright youngsters, was fused with an obsessive drive to win. In the late 1950s, from his office on Gresham Street, he wrought a transformation that introduced a much more cutthroat approach and earned him notoriety and a degree of fame on both sides of the Atlantic. The fine details of the Aluminium War of 1958 and 1959 do not matter much now. One of Warburg's clients – Tube Investments, run by Sir Ivan Stedeford – in league with an American company wanted to buy British Aluminium. Warburg organised the (secret) buying of shares and associated media manipulation to shame the members of the British Aluminium company's board, which was chaired by the august figure of Lord Portal, the wartime chief of the air staff. Even though Warburg's clients were making by far the best offer, the board of British Aluminium did not want the mere shareholders – the owners of the company – to know it. Warburg and Stedeford outwitted Portal and won control of British Aluminium, causing a sensation. In taking on the other merchant banks and the board of a large British company in this way, Warburg had defied the City's supposed code of ethics in which these matters were supposed to be dealt with quietly between friends and certainly beyond the purview of the press. He had only been admitted to the hallowed Accepting Houses Committee in 1957, when Warburg bought Seligman, yet here he was, soon afterwards, unleashing the first hostile takeover in the City's history. Critics accused him of lying, or at least of not being entirely frank in his dealings. Some rivals thought it was the absolute limit. Kenneth Kleinwort described it later as the moment when 'Americanised methods started to be applied in the City, and the atmosphere started to become less smooth, less gentlemanly than it had been in the past . . . the wave of toughness started to hit the City.'[6] Warburg was even described by others as a 'shit', which was saying something considering the low regard in which the rest of the City was held by many Britons.

The predations of the outside world, and the bad publicity from the Aluminium affair, which demonstrated how loftily shareholders were sometimes treated by the traditional City Establishment, did prompt the beginnings of a rethink though. Perhaps the City needed to explain itself a little better, particularly at a moment when the Establishment was under such scrutiny from satirists challenging the old conventions. When the BBC wanted to make a documentary series about the City – called *Men and Money* – cooperation was granted and the resulting films first aired in 1964.[7] The crew was allowed to film on the floor of the Stock Exchange and behind the scenes, and at the Bank of England the Governor, Lord Cromer, gave his first television interview. Cromer was a member of the

Baring banking family who had married a Rothermere, from the newspaper dynasty. In his interview for the documentary series he explained the workings of the Bank, and other episodes gave an insight into the Lloyd's insurance market and the world of economists, analysts and financial journalists. It asked if these experts really knew what was going on. Brokers at the sugar market, based in Plantation House, were also filmed shouting their orders promising to buy future contracts. At the Stock Exchange in Capel Court, the floor at work was recorded from a safe distance alongside the only women then allowed near it, who were guides in the public viewing gallery.

'Although the City is international, the romance of the market place is deceptive,' noted the scriptwriter Paul Ferris in 1964. 'In many ways it is a rigid little society, formal and exclusive.' The truth of that observation was illustrated in the same period in the disgraceful treatment of Lord Mancroft, a Conservative politician decorated during the war, who was forced to resign from the board of Norwich Union in 1963 because he was Jewish and newly powerful Arab investors abroad had threatened a boycott. When the Norwich Union board changed its mind, following an outcry in the newspapers, it was too late. Mancroft refused to return. As The Spectator put it in December 1963: 'He is quite right and he alone emerges with any dignity from this wretched affair.'[8]

While old attitudes remained – in the form of periodic outbreaks of anti-Semitism and the virtual absence of women – the key outsider turned insider launched an innovation that made 1963 a pivotal year in the fortunes of the City and in financial history. In the Eurobond, Warburg and his team produced something that was to have enduring consequences for the future of international finance and what came to be called globalisation. It may sound like a dry technical measure, but its introduction in London on 1 July 1963 turned out to have explosive consequences that did as much as anything – until the revolution of the 1980s – to open up London. The Eurobond (nothing to do with the euro, the European single currency, which came much later) was simply a way of companies raising money to finance projects and pay for expansion. It meant an Italian construction firm or a German car manufacturer could thereafter tap into the reservoir of dollars in London and elsewhere that had accumulated thanks to the dramatic increase in international trade in the aftermath of the Second World War and American spending on reconstructing Europe. The resulting Eurobonds – debt – could then be bought and sold by investors. The catalyst for this was a decision by President Kennedy to crack down on American financiers investing too much abroad rather than at home, when he introduced in 1963 what he termed an interest equalisation tax, which all but shut down US interest in speculation abroad.

Siegmund Warburg in his office in the City. A German immigrant fleeing the Nazis, in the 1960s he was a leading force in the re-emergence of London as a financial powerhouse.

S.G. Warburg spotted an opportunity and approached his friend Guido Carli, the Governor of the Bank of Italy, to request the name of any Italian firm that might want to try the Eurobond first. According to Peter Spira, then the most junior member of the Warburg team working on the project, Carli suggested the Italian steel company Finsider.[9] When complications meant that Finsider could not be involved, Carli next suggested Autostrade, which was looking to raise funds for the completion of the A1 motorway that runs from Milan to Naples. The resulting deal was managed by Warburgs, Banque de Bruxelles, Deutsche Bank and Rotterdamsche Bank and it was quoted on the Luxembourg stock exchange, for tax reasons. With that $15m deal, constructed in London with the help of City brokers, accountants and legal firms, the Eurobond was born. The business was swiftly copied by other merchant banks and grew rapidly, with London as the main centre and bonds issued in a wide range of other currencies and combinations. By the end of the 1960s, $3bn of Eurobonds a year were issued. In 1980 it was $26bn; in 1986 $185bn; in 1989 $224bn; and in 2013 $4 trillion.[10]

Warburg's initiative was visionary, and the result was not only the creation of a newly internationalised market which London came to dominate. The innovation and lure of profits also made the City increasingly attractive to foreign banks, principally those from Japan and the US. There had been small numbers of Japanese bankers in London in the late nineteenth century, when the Yokohama Specie Bank (later the Bank of Tokyo) opened in London in 1884, and a few more in the 1930s.[11] Following the cessation of hostilities in 1945, the Japanese returned with six banks opening London offices between 1952 and 1956 to facilitate trade with Europe for Japanese companies. A few more opened in the 1960s and there was considerable nervousness about dealing with the Japanese so soon after the end of the Second World War, but gradually relations eased and London became a key Japanese outpost. As a young girl, Huruko Fukuda had a unique perspective when she arrived in London in the early 1960s, thanks to her father's latest diplomatic posting to the London embassy as the representative of the Japanese finance minister.[12] The family's first glimpses of fog-laden London were not encouraging, but she settled, going to Cambridge to read history (where she booked the band Pink Floyd to appear at a ball). She became an expert on trade and then, initially ashamed to tell her wealthy family that she had lowered herself to stockbroking, embarked on a successful City career, first with Vickers da Costa and then with James Capel. Links between the London Stock Exchange and Tokyo had been forged from the early 1960s and in the mid-1960s the first Japanese bond in London was issued.

In 1964 there were only fourteen US banks with operations in London, yet by the mid-1970s there were more than fifty. America and Wall Street had serious advantages, and from the wreckage of the Crash, the Depression and the 1930s it emerged even stronger as the leading world economy thanks to the dominance of the dollar, the power of the American war production machine, the expansive corporate culture, advances in science and technology and the appetite of consumers. This created myriad opportunities on Wall Street, and in the smaller financial centres and cities across America where smaller banks and brokers plied their trade to local investors.

But London had a niche that made it once again a potential hub, or a bridge between other financial centres. As a result, the total number of foreign banks in London in the 1960s almost doubled. London – between New York and Tokyo – was in the perfect time zone for trading and it also had the English language, long-held expertise in foreign exchange and financing trade, and a framework of institutions in place stretching back several centuries. History and the promise of the future, in an increasingly international financial scene that would depend on technology and ease of communication, both favoured London. It looked as though it might be possible for that long process of isolation and decline – relative to Wall Street – that had begun in the shutdown of 1914 to start coming to an end. It was as though the City as an international centre and innovator was, tentatively at first, reconnecting with its eighteenth- and nineteenth-century roots. By the mid- to late 1960s it was possible to imagine that London might one day reclaim its status as the premier financial capital in the world.

For the new migrants from Japan, America or the European mainland, 1970s London could be a shock to the system. Henry Angest, an ambitious young Swiss banker, thought he was entering a Stygian world. 'It was a hardship assignment,' he says more than forty years later. 'The food in London was inedible for a Swiss. I noticed that the place was grimy and the streets were full of potholes. Many clever graduates went abroad in the brain drain and in Britain it seemed to take a year to install a telephone. It was a really backward country.' Charles McVeigh, arriving to set up shop for the New York securities house Salomon Brothers, had a slightly easier entrée. He and his wife purchased a home in Cheyne Walk, Chelsea, and settled in thanks to social introductions that came through the firm. McVeigh soon set about expanding Salomon in London, and Angest began a career that would lead to him buying and building up the private bank Arbuthnot Latham.

Left to right, Muriel Wood, Susan Shaw, Hilary Root, Anthea Gaukroger and Audrey Geddes, five of the first women members of the London Stock Exchange in 1973.

At the Stock Exchange, the battle for acceptance was hardest of all for women, until a campaigner, Muriel Wood, and several colleagues fought in the early 1970s for admission as members. A few worked for brokers and jobbers in the office, but without being members they could not rise to the rank of partner or trade on the floor of the Exchange. In keeping with the attitudes of pre-1980s society, a few of the old guard among the Stock Exchange membership excelled themselves when it came to the excuses offered as to why no woman should be admitted. Women would change the unique atmosphere. The Stock Exchange was more a private club than a conventional place of business, one letter writer to *The Times* claimed, a point contested by his pro-modernisation son who wrote to the newspaper to challenge his father's argument. This being Britain, others were particularly worried about the lavatory situation. The only woman to have ever walked across the floor was the Queen. What if, asked one member, one of the women needed to use the lavatory? There were lavatories nearby, responded the campaigners, who eventually won the day.

On Monday 26 March 1973 they started work, with the media on hand to record the historic moment. Susan Shaw was the first to go onto the floor, shortly after 9.30am, accompanied by Richard Bradshaw, her boss, who had backed the campaign to admit women. 'I didn't know what to expect. But actually it was amazing,' she said. 'People suddenly came up, and shook my hands, and said "Welcome, welcome" and "Well done", and I got kisses on the cheek from someone I knew.' Jane Partington, who worked on the floor shortly afterwards, found the environment much less congenial.[13] When she spoke sharply to a colleague, she was asked if it was the 'wrong time of the month'. The women had to be tough because, as Partington recalls, they were harassed by some of the brokers and jobbers and given unwelcome nicknames: 'I was the Night Nurse – there was Sweaty Betty, Super Bum, the Grimsby Trawler, the Road Runner, Stop Me and Pick One. They were very cruel.' The old tricks, the ragging and setting fire to newspapers, looked badly out of date and ludicrous in what was supposed to be a modern financial centre.

Elsewhere, 'voracious London' was sucking in new domestic entrants. At the American firm Salomon Brothers, where Charlie McVeigh worked, Valerie Thompson was one of the first of a new breed of potential traders. For her, the City represented escape and potential fulfilment after a difficult upbringing in Dagenham, Essex, which had been marred by poverty. With no exam qualifications she learnt to trade helping her greengrocer father, next got a job as a filing clerk for the stockbrokers Hitchens Harrison, and had the gumption to wangle a post as a telex operator at another firm, Vickers da Costa, despite not knowing how to operate the machine. Thompson learnt quickly, and when she was turned down for a post at Salomon she found out the name of the company's boss in London and called him direct. The job was hers. Thompson turned out to have an instinctive grasp of numbers and was eventually thrown into trading, after a stint making the tea. With no prior experience, she was suddenly the firm's Deutschmark trader in London: 'There came a point when I was taking positions in Deutschmarks and guilders and I had the idea that I would sell short and it went badly, horribly wrong. I sat there thinking, God! I've got to tell someone about this.'[14] Her boss was forgiving, and Thompson gained a valuable lesson about trading, namely knowing when to cut and run having made a mistake. In 1980 she was dispatched to New York, and along with her young daughter and nanny, was put up in an apartment in the Surrey Hotel on Fifth Avenue. It was a long way from Dagenham.

The City was not alone in feeling the impact of dramatic social changes during the 1970s, of course. Other British professions and walks of life were being opened up and exposed to outside influences. But the Stock Exchange itself seemed to have changed least of all, even if outwardly it had acquired a sheen of modernity thanks to the construction of the Stock Exchange Tower, opened by the Queen in 1975. The old Capel Court building, cavernous and forbidding, has been pulled down in 1966 and its replacement, at twenty-six storeys high, helped begin the move towards taller towers in the Square Mile that was initially resisted by traditionalists. But inside, despite the shiny space-age surfaces in fashionable cream and beige, the Stock Exchange still functioned according to a set of rules that looked increasingly obsolete. When Labour, under Harold Wilson, returned to office in 1974, rumours surfaced that the government had finally had enough and that reform was coming to the City.

The Wilson–Callaghan government of 1974–9 is often singled out for criticism, much of it justifiable, for the role it played in Britain's economic decline, but it is worth remembering the full technicolour horror of the inheritance left behind by Edward Heath's outgoing administration in 1974. A global oil shock in 1973 that put a rocket under prices and wage demands would have been difficult enough to contend with, but the Chancellor, Anthony Barber, had earlier embarked on a programme to liberalise lending, scrapping the ceiling controlling how much banks could lend and introducing a policy called Competition and Credit Control. Wilson commented that he did not realise Heath had a sense of humour until he appointed Barber as Chancellor following the sudden death of the widely respected Iain Macleod in 1970.

Even though O'Brien at the Bank of England had grave concerns that Barber and Heath did not know what they were doing, he was too slow to act. The money supply duly surged – meaning the amount of money in the economy rose dramatically as banks created credit and lent more – which propelled house prices upwards, at the rate of almost 50 per cent in one year in London, and created a stock market bubble based yet again on wild speculation. The outcome was a classic British smash in 1973 and 1974, featuring plummeting industrial profits, a series of strikes and the secondary banking crisis, in which small lenders had to be bailed out by the Bank of England and Slater Walker's Jim Walker, who had until then been the darling of the financial press, got into severe difficulties. The stock market crash was bad enough in Wall Street. In London, prices fell by 63 per cent in 1973/4 and there began a period of many months in which nothing moved and deals evaporated. The impact on employment and pay was severe.

It was in this difficult climate, with profits obliterated and the incoming Labour government increasing taxes at the uppermost level to 98p in the pound, that the City first faced demands for reform. The director of the Office of Fair Trading, Gordon Borrie, later a Labour peer, was particularly determined and made it clear to Wilson that there must be action. If other industries were subject to legislation aimed at tackling anti-competitive restrictive practices, and were subjected to necessary lectures on modernisation and innovation, then why should the City exist in its own bubble, defending cronyism and its own closed shop in the name of tradition? City elders sniffed class war in the air and when Sir Nicholas Goodison was elected chairman of the Stock Exchange in 1976 he swiftly had it confirmed that the government was going to bring the market's rulebook within the purview of restrictive practices legislation. At first the notion that the Stock Exchange faced potential prosecution by the government seemed faintly preposterous. Says one stockbroker of the period from an aristocratic, landed background: 'You must remember that the City kind of worked as it was. Don't ask me how or why. It just did, because it was a small group of people who would not stand for bad behaviour. The word would go round. That chap's dodge.' But wasn't it a cartel protecting the interests of a small elite? 'Yes, that was the problem. The City was for old British families protecting their wealth and looking out for each other.'

The contrast in that respect with mid-1970s Wall Street was stark. Reforms introduced there on May Day in 1975 destroyed the system of fixed commissions enjoyed by brokerages and gave investment banks such as Goldman Sachs and investment companies the chance to compete for more business. It sparked creative destruction, wiping out cartels and creating an increasingly go-go climate in which supposedly high-minded analysts at the brokers and in the banks had to start operating virtually as salesmen, identifying companies worthy of investment to attract customers and to generate deals. The potential for conflicts of interest only became fully apparent later, but in the late 1970s it looked simply as though New

York was gearing up for a new wave of innovation in the decade ahead. Shouldn't Britain follow suit? Goodison agreed that modernisation was necessary, but he and his members were concerned about the risks. He attempted to intercede with Roy Hattersley, the minister for consumer protection, and went to see him in his office in Whitehall to explain that a court case and a sudden judgment against the Stock Exchange could cause complete chaos. It would be impossible, he told the minister, to guarantee the stability of the markets. Hattersley was adamant that he would not countenance government intervention to halt any case, however. There must be no favours for the City.

By then the Labour government, led by Jim Callaghan following Wilson's retirement in 1976, had much bigger problems to contend with than the fate of the Stock Exchange. Hattersley was present on 1 December 1976 when the cabinet discussed what to do about the perilous position of the UK and the terms under which an emergency loan from the International Monetary Fund might be arranged. Various solutions were proposed to deal with Britain's woes, although the depth of despair is apparent in the Cabinet Secretary's note of the conclusions that day: 'A go it alone policy was not viable . . . rising unemployment was inevitable.' There was worse to come as the mistakes and mishaps of the previous decades by administrations of both major parties caught up with government. It had been Callaghan himself who was instrumental in blocking effective trade union reform in the late 1960s. Now the unions repaid him by destroying his government with a wave of strikes and unrest in the Winter of Discontent of 1978/9. Callaghan and the Chancellor, Denis Healey, attempted to bring some order and restraint to public spending, but the collectivist, paternalistic settlement that had come in with Attlee in 1945 was breaking up. It looked as though dilapidated old Britain was at risk of sinking quietly into the sea.

Much of the country's rather tired governing class seemed ill equipped to cope with the collapse of post-war certainties and the emergence of new ideas, as though it was scarred by the trauma of successive devaluations of sterling since the war and the decline in status this indicated. The final collapse in 1971 of the Bretton Woods Agreement, when Richard Nixon ended the system by which leading currencies were pegged to the dollar and physical supplies of gold in Fort Knox, was another change that seemed technical but its implications were revolutionary for countries such as Britain. Exchange rates would float, capital would begin to be much more mobile, moving to wherever investors saw a potential return, and the financial innovators of Wall Street were on the verge of inventing seemingly exciting products and ways of packaging and selling ever-larger amounts of debt for companies and countries. The future, the 1980s, looked to the alert as though it was going to be about openness to this coming tidal wave of money. Thanks to a long history of innovation, and its international outlook best expressed in the development of the Eurobond market by Warburg and others, the City of London was surely well placed to prosper.

First, though, the Stock Exchange would have to negotiate its way delicately around a new government headed by Margaret Thatcher, which came to office in May 1979. On 9 February, Borrie and the OFT had referred the Stock Exchange formally to the Restrictive Practices Court, setting in motion potentially years of legal action. Somehow the Stock Exchange needed to get out of this infernal court case. That shouldn't be too difficult. A woman – especially a Tory woman – wouldn't be too difficult to manage now, would she?

PART TWO
FRICTION

You say you want a revolution: accompanied by Sir Nicholas Goodison, Margaret Thatcher visits the London Stock Exchange in February 1979, three months before she won power.

5

DISCORD AND HARMONY

'I regret to tell the House that I cannot meet the request of the Stock Exchange.'

John Nott, 23 October 1979

By temperament and outlook Nicholas Goodison was an unlikely 1980s revolutionary. As the author of *English Barometers 1680–1860* (published in 1968), the chairman of the Stock Exchange was happiest of all immersed in the study of furniture, clocks and music. His career before the Thatcher era did not suggest insurgent tendencies either. After Marlborough School and King's College, Cambridge, in 1958 he joined the family City firm H.A. Goodison & Co., later Quilter, Goodison, rising to become a partner four years later. Four years after that, the same year his work on English barometers appeared, he was elected to the Stock Exchange's governing body, the Council. As one of several 'young turks', he did think the institution needed to liberalise, and he subsequently faced some resistance as chairman of the Planning Committee from older members who did not think there should be anything as racy as planning, but Goodison argued that change should be evolutionary and carefully considered. The rules on allowing members to trade overseas were relaxed somewhat, women were admitted in 1973. Those who accused the Stock Exchange of being a club were wrong in their diagnosis, thought Goodison. It was, he remembers four decades later, 'very genial, very nice', with interesting people. 'But people didn't really appreciate what the Stock Exchange was. Although it was a mutual understanding of 4,500 members, it was also the only regulatory body in the industry.'

Indeed, the City had its own delicate eco-system that had evolved over centuries. The Stock Exchange was the province of broking and jobbing firms, buying and selling shares and securities. It had no reach outside that realm of activity but beyond the Square Mile it had long been the most famous manifestation of the City. The Bank of England had no formal responsibility for the Stock Exchange or its dealings, but as the institution responsible for the issuance of national debt and its trading, the Bank relied on the Stock Exchange and kept a paternal eye out for excesses. The merchant banks, and the clearing banks, could not afford to offend the Bank of England either. It sat at the centre of a complex, inter-twined network of obligations and duties. The non-statutory Takeover Panel was also there from the late 1960s to police City takeovers and impose some order on companies and stockbrokers keen to do deals.

Having been elected as chairman in 1976, at forty-one the young-est occupant of the office, Goodison's attempts to explain the deli-cate nature of the Stock Exchange's role in this very British network to Labour ministers were a failure. Gordon Borrie, the head of the OFT, declined to agree a compromise, and many of Goodison's colleagues on the Stock Exchange Council felt that they must defend the existing arrangements. The old separation between brokers and jobbers offered the customer some protection from conflicts of interest, because the client knew that their broker had a sole respon-sibility to buy their shares at the best available price, and could not collude with the jobber. Customers feared that changes would mean competition and pressure on profits. If reform on the model of Wall Street was introduced – moving to so-called 'dual capacity' in which brokers and jobbers were effectively merged and scrapping minimum commissions on share trading – the customer might find their costs reduced, lowering profits.

Goodison and his colleagues were trapped. Realising with grow-ing horror how damaging and messy a potential court case would be if Borrie was allowed by the government to proceed, Goodison decided to try Sir Harold Wilson, by that time out of office. In

October of 1976 the newly installed Labour Prime Minister, Jim Callaghan, needing to give Wilson something to do, had asked him to chair a Committee to Review the Functioning of Financial Institutions, in an effort to examine how savings might be increased and industrial investment encouraged. Goodison suggested to Wilson that a new inquiry should be established to work out how to protect what was best about the City while introducing sufficient reform to satisfy the demands for change. 'Wilson was sympathetic,' says Goodison. 'Not at all hostile.' But the Stock Exchange chairman was wasting his time. There was no further inquiry and when Wilson's report was eventually published much later – in June 1980 – it was rendered irrelevant. By then the world had moved on, the era of Callaghan and Wilson was dust, and Margaret Thatcher was in Number 10. What mattered was persuading the Conservative leadership of the City's case.

This was to prove more difficult than it looked. Considering the scale of the changes that ended up being implemented by Thatcher's ministers, to the great benefit of many stockbrokers, jobbers and bankers, it is ironic that the Tory leader's initial early experiences in the Square Mile were not remotely conducive to friendly relations. Her official biographer Charles Moore records that on 4 February in the middle of the Tory leadership election of 1975, in which she defeated the incumbent Edward Heath, she went for lunch at N.M. Rothschild and had a tough time.[1] Several pro-Heath members of the Rothschild clan refused to attend and on the way back to Westminster she told the recently elected Tory MP, Norman Lamont, that she did not want to be taken 'to that red bank again'. The irony is that the Rothschilds and other merchant banks did extremely well later out of their role in arranging the Thatcher government's privatisation programme in the 1980s. But in the 'small c' conservative City of the mid-1970s she was not yet the warrior queen beloved of investment bankers and rapacious tycoons that she would become a decade or so later. In 1975 she was just the woman who had dared to cause trouble by taking on Ted Heath, the chap who led the Tory tribe, even if he was a chap who had presided over an economic cock-up of epic proportions in the early 1970s.

Thatcher's ideological re-engineering of the Tory Party had in the mid-1970s barely got underway. Although the think tank that she and Keith Joseph founded in 1974, the Centre for Policy Studies, was established to promote 'freedom and responsibility', it and the colleagues she trusted took time to develop a specific free market programme of policies. Her leadership was doubted by many of her old-school Conservative colleagues, and although a clear direction was apparent to her supporters, much of her time was spent seeking to reassure sceptical voters that she had the mettle to be prime minister. Following the calamities of the decade, and particularly after the Winter of Discontent, there was a sense of expectation in the City as the 1979 general election approached, and the Conservatives championed the urgent need for an economic renaissance and pro-business policies. Thatcher was received warmly in February that year when she visited the Stock Exchange and was given a tour by Goodison. That spring there was also a mini-boom in the market as share prices rose in expectation of a Tory win. Investors were also buoyed by the possibility that Britain's North Sea Oil deposits would make the years ahead easier to navigate, creating tax revenue for the Treasury and providing profits for investment. The Conservative manifesto put in front of the country in 1979 made no specific mention of the City itself, but it did emphasise the need for wealth creation, limiting taxes on capital and expanding share ownership.

Any hopes harboured by the City's senior figures of being given a smooth ride by the Thatcher administration did not survive early contact with the new government, however. On 22 May, with the government just eighteen days old, Goodison discussed the possibility of an exemption for the Stock Exchange with Sally Oppenheim, the new Minister of State for Consumer Affairs at the Department of Trade. Their conversation sparked an exchange of letters between the department and the Bank of England on whether or not Goodison's wish should be granted. That spring, John Nott, the no-nonsense Secretary of State for Trade, seemed unconvinced when they met several times in Whitehall. A colleague of Nott's remembers his scepticism: 'John thought Nicholas Goodison was looking to do a cosy deal. He wanted nothing to do with it.'

The truth is that Nott, a former merchant banker, had regarded a deal exempting the Stock Exchange as theoretically feasible, even desirable, but he felt it was now too late. On 30 May 1979 he wrote a long note to Geoffrey Howe, Chancellor of the Exchequer, detailing his thinking.

> We have, somewhat reluctantly, come to the conclusion that, if the legal proceedings before the Restrictive Practices Court had not already begun, following the rejection by Mr Hattersley (the former Labour minister) of the Stock Exchange's early request for exemption, it would have been right to exempt the Stock Exchange . . . However, the situation is very different now that the reference has been made.[2]

Any exemption would involve interrupting legal proceedings. Nott thus concluded: 'I do not believe therefore that we could justify giving special treatment to the Stock Exchange at this juncture.' Howe disagreed, and in a memo sent the following day from Number 10, the Prime Minister's staff advised Nott that the Chancellor wanted to discuss it as soon as possible after the looming Budget. Howe's view was that the Restrictive Practices Court was entirely the wrong forum to consider the future of the Stock Exchange. Could they not set up an ad-hoc committee or reconstitute the Monopolies and Mergers Commission?

Keith Joseph, the Secretary of State for Industry and one of the architects of free market Thatcherism, also became involved. He wrote to Nott on 6 June, indicating that he was not persuaded of the case for exempting the Stock Exchange and had no faith in the Monopolies Commission either. That summer, civil servants produced papers on the subject and by July, Howe, who was worried about the potential impact on the markets, was suggesting a compromise, in the form of either a stay of execution if the court judgment went against the Stock Exchange or openness to suggestions for reform. On 16 August, Nott wrote to Howe accepting his suggestion. The result – the bottom line – of the discussions in Whitehall was that the court case would go ahead, and Goodison had failed to shift opinion. For all the myth of Thatcher driving every aspect of government, the involvement of the Prime Minister had been limited. In her handwritten note scribbled on a memo, explaining that Nott would announce the next day that the Stock Exchange would be allowed time to implement the judgment if it lost, she said that she was content: 'Yes – it is a good compromise on practical grounds.'

The disappointed Stock Exchange chairman was duly notified by Nott, and in the Commons on 23 October 1979 the Secretary of State confirmed it publicly, responding to questions from Tory MPs during a debate on the competition bill.[3] There had been, he said, a great deal of correspondence between Goodison's colleagues and ministers. 'I regret to tell the House,' said Nott, 'that I cannot meet the request of the Stock Exchange.' He defended the role of the Restrictive Practices Court and indicated that the Stock Exchange would have a grace period in which to make changes following a court judgment that went against it. The implication was that the City was heading for a kicking in court and had best get used to the idea.

Another factor was the quixotic personality of the Prime Minister herself, frequently misread on the question of the financial revolution associated with the ideology carrying her name. One of the great myths – fostered by the privatisations and reforms she introduced from which flowed great wealth to an old and new City generation – is that she was always a natural supporter of the Square Mile and its grandees, and deliberately designed a deregulatory cornucopia of delights to please them. This was not the case. Says an advisor to Thatcher from the early 1980s: 'Margaret looked at the City and saw a self-satisfied old boys club that was rigid and stuck in its ways.'

The grocer's daughter, the mercurial Methodist who had developed into a sophisticated political operator determined to shake

Britain out of its torpor, was hardly a natural ally of a bunch of men who had been in positions of authority during the UK's economic decline. They were judged undynamic; many of them had been to school together and sat on each other's boards; and now they were behaving like the leaders of an upmarket trade union. Her closest friend and most solid supporter was not of the City either. Her husband Denis was affluent industry, not City, and these tribal distinctions mattered, a lot, in the anthropological jungle of late 1970s and early 1980s Britain. Denis had taken over the family paints and chemicals business after serving in the Second World War, and when it was sold he served on the board of Burma Oil and several other firms involved in businesses such as waste management. His was the world of smart suburban golf courses, strongly held right-wing views, and gin and tonic with a stiff measure. As in a Venn diagram, the two tribes of City and British industry overlapped socially and commercially, of course. But the City – the Bank of England, the floor of the Stock Exchange and the network of brokers and jobbers – was not the natural terrain of the Thatchers.

The idea that Thatcher was actively seeking to do chums favours is not borne out by the correspondence of the period either. Goodison wrote to the Prime Minister on 6 November 1979 to express his regret at the decision by Nott, and to complain that he had not been consulted. His note gives an indication of how difficult the City was finding it to process a lack of cooperation from the leadership of a party that it had hitherto regarded as an ally. 'I really was astonished by the Government's failure to respond to our repeated requests for discussions before the taking of an adverse decision', wrote Goodison. 'As you know, I am a keen supporter of your Government. I am very sorry that I had to criticise it publicly for taking this decision without any consultation whatever with us. I had no choice, which was a very invidious position to find myself in.' An official wrote a covering note saying that Goodison's claim of a lack of consultation 'does not stand up'. Would the Prime Minister respond or would she like it passed to Nott? 'Alas, I shall have to reply', Thatcher scribbled. She sent a polite but firm response to Goodison. The Stock Exchange would have time to implement any changes, she wrote on 22 November 1979. Any suggestion that he had been ignored by ministers was not correct, she insisted.

The new government had more than enough to deal with without worrying about the bruised feelings of stockbrokers and jobbers. Indeed, the economic situation in which the UK found itself was dire. The Chancellor, not known for being excitable, had described it in stark terms in his first Budget in June 1979.[4] A depressingly familiar feature of the first Budget speech by new chancellors taking over after a change in governing party in the previous fifteen years, explained Geoffrey Howe, was that every one of them had found cause to complain, with more or less justice, about the pitiful state of their inheritance. 'The House will understand,' said Howe,

> in the light of the most recent evidence about inflationary trends, monetary growth, Government borrowing and the deteriorating trade balance – not to mention the post-dated cheques for public sector pay that I found on arrival at the Treasury – that I am certainly in no position to discontinue the tradition of my predecessors.

It was not only the fault of the previous Labour government, said Howe. Britain's decline had deeper roots, in the failure of the broad consensus that had existed between the two major parties since the Second World War: 'Are we not driven to the conclusion that the notions of demand management, expanding public spending and "fine tuning" of the economy have now been tested almost to destruction?'

The mild-mannered Howe announced measures aimed at restraining public sector spending, fighting inflation, controlling the money supply and reforming the taxation system. VAT was almost doubled, the standard rate of tax was cut and the top rate of income tax fell from 83p in the pound to 60p, giving a large boost to the take-home pay of the better-off in the City and industry and sending a signal that wealth creation – for some – would be the leit-motif of the Thatcher governments. As the economics commentator David Smith put it: 'The 1979 budget was big and bold. Rarely has a government set out its stall, and its philosophy, so clearly.'[5] But the announcement that most merited such acclaim concerned the abolition of restrictions on taking money in and out of Britain. The decision would supercharge the changes underway in the financial markets. This was a revolutionary decision.

Inside the Treasury, officials had picked up one important clue during the 1979 election campaign about the transformative nature of what was coming. Before the election Nigel Lawson, as a member of the Conservatives' shadow Treasury team, had written a regular column for *Financial Weekly*, in which in his final contribution on 20 April 1979 he advocated the abolition of exchange controls – then the international norm – apart from in West Germany, where they had been scrapped by the pioneering finance minister Ludwig Erhard after the Second World War. In the UK's case, exchange controls were used to conserve the country's foreign exchange reserves and to improve the balance of payments, which restricted money leaving the country. It also hampered investment. Introduced at the outbreak of the Second World War, when the government needed all the currency, gold and securities it could lay its hands on, the most draconian restrictions were relaxed and then reintroduced from 1947, with certain controls reintroduced at points of crisis when the government judged that too much money was leaving the country. For the British tourist in 1979 this meant they were restricted in how much they could take out of the country on holiday; for British companies it presented barriers to investing abroad; for foreign companies it made the UK highly unattractive, as once their money was invested it might be difficult to get it out; for the Stock Exchange it limited the scope for international trade.

Lawson was convinced that the economy needed to be more open to flows of money in both directions. British companies that invested abroad might prosper and reinvest profits at home or earn returns for their shareholders, he believed. Foreign investors would bring money, jobs and new expertise. When Lawson arrived at the Treasury in May as Financial Secretary, working for the Chancellor, he was surprised to be told that senior Treasury and Bank of England officials were expecting abolition of exchange controls, having attached too much authority to his article in *Financial Weekly*. Senior officials in the Bank of England agreed it was time Exchange Controls went, but in the Treasury the officials were opposed.

Like several of the boldest, defining acts undertaken by the Thatcher government, and ever since associated with her name, the exchange controls move was not actually her idea and she took some persuading that it was sensible. Howe had long been in favour theoretically and took the final decision, although he too had concerns about the practical implications. A quietly spoken and at times Eeyorish figure, Howe was capable of seeing a problem from eight different angles. In contrast, Lawson was much more 'Tiggerish'. After all, he had been a Fleet Street financial journalist and then an iconoclastic editor of the *Spectator* magazine from 1966–70.

Opponents feared that abolishing these controls would cause capital to flood out of the feeble UK economy as investors went in search of more prosperous climes, in turn causing a run on the pound. When Howe asked Lawson and officials to examine the possibilities, they judged that such a crisis was unlikely because the markets had faith in the new government and sterling was safe since its newly acquired status as a petro-currency made it more attractive, strengthening the pound. But Howe wanted to proceed in careful steps, with the first taken in the June Budget. The limit was raised on how much British travellers could take abroad and all investment by UK companies up to £5m was allowed automatically without the need for approval from the government. The following month, all restrictions on foreign direct investment were scrapped and investors – operating principally through banks and City firms – could invest in securities (stocks and bonds) abroad. In early October, Lawson pushed for full abolition, leaving Howe to persuade a 'hesitant' Thatcher. At the subsequent meeting of the cabinet, only the Environment Secretary, Michael Heseltine, objected, on the grounds that the wealthy would take the money out of Britain and buy nice houses on the Côte d'Azur. On 24 October 1979, Howe told the Commons that he was going for full abolition:

> There will from tomorrow be full freedom to buy, retain and use foreign currency for travel, gifts and loans to non-residents, buying property overseas and investment in all foreign currency securities . . . Portfolio investment will be wholly freed, and the requirement to deposit foreign currency securities with an Authorised Depositary is abolished. Foreign currency accounts can be held here or abroad. Passport marking for travel funds can now be abolished.

Howe's Labour opponents were appalled. Denis Healey, the Shadow Chancellor, responded that while there might be a case for some relaxation, abolition was a 'reckless, precipitate and doctrinaire' action which the government would soon regret. These concerns were understandable, if misplaced. The British were too used to exchange controls. In the Treasury, a team of 25 officials, and in the Bank of England 750 staff, managed and policed the restrictions. In many other countries something similar was then the norm and the notion of private money washing across continents, unimpeded by the intervention of government, seemed somehow illicit. Such a free flow was, of course, precisely what had happened in the late Victorian period, when the City and British investors sent a tsunami of capital abroad in search of profit, funding foreign railroads and industry. This time ministers hoped that capital would flood in from foreign investors, and that British companies would look abroad for opportunities.

Labour's opposition to the change persisted and in the party's 1982 pamphlet 'Investing in Britain', the City was singled out for criticism. 'Since the abolition of exchange controls, institutions have invested far too large a proportion of their funds abroad.'

Investments, the party said, had been insufficiently concentrated on the needs of the domestic economy, a theme which still surfaces periodically. In the party's manifesto for the 1983 election, dubbed afterwards the 'longest suicide note in history', Labour proposed the establishment of a Securities Commission to regulate the institutions and markets of the City, including the Lloyd's insurance market. Banks would have to submit detailed investment plans to the government explaining how they would help businesses of which the government approved, and if they did not cooperate they would be nationalised. Ironically, after Labour went on its long ideological journey following defeat in 1983, its leaders Neil Kinnock, John Smith, Tony Blair and Gordon Brown embraced the City and accepted that capital should be globally mobile, before the party ended up nationalising two banks, RBS and Lloyds, in the midst of the 2008 financial crisis. In the early 1980s, that calamity lay long distant in the future.

The warnings on Exchange Control abolition did turn out to have been overcooked though. Following a slow start – and a reverse during the economic convulsions of the early 1980s as industry was hammered by the effects of a strong pound and the high interest rates applied by the Conservatives to squeeze out inflation – foreign investment in the UK rocketed. Precise figures on inward investment have to be treated with caution, but the trend is clear. It is estimated that in 1975 total investment by foreign firms and investors was £260m; in 1979, £480m; 1985, £1.3bn; 1990, £3.2bn; 1995, £5.1bn; and 2000, £25bn.[6] Not all of this was down to the decision taken by Howe on exchange controls, of course. But taken together with what had developed in the Eurobond market in London since Warburg's innovations of the early 1960s, the abolition of exchange controls was one of the most significant acts of a British Chancellor in the twentieth century. The long deep freeze that followed 1914, when the free flow of capital was restricted and then frozen stiff between 1939 and 1945, was thawing.

Nicholas Goodison and some of his colleagues at the Stock Exchange grasped the significance of what Howe had done. He knew that if the UK was opening up to foreign investment, and foreign competition, then the City was bound to feel the effects. But how to harness this opportunity when any hope that a gentleman's compromise with ministers might be feasible had been abandoned and it seemed that Margaret Thatcher was content to see the Stock Exchange confronted in court?

That year, in September 1982, there was more pressure applied on the Stock Exchange when a brash new rival on the American model opened on a historic City site. LIFFE – the London International Financial Futures Exchange – took over the Royal Exchange building, on the site that Gresham had chosen for his Exchange in the sixteenth century. Under the roof topped with the Gresham-family gold-grasshopper weathervane, traders wearing bright multi-coloured jackets gesticulated and shouted their trades. The cacophonous enterprise was based on the Chicago-based futures markets, in which traders bought and sold futures contracts for commodities or shares, enabling suppliers and purchasers to insulate themselves from future fluctuations in price. An investor agrees to pay the seller if the price of a large consignment of a commodity – tea or coffee, say – falls below an agreed price. If the price goes above an agreed ceiling, the investor keeps it and makes a profit. It gives the producer certainty by reducing price volatility. The market soon broadened out beyond foodstuffs and into futures contracts on all manner of financial products. Assorted working parties from London had visited Chicago to discover how it worked, and Brian Williamson and John Barkshaw readied LIFFE in London. Unlike at the Stock Exchange, in which membership was hard to get and jealously guarded, LIFFE welcomed all comers, including banks and securities firms from abroad.

Nick Durlacher of the jobbers Wedd, Durlacher was one of those deputed to work at LIFFE when the firm decided that it should try this exotic new market. He was deeply disappointed to be leaving the Stock Exchange floor and, having never heard of futures markets, went off to the US to find out. What struck him most there was the noise, the jostling and the shouting. In the

London Stock Exchange you waited your turn. Not in a futures market. The night before the opening, there was a party in the Guildhall, the ancient seat of the Corporation of the City of London, at which the Bank of England Governor, Gordon Richardson, made a speech congratulating the innovators who had created LIFFE. He also rang the bell at 10am the next morning to get trading underway. Compared to the Stock Exchange, it was a bear pit. The new breed of traders tended to be young, below thirty-five, and the mix was, if not 50–50 male/female, at least close to that. Compared to the excitement at LIFFE, the long-established Stock Exchange round the corner risked looking like the genteel cousin or relic of a bygone age.

Inside the Bank of England, one of the most senior figures soon realised there must be a deal to be done on the future of the Stock Exchange. David Walker's early career gave him the perfect mix of experiences and contacts to be the bridge between the various outposts of the UK's financial and political Establishment. A grammar-school boy from Chesterfield, Walker joined the Treasury in 1961 with a double first in economics from Cambridge. During a period in Washington working for the IMF in the early 1970s, his views on Britain's economic situation hardened, and on his return to the Treasury he found himself working closely on the sterling crisis. Walker had been in the government car, briefing Denis Healey, on the infamous occasion in September 1976 when the Chancellor was on his way to Heathrow Airport. Healey was supposed to travel to the International Monetary Fund conference in Manila, but when they arrived at the VIP lounge, Healey and Walker discovered that the market pressures on sterling had intensified to such an extent that the Chancellor could not responsibly leave Britain. Gordon Richardson was also at Heathrow. They then had to get hold of Callaghan – with some difficulty as he was at the Labour Party annual conference – to update the Prime Minister. 'The whole thing was abandoned,' recalled Walker. 'I was invited to go back to the Bank with the Governor . . . on this day of great crisis he said well, perhaps we ought to talk about what we can do about the sterling

balances. Let's have a quiet conversation and have some lunch.'[7]
That conversation, and Walker's links with other officials, meant
that in 1980 he was offered a post at the Bank of England, first
running the economic intelligence department and then the 'life-
boat' for struggling companies that could not access funding from
the commercial banks.

As an executive director of the Bank of England in 1981, Walker
concluded that the City had to change. Here the Bank was in a
curious position. Technically it had few formal powers and the
Stock Exchange was self-governing as a membership organisation,
but the senior figures in the Bank felt a general sense of responsibility for the City and perhaps wanted to extend their remit. The
Stock Exchange firms also bought and sold the Bank of England's
gilt-edged securities, the name for UK government debt. Walker's
concern was that the City's firms were so badly under-capitalised,
meaning they lacked the clout and resources of the larger American
organisations to compete, that they would just die if nothing was
done. If the court case went ahead, the City could be tied up in
years of litigation and the malaise could damage London's reputation. Walker commissioned a young economist, Andrew
Threadgold, to write a report that drew lessons from the liberalisation that had taken place in New York in 1975. When it was
presented, Threadgold's initial 'Blue Skies' study was instrumental in coalescing opinion in the Bank of England and the Treasury.
Walker and other officials were also concerned about a ruling by
the European Court that appeared to suggest that single capacity
– the separation of jobbers and brokers – could fall foul of
European law.[8]

In the Treasury, the most senior official, Permanent Secretary
Peter Middleton, and Geoffrey Howe were also discussing how to
find a way forward, prompted in part by the work of the Bank. A
meeting was convened at Number 11 Downing Street on 10.30am
on 6 May 1983, three days before Thatcher went to the Palace to ask
the Queen for a dissolution of Parliament and a general election.
Around the table that day were Howe, Middleton, Gordon

Richardson, David Walker, and Arthur Cockfield, the Secretary of State for Trade. Cockfield was notoriously self-confident, an attribute that did not endear him to all of his colleagues. He ended up almost by accident being one of the most consequential and least mentioned figures in the Thatcher era. In 1984 she appointed him as a European Commissioner, where he played a leading role in driving through the single market, and in the process in Thatcher's eyes going irretrievably native in Brussels, to such an extent that he was not offered a second stint. At the meeting in Number 11 in May 1983, Walker saw that Cockfield was one who got the City and grasped what needed to happen. Cockfield advocated a potential compromise, centred on the abandonment of fixed commissions. It was agreed that this mess was at least partly down to the Stock Exchange's handling of the matter. There now needed to be private discussions with the Exchange, and the Treasury and Department of Trade were tasked with producing a negotiating brief. That meeting before the election was pivotal.

On the day after the 1983 general election when Thatcher was returned to office with a landslide, Goodison got encouraging news. Cecil Parkinson was appointed as Secretary of State for Trade and Industry and Goodison sent him a letter making a plea for talks. Would Goodison like to pop round to his office for a chat? He would. Parkinson had encountered the City earlier in his career as an auditor and while he recalled that he had been unimpressed and suspicious of the old set-up, regarding it as too much of an old-boy network, he saw the value in reinvigorating the City with a burst of reform and modernisation. The amenable Parkinson had consulted Nigel Lawson, newly appointed to take over from Howe as Chancellor, who told him that the compromise with the Stock Exchange was a positive development, as long as the promises of reform were real. David Walker found Lawson to be an enthusiastic advocate of change. The new Chancellor had the City in his blood. Lawson's father had been a tea broker in the City and his grandfather had been a senior partner in a stockbroking firm. As City Editor of the *Sunday Telegraph* in the 1960s Lawson had been there when Jim Slater was hired as share tipster, the same Slater who went on to have such a controversial career and then a sensational smash in the early 1970s when his Slater Walker empire got into difficulty. Lawson came to the job with few illusions about the City.

Goodison travelled to Parkinson's office and surprised the new Secretary of State by agreeing instantly to the outline of what was proposed. In a series of subsequent secret meetings they agreed the beginnings of a historic settlement. Fixed minimum commissions on share trading would be scrapped by late 1986, and further reforms would be introduced, including a system of appeals for those turned down for Stock Exchange membership to ensure that the 'old-boy network' could not block those it regarded as socially unacceptable. The question of dual capacity – abolishing the separation between brokers and jobbers – was parked for now, in recognition of the difficulties Goodison faced with traditionalist members of the Stock Exchange when it came to implementing any changes.

Parkinson next had to convince the Prime Minister that enough had been conceded by the Stock Exchange to merit the suspension of the potential legal action by the government. Writing on 12 July 1983, Parkinson deployed his considerable charm in a six-page memo in an attempt to persuade Thatcher that it was a good idea. 'New factors have now appeared. One is that Sir Nicholas Goodison has come to accept the necessity of some changes, and is prepared to negotiate.' That was a little harsh on Goodison, who had long accepted the need for changes but merely objected to the prospect of a difficult court case. But Parkinson was preoccupied with the Sara Keays affair, which was soon to be revealed in the newspapers, and it fell to Lawson to reassure the Prime Minister. On 21 and 22 July at the Stock Exchange Tower there were two days of closed discussions by the ruling Council, following a leak to the *Guardian* newspaper that suggested a settlement was being discussed. The Council voted unanimously in favour of settling.

At the final moment, the process was almost derailed when Willie Whitelaw, Deputy Prime Minister, expressed concerns in cabinet. Wouldn't it look as though the Tories were looking after their friends in the city, whose donations had helped the Tories to their recent election victory? Lawson had to make a strong case, explaining that it was not only the right course of action, it was also early enough in the Parliament for it to be forgotten later. That argument prevailed and the next day, on 27 July, Parkinson made an announcement to the Commons, in which curiously he said that while fixed commissions would go, separation between brokers and jobbers would for now be maintained, a position that did not endure for long. The reaction to the retreat of the Restrictive Practices Court, both from the Labour opposition and even from Tory-friendly newspapers, was scathing. It was, said Peter Archer, MP for Warley West, a slap in the face for the director of the OFT: 'Is the Secretary of State asking the House to accept that a deal between cronies in a smoke-filled room is a substitute for a full public inquiry into how public interest is affected by a major institution such as the Stock Exchange?' The *Daily Telegraph* on its City pages said that a government theoretically committed to competition had abandoned its own guardian of competition policy. The contrast with the destruction being experienced by British industry, which had its worst year since the Second World War as factory after factory closed, causing unemployment and distress, could not have been more pronounced. *The Economist* spoke of the Square Mile having been done a favour by its chums. But Tory ministers had, over four years of difficult negotiations, gradually arrived at a position where the City could rethink how it did business and open up to more outside competition. It might make it feasible for financial services to expand rapidly as the old manufacturers sank into the post-industrial wasteland. The City could be a beacon amid the gloom and national introspection. 'The truth,' says a Thatcherite minister of the period, 'is that I think they didn't know quite what they were doing. They didn't realise what they were unleashing.'

6

SELL

'We took the Concorde and were in the Merrill Lynch New York office by nine-thirty in the morning and by ten o'clock were back on the street, figuratively speaking, cheques in our hands for the unexpired terms of our three-year contracts. We took the twelve o'clock Concorde and were home for dinner.'

Sir John Craven

In the autumn of 1983 the partners in most City firms faced a choice. If they were lucky, the outfit which they had joined many years previously perhaps had an august name and a serious reputation rooted in many decades of trusted trading in shares or government gilts in the network of firms clustered around the Stock Exchange. Being a partner meant they were co-owners of the firm, a status which came with obvious advantages and disadvantages. They won when the firm did well. But their money, even their house, was on the line in a difficult year of trading, which made it sensible to pay attention if any of the firm's younger, racier types claimed to have discovered an ingenious way for the firm to make more money. If the theoretically bright youngster was badly wrong about his suggested technique or trade, the partner stood to lose a lot personally. The partner had a strong incentive either to pay attention when risky ideas were mentioned, or to foster a generally conservative approach and clearly established hierarchy so that his staff would not cost him his house in Surrey. But 1983 and 1984 were good years on the Stock Exchange, with prices rising. London was once again opening up to the world. The Americans and

Japanese who had arrived in the 1960s and 70s were scaling up their operations. The Stock Exchange stood to be transformed and while partners might be proud of their firm's high standing, tradition would only get you so far in the new era. But the firm they part owned had experience, contacts, wisdom and insight into the working of the markets at just the right moment when Wall Street and Tokyo were looking to London, partly because of its perfect position in the international time zone halfway between the two rival centres, and partly because of the early glimmer of reflected glamour from its trailblazing free market, reformist government. Suddenly, the old firm in which the partners had worked their way up was potentially rather valuable to new outside shareholders. And even if it were not, there was a chance it might seem convincingly valuable to potential purchasers for long enough for a foreign or a British bank to sign a large cheque for the partners. What would you do?

That was the question facing hundreds of partners in the second half of 1983 and in 1984. The City and its dining rooms and drinking dens buzzed with incessant gossip about who would be bought and for how much, as the senior figures tried to make sense of what was coming and ensure they made the right decisions. The confusion was understandable. It wasn't as though the agreement of July 1983 between Goodison and Parkinson, with the Bank of England guiding the way, laid out any detailed plan for what everyone involved should do next. The looming revolution posed an assortment of challenges, some of them bewildering. The best stockbroking and jobbing partnerships were targets and the merchant banks – which traditionally simply advised clients doing deals and placed customers' orders to buy shares or securities via independent brokers – were about to find themselves up against American banks that combined all these activities under one roof with much bigger resources. Merchant banks such as Warburgs, Schroder's, Lazard, Barings and others had to consider whether or not they wanted to buy stockbroking and jobbing firms, and integrate them into their businesses. But how might it be done? Who should they buy and for how much? The risk of getting it wrong could involve extinction and the premature death of a long-standing City firm. Get it right and a large villa on the Côte d'Azur and a mortgage-free existence was in prospect. There was going to be a lot of money to be made very soon.

What almost everyone in authority at the time could agree on was that the UK firms were under-capitalised for an increasingly international business. The fear was that they were way too small, with too little money, to compete with the Americans and Japanese. Where those in authority differed was over the extent to which British ownership mattered. At the Bank of England, that guardian of British economic prestige, David Walker in particular privately encouraged the British to be imaginative in dreaming up mergers and new agglomerations of firms, in the hope that several success-ful British champions might be formed to compete on equal terms with the Americans and Japanese. With Cecil Parkinson gone quickly – following his resignation from the cabinet in October 1983 over his affair with his secretary Sara Keays – the minister who pronounced publicly on such matters for the government was Alex Fletcher, the Minister for Corporate and Consumer Affairs. Ostensibly, Fletcher and his colleagues agreed. In an interview with the *Financial Times* published on 13 December 1983 he declared: 'If we want to maintain London as a prominent market, I think it is very important that the Stock Exchange and the majority of the institutions here should remain very firmly in British hands.'

In reality, these expressions of government concern were cosmetic. How could they be otherwise when Thatcherism rested on the idea of open markets and exposing institutions to competi-tion to produce dynamism? The government had spent several years refusing to intervene in defence of manufacturing industry, and it was entering a bruising battle with the miners and trade union mili-tants. It could hardly now try to prevent foreign takeovers at the Stock Exchange. In the Commons, when Fletcher was asked that year about the impact of potential mergers in the City he stressed that the market must take its course. 'It is a matter for the commercial judgement of the City and not for the government how the institutions best organise themselves to meet the future.'

One of the key figures in shaping how exactly the firms would organise themselves was the financier John Craven. For a firm that was to play a leading role in the birth of a new City of London, the name chosen – Phoenix Securities – was perfect. After all, the mythological bird rising from the flames – cited by the Ancient Greeks and the Romans and adopted as a symbol by the early Christians – represents reinvention, rebirth and resurrection. In the early 1980s, Craven certainly needed to resurrect his hitherto promising career. His professional life was suddenly looking cursed after he'd accepted a job at the US brokerage and wealth manager Merrill Lynch, to head their international operation based in London. It proved to be a huge mistake, although in the process Craven and one of his friends had gained a useful insight into how tough US bankers could be once the wooing was over and the new hire had turned up for work.[1] David Montagu (later the 4th Baron Swaythling) – a tough-minded and witty City aristocrat with a love of horse-racing, wine and winning in business – felt he and the younger Craven had been the victims of an American confidence trick by Merrill Lynch.[2] Montagu was already a City veteran, having chaired the family bank Samuel Montagu before it was sold to the Midland Bank in 1973. He then ran Orion, the joint-venture or consortium bank involving six foreign banks that briefly became a leading player in the European market. When he left he received thirty-six job offers, including one from Merrill Lynch. Both Montagu and Craven were led to believe that the other had already definitely agreed to join, Montagu as chairman and Craven as chief executive, and on that basis they signed up. It was a mission doomed from the moment they turned up for work in early 1980, with all of the authority residing in the New York headquarters and the culture of an American institution definitely not to their liking. Faxes containing irritating requests about office partitions, and other footling matters winged their way across the Atlantic. Montagu tended to throw the missives in the bin while Craven drafted rude replies.

The clash of cultures was even more apparent when Donald Regan, the chairman of Merrill Lynch in New York, announced that he wanted to visit London in 1980 to meet senior figures in the City and then go to Scotland to play golf. Regan was in line to become Ronald Reagan's first Treasury Secretary after the forthcoming US election, but was rather obviously out of his natural habitat on what may have been his first trip to London. A stellar Establishment guest list – including the Chancellor of the Exchequer and his wife, the Governor of the Bank of England and his wife, Arnold Weinstock of GEC, and Christopher and Mary Soames was assembled by Montagu and his wife for a dinner party at their home in honour of the Regans. 'It was,' said Montagu later, 'a spectacular disaster. Mr Regan barely opened his mouth.'[3] The then rumour that he would be appointed US Treasury Secretary, which duly happened later that year, prompted Geoffrey Howe in his thank-you letter to the Montagus to say, 'if you're right about this man becoming Secretary to the US Treasury, then God help the Western world'. Montagu and Craven wanted out. 'After eleven months,' said Craven, 'we took the Concorde and were in the Merrill Lynch New York office by nine-thirty in the morning and by ten o'clock were back on the street, figuratively speaking, cheques in our hands for the unexpired terms of our three-year contracts. We took the twelve o'clock Concorde and were home for dinner.'[4] Dealing with Wall Street and accommodating the American interest in doing a lot more business out of London was clearly not going to be straightforward.

An unemployed and worried Craven set up on his own, advising clients that included the Mexican government, the IMF and Canadian gold-miners. When he needed a name for his small business his wife suggested Phoenix. Hopefully, she told him, you'll rise from the ashes of your disastrous career at Warburg and Merrill Lynch. Luckily for Craven, his blend of skills and contacts left him ideally placed to advise City firms on how they might make sense of the changing landscape of international finance. He had seen how the Americans operated and he knew the City. His Phoenix Securities would act as advisor in more than two-thirds of the thirty marriages made by City firms as they raced to get ready for Big Bang, giving him and his small number of colleagues an enormous amount of influence in the process.

A Los Angeles bank, Security Pacific Corporation, moved first, even before the Parkinson/Goodison deal was announced. It bought a 29.9 per cent stake in the broker Hoare Govett. The rules were altered in stages to allow foreigners to buy larger stakes and then to take over British stockbrokers and jobbers. Among London's merchant banks in the early 1980s the most sophisticated players had been thinking ahead about this possibility already. At Warburg, the firm's guiding light flickered out in October 1982. Before Siegmund Warburg's death, the most influential British merchant banker of his generation had been amenable to the idea of Warburg's expanding its business, buying a stockbroker, and becoming what the Americans talked of as a fully-fledged investment bank. The old man's fear, his friends noted, was of excessive expansion and greed running riot. He had witnessed the economic and political impact of the Wall Street Crash on Germany in the early 1930s and seen the carnage it wrought. Men and women in the midst of a boom have a tendency to forget, but he could see the need for the firm he'd founded to adapt and change. In 1984, Warburg's parent company Mercury Securities bought a 29.9 per cent stake in Akroyd & Smithers, the leading jobbing firm, for £41m, a purchase followed by the government broker – Mullens, the men in the silk top hats – and the stockbroker Rowe & Pitman. The disappearance of Mullens – bought pretty much as a favour to the Bank of England, which did not want the firm that had traditionally handled the distribution of gilts humiliated – was another harbinger of change. The Prime Minister no longer wanted gilts – UK debt – to be handled by an exclusive arrangement via Mullens. It would be organised through a new office based inside the Bank of England. Warburg's purchases cost a total of £200m.

There was a further freedom that did not apply in the US. In Britain, without the separation between investment banks and retail banks that had been enforced, although gradually less assiduously, on Wall Street, there was also the possibility that the high-street banks could expand too and enter the securities business. A big British name, such as Barclays, NatWest or Lloyds, might buy a broker or two and seek to go beyond straightforward retail and business banking. Eventually, a small Scottish institution, the Royal Bank of Scotland, would (almost unimaginably) buy the much larger Nat West, expand its investment banking division and become, briefly, the biggest bank in the world before blowing up in spectacular fashion in 2008. All that lay far in the future.

Craven's phone was ringing with increasing frequency, as senior partners in other stockbroking and jobbing firms wanted advice on how they might sell themselves or establish new firms. Craven attempted to impress upon them that they should be careful and try to choose a suitor who might be a good match, rather than just falling for the buyer offering the most. They didn't always listen and many of the partners who stood to benefit from a sale had little expectation of staying on. They could pocket a million, or several multiples of that sum, and move on. To most of the population, a million pounds is still, today, a lot of money. In the mid-1980s it was undeniably a lot more money. It is estimated that more than 750 millionaires were created in the sell-off, with the total price paid for firms estimated as having been close to £1.5bn.

The process was complicated, partly because firms wanted to keep their discussions secret from each other. This meant it was also not always possible to get prospective buyers and targets in the same room. When Salomon Brothers in New York expressed an interest in possibly buying Wedd Durlacher, the Phoenix team suggested a fun trip to Wall Street, but it emerged that one of the most senior figures at Wedd Durlacher could not travel because he did not have a passport and had never left Britain, an unthinkable concept in finance thirty years later.[5] Wedd Durlacher was one of the leading jobbing firms, and had been run by Jack Durlacher, father of Nick Durlacher who had gone off to work at LIFFE. What Craven and his colleague Martin Smith helped secure eventually was a deal with Barclays, after talks with Kleinwort Benson got nowhere. The amount split between the partners for selling Wedd Durlacher was a pot of £100m. Barclays also purchased the stockbroker de Zoete, fusing it with Barclays merchant banking operation and creating the investment banking operation BZW. When the stockbroking firm Scrimgeour Kemp-Gee was bought by the American Citicorp, the price was £50m. The high-street bank NatWest purchased the jobber Bisgood Bishop, and the US bank Citicorp also spent £20m acquiring 29.9 per cent of Vickers de Costa, along with its operation in the Far East. N.M. Rothschild bought a chunk of Smith Brothers. The American firm Chase Manhattan swallowed Simon & Coates and Laurie Millman, two brokers.

Some firms found it difficult to decide because they had so many potential purchasers. Dundas Hamilton, the senior partner at Fielding, Newson-Smith, had to make the choice on behalf of his firm: 'At one time we had six different suitors,' he told an interviewer in 1988. 'They were American, a European bank and a London clearing bank . . . we thought we were quite a snip to be taken over. Ultimately we went to the National Westminster Bank and it turned out to be rather a tragedy.'[6] The UK merchant bank Morgan Grenfell could not make up its mind until it was too late and purchased a lesser jobbing firm, Pinchin Denny, for £21m. Already there were signs of trouble ahead, when senior Morgan Grenfell people briefed dismissively during the talks about their new purchase, describing the jobbers as looking like traders from a street market. The flaring up of class tensions between jobbers and brokers and grand merchant bankers did not suggest that a happy partnership was in prospect.

Goldman Sachs, Morgan Stanley and Salomon Brothers opted to hire staff to boost their own operations in London, rather than paying to buy an established firm, which may have been a better use of resources. Not all the old names allowed themselves to be swallowed up. Both Cazenove and Lazard decided to stand alone. Lazard stood back from the securities business entirely, choosing to remain as a merchant bank that solely advised clients, and Cazenove, the appointed stockbroker to the Queen, went its own way. The joint senior partner John Kemp-Welch, and other senior figures including David Mayhew, were determined to preserve the firm as an independent partnership. Clever old 'Caz' came up with possibly the most ingenious solution to the need for new capital, tapping twelve leading institutions for a loan of £32m that gave the investors zero influence on the firm but bolstered its position.

The sums seem small now relative to what followed in term of profits, losses and mega-deals in the next few decades, but the stakes at the time were high for a good reason. What only an insightful few understood at the time was that the entire basis of international finance and the business of money was changing dramatically, presenting new opportunities and challenges not just in shares, but also for those who traded in government and corporate debt, and increasingly from the 1980s, bonds made up of pools of mortgage debt. The roots of that revolution lay in President Nixon's decision in the early 1970s to uncouple the dollar from gold. Until that point, a dollar was worth a fixed amount of gold and was theoretically redeemable for said gold. The Americans had taken over leadership in the currency field from the British as the US economy surged to dominance in the twentieth century. Finally ending the connection to gold meant the dollar and other countries would be worth purely what the market decided. A central bank could print or create as much as it wanted, as long as (and this was a vital caveat) those in the market place buying and selling the debt – investors, traders – believed the government in question was good for it. This new post-gold approach facilitated a debt and credit explosion in the world's largest economy that was already well underway by the early 1980s. In 1970 the total debt of the US government stood at $370,918,706,949.93 (almost $371bn). By 1980 it was nudging $1 trillion at $907,701,000,000. By the year 2000 it was on its way to $6 trillion at $5,674,178,209,886. There was a brief flurry of excitement when it seemed under President Clinton and then in the early years of the George W. Bush first term that the US government debt pile might diminish or even eventually disappear. As I write, it is heading for $20 trillion.

Of course, that government debt fluctuates as a percentage of GDP – the output of the economy – as the economy grows or suffers a recession, and it is also eroded by bouts of inflation. Debt is necessary. It has been the fuel of economies, even before William III's allies established the Bank of England to lend the Crown money to rebuild the English navy. In good times and bad it can help power growth. The US economy has grown strongly since the 1970s despite its periodic detours into disasterville. But it wasn't just government debt that shot up. Private debt was growing sharply too, as homeownership was extended and access to credit cards went from being the preserve of an elite to a staple of life on main street. In the US, the government also underpinned home owner- ship through a network of state subsidies. There were attempts to check this debt expansion, such as when the tough-minded Federal Reserve chairman Paul Volcker, a Democrat appointed by President Carter in 1979 and reappointed by President Reagan four years later, instituted a credit squeeze in 1981 to reduce the money supply and bring down inflation. But while that initiated a lull it did not seri- ously impede the tidal wave of debt and opportunities for trading it.

Put that together with the innovations that had their roots in London in the Eurobond market – companies borrowing to fund expansion, restructuring or infrastructure – and the scope was immense for financiers buying that debt, distributing it and making a profit funnelling it to willing customers (the object of bond trad- ers' derision) who wanted the stream of income (the coupon) that a bond paid or the chance of selling when the price improved. Acting as the conduit between those who needed to sell the debt of govern- ments and companies, and investors seeking to buy them, put the hungriest firms at the apex of a rapidly expanding market.

The 1980s is often talked about in popular parlance as though the Reagan and Thatcher marketplace revolution was mainly about equities – stocks and shares in individual companies – but that was only part of it. Debt was a key element of the story. As the numbers got larger, the slice that firms and their traders could take and pay themselves got bigger too. In the early to mid-1980s the two would fuse together, debt markets and stock markets apparently in perfect harmony. Finance or debt was readily available for companies wanting to construct takeovers, and rumours or confirmation that a company might be in line to be bought pushed up its share price. This had long happened to an extent, but the scale was now mind-blowing. A Mergers and Acquisitions (M&A) boom in which household names would be sold or restructured – on borrowed money, leverage – was gathering pace. The junk bond business – which began with the aggressive trading of the high-risk low-grade debt of firms that traditionally had been looked down on by Wall Street because they were small and unglamorous – was also getting going in the US. On parts of Wall Street this climate produced quasi-criminal chicanery, and in some cases outright criminal behaviour in breach of the securities laws introduced in the 1930s. The scale of the money to be made in late 1970s and early 1980s New York increased the value of inside information about companies' intentions and tempted the greedy to trade it for gain.

Even on the legal side of the line, the Americans had understood the implications of the debt explosion earlier and better than anyone. In Michael Lewis's hilarious account of life at Salomon Brothers in the 1980s – *Liar's Poker* – he explains how bond traders became what the novelist Tom Wolfe later termed 'Masters of the Universe', cursing and shouting their way to mastery, crushing rivals and generally behaving like a highly unpleasant and money-obsessed version of the Muppets. Bafflingly, the sharp-eyed Wolfe was allowed onto the forty-first floor at Salomon Brothers in New York to undertake his research for the 1980s novel that would become *Bonfire of the Vanities*. We should be clear: the worst excesses of those he observed might have been reprehensible, but the men (mainly men) doing it weren't stupid. The governments of the Western world were taking a punt on debt, both public and household, and the bond traders and salesmen were responding rationally to the appearance of a giant gold-plated opportunity. American investors searching for higher returns were also becoming increasingly interested in the outside world and in buying up shares in foreign companies. American international pre-eminence in politics and culture was reflected in the internationalisation of its financial markets. The business of money was becoming less constrained by borders, which is illustrated by data from the US Federal Reserve. In 1965 the total US holdings of foreign corporate equities (shares in companies) were tiny, just $5bn's worth. In 1975 it was $9.6bn. By 1985 it would stand at $44.4bn. It kept on going, hitting $790.6bn in 1995 and almost $7 trillion in 2014.[7]

These epic forces were being unleashed as London got ready for Big Bang. Lewis, the unlikely bond salesman with a degree in art history, had, he acknowledged, lucked himself onto the graduate trainee scheme at a point when Wall Street was in transition. Banks and brokerages that had traditionally drawn much of their talent from the shop floor, promoting boys from the backroom, now wanted to hire as many high-achieving graduates from the leading American universities. This was not difficult. Such graduates had heard there was a lot more money to be made on Wall Street than in other industries, and fought to get themselves hired.

The firm Lewis had joined, Salomon Brothers, had had a relatively small operation in London since the 1970s, although in the 1980s under Charles McVeigh it was keen to grow. It was there that Lewis was posted, to a cramped office with a view of St Paul's Cathedral and not much else. It was Salomon that had also given Valerie Thompson, from a very different background, her break. Like the old-school traders on Wall Street, she had come up through the administrative route without formal qualifications. What mattered was that she was bright and ballsy with an instinct for numbers and the psychology of trading. Both graduates and the autodidacts of the trading floor could prosper, it seemed. What counted was ability, and profits.

In London, there was certainly suddenly a lot more money around and the pace of promotion, as well as excitement, was quickening. Davina Walter was in her early thirties when she was poached by Henderson in the mid-1980s to become a fund manager. On Wall Street, the stealing of staff and offers of vast salary increases was more aggressive at that point, as New York had a head start following its reforms in 1975. In contrast, Walter didn't want to offend her boss at Cazenove, who in the event was very civilised and understanding about her move. He was married to a Henderson. 'When I joined Henderson's I was employee one hundred and seventy-nine or eighty. Within two years there were over six hundred people.'[8] But not all poaching could be quite so polite. The booming jobs market created obvious opportunities for an innovative new generation of head-hunters who were prepared to be more audacious. Philippa Rose launched her recruitment agency in 1981 when she was only twenty-one. Rose had worked for less than two years in corporate finance at Kleinwort Benson and then for a recruitment agency. When she thought she might go mad interviewing any more secretaries she worked out how to start a business, and her employer invested £8,000 for 40 per cent of her new company, with Rose and her father scraping together the rest needed. Her targets were the brightest fellow youngsters who had joined the City, then realised that they were unsuited to their role and in need of a more lucrative challenge in another bank or firm. She offered to match them to the right institutions. The approach was daring and iconoclastic. Rose refused to deal with HR departments and went straight to department heads and CEOs, developing close relationships with them. In year one she made a profit of £11,000 and expanded her team. 'From there the trajectory was vertical for twenty years,' she recalls.

Ross Jones also enjoyed a rapid rise, though in his case it was through staying with the firm he had joined in 1977, despite having no real idea what it did. The answer was that Gerrard & National and the other discount houses provided liquidity to the market, as they had always done, lending it to the banks when they needed it and mopping up a profit, although they were also diversifying and turning themselves into fully-fledged investment houses that looked after more money for clients. Jones rose quickly and in 1984, on returning from a posting in Spain, he was appointed assistant director, making him senior to his former bosses. He was put on the gilts desk to learn and it was very exciting. His salary rocketed; he bought a flat and got his first car: a Porsche. Six months later, his salary was raised again and six months after that it more than doubled.

The head-hunters and fast-rising young professionals, traders and bankers would soon be known by a new word. In 1984 the term 'yuppie' was only beginning to enter the mainstream in the UK, although it rapidly became the catch-all nomenclature for young City workers, advertising executives, people wearing red braces, London estate agents or anyone who seemed to be suddenly earning a great deal of money and spending it ostentatiously on German cars, champagne and property. The yuppie as a species (meaning young urban professional) was first identified in the US in 1980 by Dan Rottenberg, an American journalist, writing a feature for *Chicago* magazine about the phenomenon of urban regeneration.[9] He noticed that affluent young professionals were declining to follow their predecessors to the suburbs, choosing instead to reclaim run-down but potentially valuable properties in the city. They sought urban excitement and were prepared, in numbers, to take over and renovate entire neighbourhoods. Yuppie was a good nickname that evoked an obvious contrast with the dazed, anti-materialistic ethos of the late 1960s and early 1970s hippie. A fair few yuppies in the US had been hippies first, before they got jobs and joined banks, or brokerages, or became architects or media executives.

In London, the word took on different class-based connotations, until there was confusion. Were City yuppies *arrivistes* or aristos on the make? The caricatures would overlap and by the middle of the decade it was a reliable, easy standby for any television news crew looking for a way to illustrate a package for the evening news about class, or the north–south divide, or the decline of manufacturing, to find a City wine bar and film the shenanigans. After hours it was not difficult to find people laughing and drinking champagne. Inevitably, their brighter colleagues declined to say anything. But some of the bolder and brasher types were prepared to burble on camera about how much money there was to be made.

This was one of the curious aspects of the period. On the one hand the smorgasbord of opportunity lent itself to largesse, celebration and intoxication, either to cope with the excitement or to come down afterwards. 'Some of my colleagues, not all, some, were coked up pretty much continuously,' is how one wealthy veteran, then a trader, remembers it. Simultaneously, it produced a shift to seriousness as the hours started to get longer in preparation for Big Bang and the need for a clear head when handling everbigger numbers became obvious. For that reason lunch had had it, or at least the old-school alcohol-fuelled lunch was on the way out. Not everyone drank pre-Big Bang, of course. David Mayhew, of Cazenove, decided in the 1970s that he would forgo alcohol during the working day in favour of clarity. But abstinence was not the norm. John Craven recalled lunches in Hambros' partners room before the 1980s: 'Partners would drift in and out. There was wine and port and no business talked at all. It was the atmosphere of a languid country-house lunch on a Sunday.'[10]

The old-school British moneymen already had long had a reputation among their American cousins for laziness, and those late starts and languid lunches were the nub of it. Never has the different meaning attached on either side of the Atlantic to the word 'pissed' mattered more. American firms pushing into London were not going to be very pleased – they would be pissed – if their staff went native and got pissed at lunchtime. Some Americans attempted to try the London way of lunching, although their efforts seem to have been driven as much by an anthropological interest in meeting the pickled specimens of the old City. Who really wanted to be 'out to lunch' when the office in New York rang demanding to know about a deal or a trade? When it was lunchtime in London the day was only kicking off on Wall Street five hours behind.

But that is not to imply the Americans were dull. Robert L. Hamburger had first arrived in 1971 with Chase, spending time in London and Rome, where in two years he dealt with the Vatican's account and while playing golf with the priest who ran the Vatican Bank said he learnt more about banking then than in the other forty years of his career combined. 'The American banker called Bob Hamburger. You couldn't make it up,' says one of the leading figures in London investment banking. Hamburger joined Goldman Sachs in 1979 and was part of the team in the 1980s that turned the institution from Goldman Who? – in London terms – into an investment banking behemoth. He later set up on his own as an advisor in M&A, bought a racehorse and subsequently published a number of erotic novels, including *Angels and Felons* and *My Saucy Wife*. There were many things that leading bankers or stockbrokers in London did pre-Big Bang, but writing erotic novels was not high on the list.

The adjustment to a more aggressive American approach was tricky for the Brits. Philippa Rose's clients who were placed with US banks in London could scarcely believe the difference in ruthlessness. They were shocked by how different the mentality was: 'The Americans were all about the deal. The British were about trying to offer the best advice. The Americans were "bugger that" we want the money.' A leading gilt-edged market maker of the period was most unimpressed with what he encountered: 'The morality – or the lack of it – of the American investment banks had to be seen to be believed. It was disgusting.' But the Americans did not arrive fully formed. As David Mayhew saw it, the Americans were still learning about the London outlook and the different attitude to risk. Although the Brits might have seemed more laconic and laid back, they were used to being a little more freewheeling and unsupervised in their dealings. Unlike the Americans, the Brits were not – yet – locked in by the bureaucracy of risk managers and compliance people with which US banks and brokerages were well stocked, because so much American business was regulated by law, a legacy of public disgust over the Great Crash of 1929. The Brits, used to self-regulation and some insider trading masquerading as wisdom, liked risk more than they let on. And while all the chatter was of London needing an injection of American dynamism, where had the Eurobond market come from anyway? Not Wall Street. One of the single most important innovations in the markets in the second half of the twentieth century, which had mushroomed into an international multi-trillion dollar business, came from London in the 1960s. It had not happened within the Stock Exchange, of course, which added to the sense that Nicholas Goodison's colleagues had rather missed an opportunity. Now, the stockbrokers and jobbers had to get on and catch up.

At the Stock Exchange, Nicholas Goodison and his colleagues knew they did not have the luxury of time. What had sounded in July 1983 like a long-distant date – the three-year deadline for reform – was racing in. At the same time, a switch to screen-based trading was planned, moving trading from the traditional floor of the exchange face to face towards traders using the prices on their screen and buying and selling by telephone. George Hayter, head of the Exchange's information services division, and his team were trying to build something that could cope with the anticipated enormous increase in trading volumes. The original intention had been to start afresh, and construct a bespoke computer system. In 1984, Hayter explained why that would not be possible. 'There is a wide river to be crossed and time only to build a Bailey Bridge,' he said in a reference to the temporary structures favoured by Allied engineers in the Second World War.[11]

There would also be a D-Day, it was decided by the Stock Exchange Council: a single day, an appointed hour in 1986, on which it would all happen, rather than the switch to screen-based trading being phased in. Who first uttered the phrase Big Bang to describe it, in the context of the City rather than physics? Some credit Martin Jacomb (of Kleinwort Benson, a director of the Bank of England and later a director of Barclays). David Walker of the Bank of England thinks it was Douglas Dawkins at the Bank of England who first said: 'This is a cosmological event, a Big Bang.'

Either way it was agreed that it was best to do it all at once and create an impact. The wider financial revolution was also, if truth be told, already underway. The Thatcher government needed the City's help to implement what had grown from being a vague aspiration in opposition into a full-scale privatisation programme. And that meant shifting a lot of shares. In the summer of 1982 the government had announced its intention to sell British Telecommunications in 1984. The City had the venue, the expertise, the interest from American investors and the ability to move large amounts of capital in and out of the country since the abolition of exchange controls. The government had state-owned industries and billions of pounds in assets that it was ideologically committed to selling. Together, Thatcher's ministers, the merchant banks, stockbrokers and advertising agencies were about to push through some of the biggest sell-offs in the history of capitalism, in the process transforming the structure of the British economy and executing a manoeuvre that would be copied around the world.

7

OPPORTUNITIES

'If you see Sid . . . Tell him!'
Advert promoting the sale of British Gas shares to the public

Once it became clear that Mrs Thatcher's plans were going to be aligned with the interests of the dealmakers in the Square Mile, the scepticism among parts of the City's elite began to fade. The tricky negotiations on the future of the Stock Exchange were one thing, and Thatcher the outsider had needed to be assured in 1983 by her Chancellor Nigel Lawson that the agreement with Goodison and the Stock Exchange was not a stitch-up perpetrated by an old-boy network. But the Stock Exchange was not the City; the Exchange was one element, albeit an important element, of a much larger financial machine that the government needed to access. The Tories now required its help to implement one of the most daring and transformative programmes of the era, namely the privatisation of large parts of British industry and infrastructure.

Since the nationalisations undertaken during and shortly after the Second World War, the government on behalf of the taxpayer owned Britain's largest oil company, the airports, the national airline, a national steel company, gas, water, the telecommunications monopoly, British Rail, and much more besides. The workforce of the nationalised industries in the early 1980s was an astonishing 1.75m strong and between them they produced 10 per cent of national output. Several governments since the 1950s had attempted sell-offs, and there was limited denationalisation and then renationalisation, but state ownership seemed to be a fixed feature of the British landscape. A handful of Liberals and a few Conservatives explained that this was unhealthy. Despite David Howell MP, the future father in-law of Chancellor George Osborne, penning a Conservative pamphlet in 1970 in which the term 'privatisation' was first used, it remained a remote aspiration. The Heath government's subsequent failure all but killed off such thinking for a while and amid economic chaos Heath partly nationalised the air engine company Rolls-Royce and assorted shipyards. In 1975, following the return of Harold Wilson to Number 10 the previous year, the government had even acquired the controlling share of a large and broken-down car manufacturer in the form of British Leyland. The company rapidly became a byword for British decline. When the Prime Minister James Callaghan needed new official cars, two Rovers 3.5 were ordered from the company. Once thirty-four mechanical faults had been fixed and the cars had been made bomb-proof they were ready for Callaghan's use on official business. His advisor, Bernard Donoughue, recorded in his diary what happened when one of the cars was taken for a spin in the summer of 1978: 'He [the Prime Minister] decided to open the window for some fresh air and pressed the button which does this electronically. The result was that the window immediately fell in on his lap.'[1] Callaghan and his broken car window symbolise perfectly a late 1970s creeping national decrepitude that Thatcher was determined to address.

Despite the shortcomings, to many on the Left the continued existence of nationalised industries was a matter of pride, reflecting the dominance of collectivist thinking and the noble elevation of fuller employment above efficiency and the profit motive. To the small group of Thatcherites who won control of the Tory Party in 1975, excessive state ownership of industry was instinctively an abomination, a manifestation of government control giving customers a poor deal and hampering competition, investment and innovation. That said, they did not know how, exactly, to proceed. The first Thatcher administration arrived in office without a fully worked plan in May 1979, and during the run-up to the general election when Thatcher's shadow cabinet discussed the possibility of 'denationalisation' it was agreed not to make their early thinking public. Once in office, senior figures in the government, the Chancellor Geoffrey Howe and a handful of other ministers including Howell at Energy, John Nott at Trade, Keith Joseph, and Nigel Lawson working for Howe at the Treasury, were determined to push forward on the subject from the start.

Another much more junior but significant figure in the development of what became mass privatisation, someone who pushed the idea in Thatcherite circles, was John Redwood, then working in the City. While Redwood was academically highly gifted – a fellow of Oxford's All Souls no less – it is fair to say that he is not famed for his social skills. That other-worldly awkwardness gave him a remorselessly logical way of looking at the world that would later earn him the newspaper nickname of Spock. But it did give Redwood an advantage in one important regard, in that he did not care for convention. If the nationalised industries were unprofitable, creaking under the weight of their bureaucratic inefficiency, bedevilled by catastrophically poor industrial relations, then why not admit it clearly and sell them back into the private sector? That was the central premise of his influential book – a long forgotten text that endeared him to the Thatcherites – published in November 1980. In *Public Enterprise in Crisis: The Future of Nationalised Industries*, Redwood mapped out the beginning of a way to return such industries to the public sector by selling them, via the City. The Redwood link was important because he was at the merchant bank N.M. Rothschild, the bank that Thatcher had dismissed as 'that red bank' when she got a hard time during lunch there in 1975. That moment of awkwardness now forgotten, N.M. Rothschild would eventually become one of the institutions handling privatisations for Thatcher.

As it became apparent that Thatcher's ministers were serious about the scale of what was going to be attempted, the merchant banks and Stock Exchange firms readied themselves to assist. In that regard, N.M. Rothschild had several advantages. Not only was young Redwood – more Thatcherite than Thatcher – an evangelist for the privatisation message; more importantly, Evelyn Rothschild, the kingpin of the institution since his cousin Jacob had left N.M. Rothschild in a dispute over strategy in 1980, had hired the highly experienced and well-connected Michael Richardson from Cazenove the following year. Richardson had a direct Thatcher connection in that their sons had been at Harrow at the same time. His appointment was described by David Scholey at Warburg as the worst news he had received all year, because he knew it would bring Rothschild so much business.

With his charm and willingness to deal with some questionable figures such as the crooked media tycoon Robert Maxwell, Richardson was made for the high pomp of 1980s deal making. The City was the family business – insurance in his father's case – and when Michael bailed out of Cambridge after a few months he had gravitated towards money and markets, forging a career at Panmure Gordon in the 1960s, where he first represented Maxwell. That association led to him being ostracised when Maxwell's shady dealings over Pergamon were condemned to such an extent that Maxwell was judged famously in a Board of Trade inquiry as 'not a fit and proper person' to run a public company. The Maxwell connection did not put off Cazenove from hiring Richardson, and he was there until 1981 when he failed to make senior partner. Evelyn Rothschild swooped and offered him the post of Managing Director at N.M. Rothschild. Richardson was, according to Nigel Lawson, at first sight too suave and smooth to be true[2], but his courtesy and good manners made him an exemplary networker in business and politics, someone skilled in bringing in new business at just the right moment with the Thatcherites in the ascendency.

Not everyone in the City was impressed with Thatcher and anxious to assist. David Montagu, Baron Swaythling, was so appalled by the behaviour he witnessed at a meeting, and her rude treatment of officials and colleagues, that he declared he would have nothing more to do with her. At Cazenove there had always been more enthusiasm for Thatcher. Indeed, the firm had on the quiet helped finance her office in opposition when she was finding it difficult to raise funds. There was much enthusiasm for what she was attempting to achieve. David Mayhew, a rising star and future senior partner, felt that complacent old Britain was a poor country sinking into bedraggled irrelevance. Opening up the City to new capital and foreign investment and privatising the state-owned industries would, he was convinced, give the UK a chance of reinventing itself.

The great 1980s state sell-off began small. Initial minor steps towards what was then known only as asset disposal were taken in Howe's first Budget in 1979 in which £1bn of asset sales were announced. Thatcher also established a small cabinet committee to prepare more state enterprises for sale. Lawson emphasised the direction in a lecture in 1980 in which he identified British Airways as being among the first candidates, although only a small number of ministers were enthusiastic. Even the then head of the Number 10 Policy Unit – John Hoskyns – did not press the case initially, despite his reputation for bold thinking. The British Airways sale was eventually postponed until much later, because the airline was embroiled in a tricky legal case[3], but when Lawson was appointed Energy Secretary in the autumn of 1981, replacing Howell, he pushed through a number of sales. On 19 October it was announced that the government planned to sell its share in the oil-producing parts of British Gas and BNOC. Already the idea was germinating that Britain's entire electricity and gas industries should be sold off when the time was right.

None of this, even enthusiasts such as Lawson admitted later, was initially popular with the British public. Throughout, the *Daily Mirror* referred to it as 'the great Tory sell-off', and not in a flattering way. It did not help that two of the early, smaller sales went badly off course in different ways. The government-owned Amersham International, selling medical and industrial research radioactive isotopes, was sold too cheaply in 1982. N.M Rothschild and Morgan Grenfell were the advisors to the government and the company, and the low price meant there was a rush for shares – meaning they were over-subscribed. On the first day the shares traded at 40p above their offer price of 142p, leaving a rather large profit for investors at the public expense. The extent of the mistake compelled a horrified Lawson to hold an inquiry. Critics said that state assets theoretically owned by all were being sold off to investors too cheaply by the City. Such concerns would be highlighted relentlessly by the opposition parties and internal Tory opponents from the rival wing of the Conservative Party who saw the Thatcherites as reckless radicals prepared to risk national division in pursuit of ideological aims. When it came to the next sale – the much bigger Britoil – Lawson vowed to avoid a repeat of the poor publicity around Amersham, and the offer was under-subscribed.

It is not difficult to work out why these privatisations mattered so much to the generation of City leaders at banks such as Warburg, Rothschild, Kleinwort Benson and Cazenove. The government selling its stakes meant work, prestige and fees. The government would select City advisors, sometimes more than one merchant bank, to help it construct the business case, arrive at a valuation and handle the sale. Together a number could underwrite the offer for fees. They could also sub-underwrite the shares to hundreds of smaller City firms, dispersing the shares via the jobbers. There was another benefit. Even if they did not get such work themselves, it might help to generate a rising market, increased volumes and a sense of possibility and expansion. Rising optimism was certainly apparent in late 1982 and 1983. In Debbie Moore, the entrepreneur behind the dance studios and clothing line Pineapple, the Stock Exchange had its first ever woman to head a company being floated, on the smaller market (USM, the Unsecuritised Market). On the day itself in November 1982, Moore was pictured standing in the middle of the Stock Exchange floor, hands on hips, looking like the embodiment of go-getting early 1980s culture. Around her stood a crowd of mostly male workers and jobbers, surveying the scene and not looking entirely comfortable. Her success only ten years after women had first even been allowed on the floor itself was a vivid example of how much had changed. Here was an entrepreneur floating her own company, and in the 'leisure' and fitness business too, a type of activity that was emblematic of the self-improvement decade.

There were other advances for women. On 1 January 1983, Mary Baker became the first ever female member of the board of Barclays

Bank. In early 1983, the Unit Trust Association also got its first female chairman in Audrey Head of Hill Samuel. Unit trusts are a simple form of investment in which bundles of investments are bought from a money manager, with the hope that the manager can outperform the market in boom and bust. Their spread – there were 500 of them on sale from various companies by early 1983 – was more evidence that smaller investors were playing the expanding market. But what hooked the newspapers were the racier initiatives that had a populist twist, which might easily communicate this strange new world of investment and shares for a new generation of everyday customers, turning what was previously a minority sport into a mainstream concern. That year – in 1983 – even a football club, Tottenham Hotspur, tried floating itself, though in typical Spurs style it missed. Unimpressed investors sat on the touchline.

The privatisation of British Telecom was on an entirely different scale, however. Since the announcement in early 1982 that the government would sell more than half of the state-run company, it had been the prospect that most excited and worried the City, and for a while it looked as though nervousness about the scale of the task might make Thatcher proceed carefully, in stages. Government ministers such as Nigel Lawson venturing into the City encountered scepticism that it could be done, or certainly not in one go, because the amount of shares being sold – in the region of £4bn (the equivalent of at least £15bn thirty years later) – was so vast. If the offer was mismanaged, or priced too high leaving a shortage of buyers, or excessively low meaning investors got too much of a bargain at the taxpayers' expense, then the privatisation programme could be discredited as a racket benefiting the friends of the Tories. If it flopped it would be said that the entire concept of getting the state out of industry was doomed.

The job of ensuring the sale did not turn into a disaster fell to Martin Jacomb of Kleinwort Benson. He was assisted on BT by colleagues including David Clementi and James Rockley. This group was relatively unusual in believing that – at a push – the sale could be managed in one go, which helped win them the mandate in 1984.

Jacomb's family background was not in merchant banking and he had fallen into it almost by accident in the late 1960s through connections. After Eton, Oxford and National Service in the Far East he tried working for his father's wool-broking business in the City and found it insufferably dull. He tried the law (and in his spare time wrote about tax for the *Financial Times*, where he first formed a friendship with Nigel Lawson). Then, on holiday with Sir Cyril Kleinwort, he was asked to join Kleinwort Benson and liked the sound of learning to be a banker. Now, in the mid-1980s, one of the showpiece projects of the Thatcher era was in his hands. That meant he would have to contend with the Prime Minister taking a close interest in the preparations. Indeed, Jacomb and his team were soon treated to the spectacle of the Prime Minister playing what he termed 'cat and mouse' with her ministers (the mice) at regular meetings in Number 10. The problem – and opportunity – was that there would be so many shares that they could not rely on institutional investors such as pension funds and asset managers buying them all. They needed the public in large numbers to buy the shares too, along with some foreign investors. Here the interests of Thatcher's ministers, seeking to spread the notion of wider share ownership, were perfectly in tune with the interests of the City as organiser of the sale and distributor of the shares.

The general election landslide over Labour in 1983 emboldened Thatcher and her supporters, and while she was not yet in the period in which she would succumb to hubris, she did have command of the field. Her traditionalist Tory critics – the Wets – had largely been bested, and there were a greater number of reformist ministers in place who endorsed her approach to transforming Britain's standing and shrinking the size of the state. In 1984 they were not only engaged in a titanic struggle with the striking miners, designed to break the trade unions; Lawson, as Chancellor, was also redesigning the taxation system to encourage wealth creation. On the other side of the Atlantic Ronald Reagan was heading for re-election on the back of a booming Wall Street, economic rebirth and a recovery of national confidence. History was flowing in a free market direction.

*Cowboys and angels: President Ronald Reagan at the
New York Stock Exchange, March 1985.*

In the UK, that sale of British Telecom was the testing ground for an entire philosophy, of popular capitalism: the idea that the benefits of the market if properly brought to bear can increase prosperity and spread it widely. Ownership, the idea of a stake for the many rather than a narrow elite, appealed to Thatcher the Methodist and grocer's daughter almost as much as it suited her political aim to build a constituency of small investors who would not want the Left let back in to take what they had earned and accumulated. An advertising campaign managed to translate those populist instincts into marketing material that talked directly to Thatcher's people – the aspirational voters who had given her such a large parliamentary majority in 1983 – by creating the notion of scarcity and a rush for shares, an approach used even more blatantly in the later British Gas privatisation. For BT, along with the TV advertising blitz, much effort was put into wooing the press in the hope that if the sale was written about in a positive manner then the readers would apply for shares. At a press conference for several hundred hacks, the privatisation was duly carefully explained and it was stressed that the price would be low enough to make the shares attractive to the individual investor.

On the nuts and bolts of the deal, Jacomb and his team ran the operation from a 'war room' at Kleinwort Benson and talked of D-Day or Impact Day. On D-Day minus one, Lawson and Jacomb met in private at the Treasury to set the price, and on 16 November 1984 it was announced that more than three million shares would be sold at an offer price of 130p, bringing in almost £4bn for the government. In another sign that bankers were learning how to utilise the techniques and showmanship of another 1980s boom-time business – advertising – the price was unveiled with the dropping of a giant banner outside the Kleinwort Benson office. Jacomb's team then had a nerve-wracking wait of several days to find out how many Britons, by sending in their applications to the operation located in warehouse outside London that Kleinwort Benson had hired for the processing of applications, had applied for shares.

The British Telecom sale was certainly ground-breaking in its ambition and success. Nothing like it had ever been attempted, anywhere. Such was the rush for shares that the issue was five times over-subscribed and 96 per cent of British Telecom staff who were eligible became shareholders in their own company. The British public had 39 per cent of the shares. Inevitably, some sold them almost straight away, taking the profit when the price rose. To critics this was 'get rich quick' capitalism in action, with publicly owned assets transferred to large institutional investors who could sell them to whoever they liked, even foreign investors. These concerns of short-termism dominated Labour criticisms of the programme, and the former Prime Minister, the Earl of Stockton, Harold Macmillan, famously in November 1984 criticised the privatisation programme. It was dubbed the 'selling off the family silver' speech by the press, although the former Prime Minister did not use that precise phrase.[4] It was a wounding attack by Macmillan, who for all his dexterity with a soundbite turned out to be wrong. Telecoms privatisation was a spur to future investment. One only needs to consider how a monopoly provider, owned by the government, would have coped with the subsequent emergence of the mobile phone and rapid innovation, to see that the UK's state-run model was best ended.

With shares and privatisation attracting all the scrutiny, another market boomed but got a lot less attention. Although the sums involved in the fast-expanding Eurobond debt markets were enormous, this was not a market whose existence was widely publicised outside the pages of the *Financial Times* and publications such as *Euromoney*. In 1985, turnover in the Eurobond market, dominated by London, was more than $1.5 trillion. This was the way of doing business that had been started by Warburg little more than two decades previously with a $15m transaction. Yet when compared to what was happening on the other side of the Atlantic, even the booming Eurobond market of the mid-1980s seems in retrospect rather orderly and British. In the stock market, Wall Street had a head start because of May Day 1975, when fixed commissions were scrapped. Just as important was the cut (28 per cent to 20 per cent) in capital gains tax made in 1981 by a Republican administration keen to encourage investors to take bigger risks which might grow the economy. By the mid-1980s, the US was well into a sustained outbreak of merger and acquisition mania that made all that had gone before seem somewhat sedate. The specialist firms of private investors – venture capitalists and private equity funds – had only really become significant following the seeding of the early growth of Silicon Valley in the 1970s, but the expanding volumes, availability of credit and favourable tax environment meant that they were able to undertake steadily bigger and bolder deals. The US investment banks had an obvious interest in these developments as potential advisors either to the target company or to the prospective buyer. These were also not necessarily corporate takeovers either, in which one established firm bought a competitor in the same field. It tended to be a firm of financial specialists buying an established manufacturing company, and deploying projected profits to pay the interest while the buyer put in very little money and set about restructuring or breaking up the purchase into sellable portions. Defenders saw private equity as unlocking value that had been hitherto unnoticed, which might then be invested to better use elsewhere in new investments. For critics, it was pure financial engineering that piled debts on previously healthy companies and caused factories to close. The era culminated with the leading private equity firm Kohlberg Kravis Roberts paying a then unfathomable $25bn for RJR Nabisco, a food and tobacco company in 1988. That year there were ninety-seven billion dollars' worth of leveraged buyouts in the US, when just eight years earlier only a couple of billion dollars had been involved. As the size of these markets and deals increased, the fortunes to be made obviously became commensurately bigger. It would be odd then, considering the lessons of financial history going back to the South Sea Bubble and the fall of France under John Law, if this excitement did not produce in some a change in behaviour and ethical attitudes.

Like all such previous booms, the M&A boom created new heroes, and in time villains, whose rise this time symbolised the spirit of buccaneering 1980s capitalism. In Michael Milken of Drexel

Burnham Lambert the movement had its marauding monarch. So valuable was the highly intelligent Milken's 'junk bond' unit to his Wall Street firm that the management allowed him in the late 1970s to take it to the West Coast, for family reasons, from where he and his small team perfected their new approach. Junk in this case did not mean worthless, it was the term given in the 1980s to the lower-graded bonds of many smaller companies that Milken argued were actually under-priced, and would eventually produce as good a return as those of blue-chip stocks. Milken not only convinced traditional US Savings & Loan companies to stuff their portfolios with his 'junk bonds', at the annual 'Predators' Ball', but he and his team also promoted their work as having a higher social purpose. They were enabling those who had until now been unable to access funding to profit.

With a vast new pool of capital swirling around, and bigger profits, the value of inside information about what might be about to happen rose too. An investment banker, if he (usually he) had lax morals or expensive tastes, might find it worth his while to discreetly trade on his own account on information acquired working for a client, depositing any profits in secret offshore accounts. Or he could pass the clandestine information on to other predators, either for profit or for future preferment. It was against this bewildering background that the authorities in London attempted to make sense of the changes that were coming to the capital and to answer questions to which they did not have anything like a clear answer.

With the City on the verge of further growth, bringing the opportunity for fraud as well as for fortune, how might finance be policed?

One of the modern nostalgic myths about the Big Bang era is that immediately before it began there were either no scandals or hardly any wrongdoing. This is demonstrably false. Disgust at the notion of some in the City making out like bandits with other people's money long pre-dated the mid-1980s. In a modern echo of the public outcry over City scandals in the nineteenth century, there

were numerous failed attempts made by governments in the 1970s
to make insider trading illegal and to crack down on those City
workers who used information to make a profit from intelligence
that was not publicly available. Insider trading, carrying a potential
prison sentence in the event of conviction, was finally made a criminal offence by legislation passed under the Thatcher administration
in the early 1980s following a further string of consumer protection
scandals. It was later made more explicitly illegal in legislation in
1985. And no wonder. The City of London police in a 1980 report
described fraud as the 'growth industry of the 1970s' because it had
increased in the Square Mile fivefold in that decade. Between 1980
and the end of 1983, the amount involved in cases under investigation by the fraud squad rose from £30 million to £115 million. That
was just what was known about.

In July 1981, ministers and officials at the Department of Trade
had been so concerned that the then Secretary of State, John Biffen,
appointed Professor Laurence ('Jim') Gower to produce a report.
Gower brought to the task a formidable legal brain, a determination
to improve consumer protection and a wealth of academic experience. During his war service he had been involved in the planning
of D-Day at Wilton House in Wiltshire and he later wrote the essential work on company law. Yet even as he took evidence, a scandal
unfolded that transfixed journalists. The revelation in 1981 of fraud
in the Manchester stockbroking firm Halliday Simpson led to the
exposure of Sir Trevor Dawson, a director of the merchant bank
Arbuthnot Latham, who was known in the City and in racing circles
as 'the Galloping Major'. His disgrace led indirectly to another City
name being bought up and revived by a foreigner. The taint of association with Dawson left the venerable Arbuthnot Latham highly
vulnerable and its grandee chairman, Sir John Prideaux, had to
accept an offer from Dow Scandia. The Swiss banker Henry Angest,
who had landed in London in the 1970s complaining about inedible
English food, was one of those who arrived with the new owners.
Piece by piece he bought Arbuthnot Latham for Dow Scandia. He
then became the owner and rebuilt it as one of the last-remaining

distinctly British small banks. In contrast, Dawson did not meet a happy end. Ruined after his role in the Halliday Simpson affair was confirmed by an inquiry, in March 1983 Dawson drank a glass of champagne and then killed himself in his flat in Eaton Square, ensuring that his estranged wife and disabled son would benefit from life insurance policies in his name.

When in 1982 Gower produced his initial findings about how to regulate the City, he was leaning towards recommending the establishment of a tough and independent Securities and Exchange Commission, with subpoena power and teams of investigators on the model that existed in the US. By the time his final report was published early in 1984 he had backed away from favouring that option, and it seemed as though the Department of Trade and Industry – by then run by Norman Tebbit – would have oversight rather than a new independent body or the Bank of England, which was seen as too much a representative of the City to be a potential adjudicator. Even this diluted version of Gower's initial thinking deeply worried some inside Number 10. John Redwood, then the head of the Policy Unit in Number 10, was particularly concerned that it would lead to the government having to assume responsibility for all the 'foibles and problems of the market place'. In a memo to the Prime Minister he described Gower's scheme as 'dangerous'. Redwood was not alone in expressing concerns that Gower was being heavy-handed. Richard Lambert, writing in the *Financial Times* on 13 March 1984, warned of the dangers of group-think. 'From Whitehall to Threadneedle Street everyone seems to have approved the Gower report', he wrote. 'But is it possible that they are utterly, completely, 100 per cent mad?' The proposals would create, in Stani Yassukovich's memorable phrase, 'an alphabet soup of acronyms and regulators' which could, in Lambert's view, prove confusing and unworkable. Thatcher herself was also concerned. When the banker and Thatcher admirer Walter Salomon (who had no connection to Salomon Brothers) gave a speech a few weeks later attacking Gower's recommendations, and sent a copy of it to the Prime Minister with a covering note, she scribbled on it an instruction to

the civil servant Andrew Turnbull: 'Andrew, can you let me have a
note on the Gower Report. WS is quite possibly right.'

Gower, Salomon said in his speech to his bank's annual general
meeting, was a lawyer of 'very high standing and reputation . . .
whose chastity has never been broken by any spell of practical experience'. The problem, he said, was that new rules would be a 'haven'
for lawyers charging high fees for advice on the regulations.
'Whenever I hear of proposals for "self-regulating" authorities and
suchlike I think of the opening remarks of the Prime Minister of
Denmark at the World Bank Meeting in Copenhagen,' said Salomon.

> We shall to evolve
> Problem solvers galore –
> Since each problem they solve
> Creates ten problems more.

This was a very Thatcherite epigram, and the Prime Minister liked
it so much she marked it with six strokes of the pen. 'Professor
Gower's propositions', Salomon continued, 'are from a practical
point of view 1) unworkable, 2) interfere with the rights of the freedom of the individual, 3) tremendously costly and 4) will build up a
vast bureaucracy.' The risk of constructing a bureaucratic system
patrolled by lawyers was that it would reduce the responsibility of
the individual to pay attention when they made investments, he
said. Salomon was by no means speaking as a typical member of the
banking Establishment defending its privileges. He had fought a
decades-long battle with the Bank of England, which regarded the
German Jew who had arrived in 1938 as unsuitable for recognition
in the City, perhaps on account of his direct manner. His outspoken
criticisms of the Stock Exchange hardly endeared him to some of
his contemporaries either. In any case, Salomon advised Thatcher
that Gower's threat to undermine the club mentality of the City
and its institutions would have unintended consequences. Her willingness to listen to a figure who stood outside the elite and advocated increased competition was another example of her being

drawn to disruptors and rebels, even if for once he was resisting change.

This row about how to regulate finance would not be resolved quickly, and the Gower Report duly disappeared into the Whitehall machine. As Big Bang neared, a battle would be fought between assorted parts of government, the Bank of England and the various vested interests of the City over where exactly power and control should lie. All the while, the Labour opposition accused the Conservatives of favouring their friends. When Tebbit made a statement on 16 July 1984 about Gower, the Labour front-bench spokesman Bryan Gould demanded that the government go further on regulation to deal with wrongdoing.

What is remarkable though is that this period is still portrayed almost exclusively as an era of evaporating regulation. Of course there was the deregulation of Britain's building societies, when they were allowed from 1986 to compete fully with banks and demutualise, and the looming Big Bang opened up the Stock Exchange to competition, but the run-up to Big Bang was characterised by the introduction of regulation, or what is termed re-regulation, to markets that had previously operated with a club mentality. As the academic Steven Vogel put it: 'The gentlemen's luncheon was replaced by the power breakfast, civilised rivalry was replaced by cutthroat competition; and discrete self-regulation was replaced by a nightmare from America: the proliferation of regulatory bodies, the endless creation of rules, and an invasion of lawyers.'[5] On that point of a profusion of lawyers, one of the most senior City figures of the period gets right to the heart of it three decades later: 'The most significant American import was not the longer hours or even the bonuses. It was the importation of the American approach to regulation and law. It is a country built on law, with a strictly legalistic way of looking at decision making.' As America's second President, John Adams, described it, what should prevail is 'a government of laws and not of men'.

In contrast, the traditional City self-regulatory approach until 1986 was distinctively English. Although it was imperfect it did rest on a fixation with reputation, a fear of exclusion by the tribe, and greater room for consideration of whether a questionable action was ethically acceptable as opposed to simply within the rules that were written down and punishable in the event of an infraction. The shift in the City to the American way produced a complete culture change that is still not much understood, even though it was by far the most consequential part of the process. The old system in London appeared to be entirely rules-based but it was British in that it allowed for a considerable amount of personal discretion and moral suasion. Says a leading British banker: 'With the Americans came the idea that if something is legal then it is OK or right. That became the simple test: legal or illegal. The thought processes required are really quite different. That was what changed. That was the real revolution.'

Add to that the rapid ongoing destruction of the partnership structure in the mid-1980s, as jobbers and brokers were bought over, and experienced, older hands departed newly rich with their share of the proceeds to acquire estates in the Home Counties or châteaux in France. Stani Yassukovich was one of those who watched in horror as, along with the timeservers, the City was emptied of many of the newly wealthy and smarter partners who knew how the place worked.

At that crucial moment, with the City being re-regulated and reimagined, the Prime Minister was conflicted in one other respect. She was a tremendous fan of swashbuckling tycoons such as James Hanson, the canny corporate raider who built a business empire out of tapping the banks and markets and then restructuring and selling on businesses. Hanson was given a peerage in 1983. The billionaire James Goldsmith was a more intellectually complicated character, in that he began the period believing in the vision of open markets and transcontinental globalisation, but as the decade wore on he became increasingly sceptical and concerned about the risks to democracy and national identity. These tycoons were glamorous figures, who because they were buying up businesses abroad were worthy of celebration in Thatcherite terms. As Hanson's adverts put it, his was a company from over here doing rather well over there, a message that echoed the Prime Minister's rhetoric of national rejuvenation. But further down the batting order, others of questionable quality were emerging who were keen to become the next great tycoons. The Cypriot tycoon Asil Nadir became a City sensation with Polly Peck, a small textile company he used as a vehicle to acquire all manner of interests. The unlikely Polly Peck for a while became a FTSE 100 company, and its eventual fall would besmirch those politicians who had befriended him.

The other side of Thatcherite dynamism it seemed was dodginess and wide-boy sharp practice. This was reflected in television and popular music when the Thatcherite ethos was attacked in a manner that would only intensify post-Big Bang. The writers of Britain's most popular television comedy of the decade – *Only Fools and Horses* – affectionately celebrated the market-trader ethos and the sense of community in a working-class London neighbourhood. First screened in 1981, by the mid-1980s it was at the peak of its popularity, with a loveable hero – Derek 'Del Boy' Trotter – defined by dubious practices and shady dealings, even if he retained a strong devotion to family. Underneath the laughter, it looked like a hymn to self-reliance and corner cutting. Everyone is only out for themselves and their mates, seemed to be the message. As the old Fleet Street joke goes: Ethics is a county to the northeast of London.

There was a counterpoint though in Band Aid in December 1984 and Live Aid the following summer, when pop and rock stars on both sides of the Atlantic played a day-long concert – creating a 'global jukebox' – to raise funds to tackle the famine in Ethiopia. For all the pious self-congratulation of some of those involved, the ringmaster Bob Geldof's insight was astute. Rock concerts to raise funds for charity were not new. George Harrison put on his concert in New York for Bangladesh in 1971, and American television had long featured 'telethons'. But Geldof and his team fused satellite technology, the techniques of London's thriving advertising industry and the glamour of the international rock elite, to blur borders and turn globalised charity into a media phenomenon. If

Thatcher and members of her government seemed bemused by these developments, and by the outpouring of donations and public enthusiasm, it fed into the developing narrative that the Thatcherites – with their privatisations and enthusiasm for growing the City – were hard-edged, uncaring and only interested in money. In time, in both the US with the election of Bill Clinton and later with the emergence of New Labour in the UK, that crude caricature would become immensely powerful. In Britain, developments in the City, and in the newly privatised utilities where management salaries started to surge, were cited by Labour as evidence of what was going wrong.

Sometimes those helping themselves to more money really didn't help themselves in terms of public perceptions. The screening in 1986 of a documentary called 'The Fishing Party' in the BBC's *40 Minutes* series involved four enthusiastic advocates of Thatcherism being done up like kippers. Their prattling was intercut with radio reports of famines, poverty and mass unemployment. The four were filmed at work in the City, at home and in Scotland fishing and shooting seagulls. As they did this they offered their views on class, politics, capital punishment, Africa, badly behaved children, public schools, marriage, money, privilege and police brutality ('stuff a grenade up his arse!'). None of this made for particularly sympathetic viewing and 'The Fishing Party' stands as a case study in why it is best never to agree to appear in a fly on the wall television documentary.

A reviewer concluded: 'Any left-wing playwright would be hard pressed to come up with a juicier collection of right-wing nitwits.' The four became, for a while, public hate figures and symbols of the arrogance and excess that critics of Thatcherism blamed on her policies. 'We were young, foolish, opinionated and should never have done it. But that's no excuse,' said Guy Cheyney, one of the participants, years later. They had been stitched up but they should have known better. One commodity broker who was invited on the fishing trip, but luckily for him was too busy to attend, was a young Nigel Farage.

The social distinctions and gradations could be confusing. Those who needed a guide to the demarcations on London's social battle-field could refer to the *Official Sloane Rangers Handbook* as a starting point. The bestseller, written by Peter York and Ann Barr, published in 1982, stemmed from a feature that ran in *Harpers & Queen* in 1975. The *Handbook* was a work of anthropological genius, identifying and affectionately lampooning the tastes and attitudes of the young upper-middle-class (aspiring to be aristocratic) tribe that resided in Chelsea and Fulham and regarded the television adaptation of *Brideshead Revisited* (1981) as an instruction manual. By the early 1980s the Sloanes had an undisputed leader in Diana Spencer, an aristocrat who married a Windsor and became the Princess of Wales. The yuppie was a more brazenly ruthless American import that arrived when the market took off in 1983–84, and could be found too in advertising and parts of the media, although there were clearly elements of overlap in Sloane and yuppie dress and behaviour. Those Sloanes or their partners who worked in the City and bought well in Chelsea or Fulham at the right moment had the best of both worlds, however. They could use the money earned in the thrusting Square Mile to recreate their English idyll by buying a country home for weekends and decorating it from Laura Ashley. The price of country houses along the M4, the motorway into London, began to rise sharply. Of course, many City workers played no part in the game playing and style wars; they were too busy getting on with their work and adjusting to earlier commutes. At a firm such as Smith New Court, the morning meeting for analysts and other key staff was shifted forward to 8.15am, meaning they had to be in long before 8am to prepare. For those who lived in the country it meant that the long journey to work started at 5am. The need for a week-time London pied à terre – and a bonus to buy it – became greater.

Among the sharpest observers of the Thatcherite tumult was a duo of unlikely pop musicians, the Pet Shop Boys. The singer and lyricist Neil Tennant had been a music journalist, while his inventive musical partner Chris Lowe, on synthesisers and baseball caps, appeared mute. Their 1986 number one single 'West End Girls' explored the theme of ambitious East End boys on the make colliding with upmarket girls from up west. A version of this Thatcherite intermingling was beginning to be enacted during daylight hours in the City, where graduates and aspirational street-wise traders worked and socialised alongside each other. In an earlier song 'Opportunities (Let's Make Lots of Money)' – first released in 1984, but re-mixed and re-released later – the band created an ironic anti-Thatcherite anthem.

It was as though almost everywhere you looked in London, and the wider southeast of England, across the classes, ambition and money itself was breaking free of its constraints, and not just in terms of the transactions arranged by entrepreneurs, companies, banks, traders, small business owners and market traders pushing knock-off Sergio Tacchini trainers. In dress, mores and willingness to talk about wealth, for those intimately involved it was an intoxicating moment of liberation. For those not invited, it looked rather different. Soon this style revolution would also acquire an architectural emblem fifty storeys high. In the east, three miles from the traditional City boundaries, a rival wrought in concrete and glass on London's docks was being planned by one of the leading Eurobond practitioners and his property consultant, an American by the name of Gooch Ware Travelstead.

8

WALL STREET ON THE WATER

'The place was a tip: 6000 acres of forgotten wasteland.'

Michael Heseltine

Gooch Ware Travelstead had an idea. In early 1985, the American property developer stood at the wharf-side of one of London's docks with Michael von Clemm, chairman of Credit Suisse First Boston's London operation. In front of them in London's East End lay the empty Canary Wharf warehouses where for decades fruit from the Canary Islands had been unloaded. 'That's big enough to take a trading floor?' asked von Clemm. Sure it is, responded Travelstead. There was certainly plenty of space and the government was in the middle of trying to redevelop the docklands area, although it was not sure how exactly, or what bigger businesses would consider moving there. You could certainly construct a trading floor, said Travelstead, but the problem was you would never get the traders to agree to move out of the Square Mile on their own, leaving behind their friends and their favourite pubs. The only way to make it work would be to move the entire Credit Suisse First Boston (CSFB) operation – the back office, the admin staff and the traders – into one big building, a tower, right there at Canary Wharf and encourage a few other banks to join in. It would be an exciting alternative to the traditional City, or at least an adjunct of it outside the ancient boundaries controlled by the City of London Corporation. Everybody needed space, Travelstead said. The pair got back into the car and agreed that with Big Bang coming they could create something here.

Thirty years later, what they envisaged and set about building has become a symbol of the power of cross-border capitalism and then, after the crisis of 2008, the striking backdrop for thousands of media graphics illustrating what went wrong with big banks. But that Canary Wharf exists at all is in large part due to Travelstead's vision. In 1985 the Kentucky-born and Baltimore-raised advisor had flown to London to help von Clemm find modern office space for expansion in preparation for Big Bang. Travelstead was a natural entrepreneur who had studied architecture at college and gone into the business of developing commercial real estate in Manhattan. He loved buildings and as the property advisor to the US bank First Boston he recommended to the group where to buy and what to build. With space in short supply in the City, von Clemm needed to locate an office in London large enough to house a computerised trading floor in the American style. Travelstead, working with his brother, had scoured the City, looking for anything suitable. They thought for a while that they had found the right place, on Lower Thames Street, down at the riverside in the City itself, but they calculated that by the time the necessary permissions were secured from the Corporation it wouldn't be worth it and anyway it probably wouldn't be big enough for what CSFB had in mind. It struck Travelstead immediately that the City of London Corporation had controlled the zoning and politics of the planning regime for too long. It presided over a situation that simply made no sense other than as a monopolistic racket that suited it and its contacts. With finite room within the City, property was expensive, or prices sometimes varied wildly from one side of the street to the other for reasons that were impenetrable to outsiders. Theoretically the foreign banks were told it was possible to keep the facades of listed buildings of the late Victorian and Edwardian period, and then to build new offices behind them, but in practice they were too narrow, and taking on such a project probably meant considerable hassle from planning officials and the press. Why not go somewhere else instead where space was not at a premium? But where?

Castles in the air: property developer Paul Reichmann and Margaret
Thatcher examine a model of the Docklands redevelopment scheme.

Travelstead and von Clemm had only considered Canary Wharf
by accident, following an earlier trip the banker had made to
Docklands on behalf of the Roux Brothers, the restauranteurs he
had helped get started in London in 1967 by arranging a loan. After
opening Le Gavroche, Michel and Albert Roux instigated a transformation in taste and quality in the London restaurant trade. In the
mid-1980s they were considering combining all their storage and
basic preparation operations in one spot. As chairman of their business, in addition to his duties at CSFB, von Clemm thought that
Docklands might be a suitable and cheap option, especially considering the rates holiday being offered by the government, available
to any business that might consider opening there. Von Clemm was
certainly one of the most glamorous and assertive figures in high
finance in London in the 1980s, someone who was well known in
banking as an early adopter of the mobile phone after the early
brick-like mobiles were first introduced in the UK (two years after
the US). The devices seemed to sceptical Britons faintly ludicrous
and destined never to catch on. The comedian Ernie Wise was hired

to make what was publicised as the first call in the UK on 1 January 1985, from St Katherine's Dock at a press event, to the Vodafone office in Newbury, which was stationed over a curry restaurant. The early phones cost around £2000 and had a battery life of as much as twenty minutes. Von Clemm was often to be seen with one of these phones clamped to his ear as he kept in touch with deals and market news on the move, in the days when it was enough of a novelty still to be a talking point. He was a highly confident extrovert who had been born into a privileged upbringing on the US east coast, studying anthropology, gaining a doctorate, spending a year living with a tribe in Tanzania and then working for a spell as a reporter on the *Boston Globe* newspaper. Following a move to London he became an early innovator in the Eurobond market in the 1960s at White, Weld, the American bank that was keen to pursue and profit from the possibilities of Warburg's innovation. Later, working with Stani Yassukovich, he originated what were known as Floating Rate Notes, creating a whole new Eurobond market in short-term debt that was tapped by developing economies. His interest in anthropology, says a friend, meant he was perpetually fascinated by tribal behaviour and the motivation of buyers and sellers. He loved to sell new products and when he wanted to push his team he had T-shirts printed with the slogan 'Buy Bonds'. That self-confidence marked him out, and even though his tailoring came from Savile Row, his lively approach stood out in London as decidedly un-English.

Perhaps that super-self-confidence was why he was not to everyone's liking. He twice clashed with John Craven, the boss of Phoenix Securities whose firm was instrumental in the post-Big Bang City. They fell out in 1978 when Craven felt von Clemm and others had negotiated a deal behind his back. Then they clashed over a house when von Clemm told their mutual friend, Charles McVeigh of Salomon, that if he ever planned to sell the Cheyne Walk property owned by McVeigh, he must tell him because he wanted it. McVeigh eventually ended up selling it to Craven instead, leaving von Clemm furious about losing out. It was the house that had once been owned by Sir Cyril Kleinwort, of the Kleinwort family merchant bank. The ownership of the townhouse illustrated the changing fortunes of the City elite, as the Chelsea residence stuffed with art and once owned by an old-school grandee was bought by the young American McVeigh and then sold to Craven, one of the British driving forces behind the Big Bang. At the other end of London, von Clemm's appetite for adventure would have long-lasting consequences. He liked Gooch Ware Travelstead's suggestion of moving the bank's entire London operation lock, stock and barrel to the Isle of Dogs so much that he gave him the go-ahead to try.

The docks that had provided so much employment in London's East End in the nineteenth and twentieth centuries, running from the Port of London beyond Tower Bridge seaward, had been dying slowly since the late 1960s. It was another story of British decline and disinclination to change. The wharves that had once teemed with men, unloading and loading consignments going to and from the British Empire, declined as the docks were blighted by clashes between management and trade unions over pay and technology. Amid those arguments the opportunity to adapt London's port was missed and deeper-water rivals such as Tilbury in Essex were better equipped to cope with the vast container ships that were increasing the amounts that could be shipped around the world. Since the 1970s, ministers and civil servants had talked about regenerating the docklands, and assorted studies were commissioned by the local authorities, resulting in several announcements made with good intentions, although almost nothing happened. This was even though the human need was pressing. Only three and half miles away from the Bank of England and the bustling environs of the Stock Exchange were deprivation, decay and unemployment around the docks on an appalling scale. A government report recorded that between 1978 and 1983 alone, 12,000 jobs were shed. Unemployment among adult males in the area in the early 1980s was estimated to be running at almost 20 per cent and many families had chosen to flee in the previous two decades, resulting in a net loss of 60,000 in the population of Tower Hamlets and 55,000 from Newham. About 100,000 people had left Southwark, south of the river, and in the parts of the boroughs immediately surrounding the docks itself there were just 39,400 residents left, although a larger population lived nearby. Only 5 per cent of the docklands residents owned their own properties and the place had, a government study revealed, few amenities, no proper transport links and not even a decent cinema.

In *The Long Good Friday*, the gritty, grimy, glamorous British gangster cinematic classic released in 1980, some of the best action takes place against this decaying docklands backdrop. Although it was a dramatic representation for the cinema screen, in terms of ambience the film's portrayal of the Isle of Dogs was judged by film critics and those familiar with the place to be absolutely on the money. This was the London of empty docks, rusting cranes, poverty and pubs, supposedly featuring cockney punters who claimed to have known the Kray Twins, even if they hadn't. *The Long Good Friday* was quite prescient too in its depiction of what lay ahead in the 1980s. Even though Margaret Thatcher was not in office when the film was written or shot, the protagonist Harold Shand, played to perfection by a young Bob Hoskins, is a Thatcherite archetype, even if his methods of business would not have been remotely to her liking. In the film, the cockney mobster Shand dreams of redeveloping the West India docks and of building a sports arena there with the help of American mafia contacts he is keen to impress. In this way he hopes to go 'legit' in the decade ahead and graduate from gangsterism to property development, although his schemes are subsequently jeopardised by gangland warfare and the murderous attentions of the IRA.

The task of regenerating the real docklands fell to Reg Ward, a public servant who was even more ambitious for the area than the fictional Harold Shand. As a law-abiding official he faced a similar if less violent problem to that encountered by Shand, in that he needed his schemes to be taken seriously when the idea of redeveloping an area so vast and deprived still sounded outlandish. The extraordinary Ward was one of the pivotal figures in the saga, someone who fizzed restlessly with ideas for schemes and struggled to contain his excitement about the possibilities. Arguably, this made him perfect for a difficult job that might have daunted a figure with a more conventional and dull approach. When he scouted around for potential investors, and invited von Clemm to take a look at the possibilities in Docklands, it started a chain reaction.

Ward, originally from Gloucestershire, was a product of the grammar-school system and as the son of a miner had been the first in his family to go to university. In a string of jobs in the public sector, he earned a reputation for being visionary but sometimes difficult if others failed to implement his bold ideas. He was appointed chief executive of the newly formed London Docklands Development Corporation (LDDC) in 1981, after Ward was said to have impressed an interview panel of civil servants with his rare enthusiasm for the project, which had manifested itself in him spending three days before the interview walking around the deserted docks painting pictures of what it might eventually look like with the application of some innovative thinking and invest-ment.[1] Some daring was just what Michael Heseltine wanted to see in relation to Docklands. The dynamic and ambitious Environment Secretary in the newly elected government led by Thatcher had introduced legislation to establish the LDDC. In his memoirs, Heseltine described what had motivated him to push ahead where other schemes had failed. Flying into London over the East End one day early in his tenure he was appalled by the view of what he termed immense tracts of dereliction and vast expanses of polluted land left behind by modern technology: 'The place was a tip: 6,000 acres of forgotten wasteland.'[2]

The chief executive and his team got down to transforming the wasteland, and despite an early attempt to remove Ward over his unorthodox management style, began planning what to do with eight and half square miles of London. The scheme for a tube or subway system linking the area with the centre of London was deemed too expensive and work got underway on a light railway system instead. Ward suggested building City Airport on the Royal Docks and it was approved. Trees were planted, 10,000 of them in year one, and 60,000 in the first four years, to 'give the impression of action' as the LDDC put it, and to make the place a little more appealing to visiting potential investors who might think, on driving there from central London, that they had arrived in a post-apocalyptic wasteland.[3]

From the beginning, the politics on the ground were poisonous, partly because the Labour Party locally was opposed to the redevelopment on the grounds that developers would benefit too much. More should be done directly to help the locals, it was said. To make matters more complicated, these wrangles took place during the bitter infighting in a Labour Party that had shifted sharply to the left after its defeat by Thatcher. Ward's deputy chairman at the LDDC, Labour's Bob Mellish, had been the MP for Bermondsey since 1950 and in the front-line of Labour's internal wars against the hard Left. He decided not to stand again and in 1983 there was one of the most viciously fought by-elections in British political history, with Mellish supporting a non-Labour candidate against the gay rights campaigner Peter Tatchell. Allegations of homophobia dominated the campaign. The infighting and conflict came at a price. Just when the LDDC needed a good working relationship with local Labour councillors, the climate was not conducive to cooperation. There was also a vocal campaign established by locals who feared opportunism on the part of developers and the consequences of disregard for the people who had lived in Docklands for generations. The place had been bombed heavily by the Luftwaffe in the Second World War, rebuilt afterwards and then slowly destroyed by a combination of neglect and failure to adapt to economic reality. By the mid-1980s some locals felt after Ward's early efforts as though they had been living on a vast building site for years, and now there were rumours circulating of a plan for an enormous development for the benefit of Americans. Were the remaining residents about to become outsiders in their own neighbourhoods, overshadowed by tower blocks built for Thatcherite financiers? Not all those complaining that this was the case were disaffected, unemployed dockers. Indeed, many of the dockers simply moved to other parts of London or out to counties such as Essex. All manner of other associated trades that were associated with the docks had also been sunk, and the social disruption was the London East End equivalent of what happened in the early to mid-1980s in the parts of Britain that lost heavy industry and coalmining. Deindustrialisation had started long before 1979 and Thatcher's election, but it accelerated in the 1980s and 90s. In 1975, 28.2 per cent of British workers were in manufacturing, by 1985 it was 23.9 per cent, and by 1993, 19.9 per cent.[4] Across the North of England and in Wales and Scotland the adjustment was extremely painful.

In London, Ward and others at the LDDC struggled to convince the remaining locals that the era of the docks was gone for good and nothing like it would be coming back. The nature of employment was changing, the LDDC pointed out politely. Locals would not necessarily be able to find work on their doorstep but the transport links being built should allow them to travel into the centre of London or beyond to seek other types of work. That might be true in time; then, to opponents of the development, it seemed, and still seems, that the security of tenure and class solidarity in the docks when they were open had been traded for temporary work and low pay for too many locals. It also looked as though the sceptics warning that this was an idea that would never get off the ground had a point. As late as 1985 it wasn't clear to the public or the government what would fill most of the space at Docklands or form the centrepiece of the development. Of course, there was room for a great deal of housing, and the first businesses to take up the government's incentives were light-industrial firms and medium-sized businesses looking for affordable accommodation. The Billingsgate fish market moved from the City in 1982 to an ugly new building close to Canary Wharf and the Westferry Printworks, printing titles that included the *Daily Telegraph*, had opened nearby in 1984. But the government that had established the organisation Ward ran wanted much more. That is why Travelstead's proposal arrived at the perfect moment. Just when the Prime Minister was keen to see the traditional City opened up to the forces of competition and fresh thinking in Big

Bang, the American property developer turned up saying that the Establishment in the Square Mile was too old-fashioned and he would build London 'a Wall Street on the water', giving foreign banks an alternative to negotiating with the stuffy cartelised City Corporation.

Following von Clemm and Travelstead's initial conversations, a consortium was formed in the summer of 1985 involving Morgan Stanley, CSFB and First Boston's property company. Travelstead – who had a 20 per cent stake – rented an office in Mayfair for his team, which was soon full of architects' drawings and models of the initial seventy-one-acre site and plans for eight million square feet of trading floors and offices. On such a large project facing considerable public and press scepticism, the endorsement of the government and a deal on building the transport links was essential. Travelstead was summoned to see Nick Ridley, the Thatcherite Secretary of State for Transport, at 11.30pm one night in the department when the Commons was sitting late, and found himself transfixed as Ridley smoked a cigarette right down until it disappeared between his yellowing fingers.

After further discussions, the consortium agreed to contribute £50m to the transport costs. Travelstead's introduction to the Prime Minister herself came from Alistair McAlpine, the Conservative Party Treasurer and a close ally of Thatcher. Born in the Dorchester Hotel, into the McAlpine construction dynasty, the Tory leader's friend and 'bagman', or party fundraiser, was fiercely devoted to her interests. The iconoclastic McAlpine guessed correctly that Canary Wharf would appeal to Thatcher, and at Travelstead's subsequent meetings, several in Downing Street and one at Chequers, she was highly supportive of the bankers' scheme. When Travelstead was worried that the planned light railway would not include sufficient capacity or stations, leaving potential commuters or workers to try to get to the Isle of Dogs from other parts of London by taking long bus or taxi journeys through the East End, and creating traffic jams and transport chaos, he told Thatcher that it could derail the building of Canary Wharf. He recalls her being clear in her advice, suggesting that for all her anti-statist credentials she was a

pragmatist who had an impeccable understanding of how government functions. Build Canary Wharf, she told him. Don't worry
about traffic jams. Create a mess, she told the developer, and then
government will feel compelled to clean it up. That's how it works.

Ward and Travelstead formed a close working partnership, which
caused the chief executive of the LDDC problems when critics
accused him of doing too much to please the American banks. But
the pair remained convinced – when few others were – that there
would soon emerge one of the largest developments in the world.
Not every senior investment banker agreed, and one attempt in
1985 to explain the vision was a failure, thanks to a typical London
traffic jam. At Salomon, Charles McVeigh, like von Clemm, was
looking for a space for a large trading floor and could not find it in
the Square Mile. The irascible chief executive of Salomon's, John
Gutfreund, was interested in resurgent London because it was
perfectly placed for further expansion due of its position in the time
zone. When he took an interest in the search for property, von
Clemm persuaded Gutfreund to drive with McVeigh down to
Docklands. They had the drive timed as taking just twenty minutes
from the City, von Clemm assured the visiting American. Three-
quarters of an hour later, with the group stuck in traffic somewhere
between Wapping and the mooted Canary Wharf site, von Clemm,
pointing out of the window at another part of the wasteland,
explained that the LDDC planned to build a lot of low-cost housing.
Low-cost housing? Gutfreund was astonished. Why the hell would
he care about plans for low-cost housing?

After the visit, Salomon decided not to join the Canary Wharf
project, instead choosing an office block more centrally located
above Victoria Station, near Buckingham Palace. There they set
about constructing the largest trading floor in Europe, at a rumoured
cost of £25m, and even installed some ornate panelling in the executive suites upstairs overlooking the vast trading floor, because the
management was convinced that visiting major clients would expect
a bank in London to look at least a little as though it had heritage.
Valerie Thompson, the trader from Essex who had risen to become

a star and the first female director at Salomon, was one of those
who moved onto the new trading floor below. When she was
appointed manager of the London syndicate department on 10 July
1986, Gutfreund sent a memo via telex to all employees announcing
it. A female colleague scribbled a note of congratulations: 'This is
super news . . . there is hope for women at the Brothers.' The move
to Victoria Plaza was not to her liking, however. It was too anonymous and excessively big, with row upon row of trading terminals.
It seemed like a vast zoo. Who were all these people she didn't
recognise? Another Salomon employee who made the move, who
Thompson did know, was bond salesman Michael Lewis, already
working part time in the evenings as a journalist, which would lead
him into writing *Liar's Poker*, the inside account that later destroyed
the reputation of Gutfreund and would forever associate the name
of Salomon with excess and egotism. When a superior tried to
threaten Lewis over a deal, he put it in the hands of the email syndicate manager, who he described as a brilliantly connected 'alley cat'.
To Lewis's amusement, she managed with a few phone calls to nix
the bully's promotion at Salomon.

In early 1986 that decision by Gutfreund to move to such a vast
space at Victoria was not yet widely seen as an indicator of looming
disaster at Salomon. It was deemed another blow to the ancient
City Corporation and an indication that its geographical monopoly
was finished. Two Corporation men who understood very well the
implications of Gutfreund's move and the Canary Wharf plan were
Michael Cassidy, the chair of the planning committee, and Peter
Rees, the head of planning. Cassidy was a lawyer who was fascinated by the City, and in his role in the early 1980s working for the
Post Office pension fund – then Britain's biggest – he saw how
markets and trading were being changed by technology. His MBA,
completed part time, was on Big Bang and when he was chosen as
a councillor to be deputy chairman in 1985 and then chairman of
The Corporation's Planning Committee in 1986, he was convinced
that the City had to modernise and rebuild rapidly or it would
continue to see banks and other firms look elsewhere. There was

already some innovation underway, of course. Lloyd's of London, the insurance market, moved in 1986 to a strange custom-built building designed by Richard Rogers that had been begun in 1978. In the fashionable style of the time, the lifts and pipes were on the outside of the building, making it look like an overblown coffee machine. The arch-traditionalist architectural critic Gavin Stamp described it as 'that naive, posturing intrusion into the City'.[5] When the Queen opened it in November that year she was more diplomatic and praised the design. In her speech she made oblique reference to the difficulties Lloyd's had suffered earlier in the decade, when an embarrassing scandal over investor protection had exposed a group of underwriters siphoning investors' money into their own offshore accounts. The Chairman of Lloyd's, Peter Miller, said at the opening of the building that Lloyd's was trying to move on and the new structure was 'an exciting contrast to so much of the boring modern architecture of this city'. He noted that it would prove practical for trading purposes. 'If it is controversial, let it never be said that Lloyd's cannot take a risk.' That was one way of putting it. Later in the decade it would became apparent just how rapacious the appetite of some of those at Lloyd's had been for recklessness and risk with other people's money.

On the site of an old station, work also started on the thirty-two-acre Broadgate development in 1985, on its eastern extremity bordering Bishopsgate. Invited by the developers Godfrey Bradman and Stuart Lipton, on 31 July Thatcher herself clambered aboard a JCB earthmover and scraped a patch of ground. Afterwards, in the marquee, or 'this great tent' as she described it, she gave a speech in which she invoked the original Victorian builders of the railways and urged the developers to be inspired by history's example to remake the City. 'We are drawing back the curtain of the future,' as she put it.[6] The Prime Minister also used a saying that sounded Methodist but which actually comes from Goethe: 'That which thy fathers bequeath thee, earn it anew if thou wouldst possess it.' The development would maintain and enhance the reputation of London as one of the greatest centres of trade and industry, she said. 'And that is the reputation I like to keep going.' She returned the following year for one of the topping-out ceremonies, and when Broadgate Circle was completed one of the signature post-modern developments of the Thatcher era was revealed. It had clean, curved white lines that imitated the amphitheatres of the Ancients, and space for cafes in which financiers wearing braces and double-breasted suits – and that was just the women – might sit sipping Italian coffee.

Across from the Royal Exchange and the Bank of England, another piece of landmark post-modern architecture was given the go-ahead in 1986, after earlier plans in the 1970s for a tower had been blocked, following complaints led by the Prince of Wales, who loathed architectural developments that altered the character of London or eclipsed the streets in which they sat. The developer Peter Palumbo tried again and the architect James Stirling designed a triangular building, clad in pink and yellow limestone cake-like stripes. Construction was then delayed for six years because of a row over the demolition of Victorian listed buildings and an archi-tectural dig during which the Museum of London thought it might have found the origins of the founding of Londinium.

Peter Rees and his team in the mid- to late 1980s realised that it would take far more than a handful of high-profile developments to rebuild the City. Cassidy had hired Rees in 1985, as deputy head of planning, although he was quickly promoted and his more conserv-ative predecessor removed. Rees was only in his thirties and full of energy and ideas about how the City should look. There was no point thinking in romantic terms of repopulating the place with more flats or apartments, he said. He and Cassidy were convinced that the City needed much better offices for banks, insurance firms, lawyers and accountants, and much bigger buildings to accommo-date the commuters that were the place's lifeblood. They ripped up the plan for modest redevelopment and, in the face of considerable opposition, and with close votes and the help of leaks to the finan-cial press, Cassidy and Rees pushed through developments and relaxed Corporation rules. There would be no restrictions on basements, meaning developers could go down as far as they wanted to put in the workings of a modern building. The plot sizes were increased to allow large floors to accommodate traders, and they tried to plan ahead as the City's streets were dug and dug again to take ever more of the cables that were needed to funnel new technology into the buildings. They set aside extra space in the trenches for future fibre-optic expansion. Within five years a third – a third – of the Square Mile's office space was replaced.

The City had been slow to start rebuilding ahead of Big Bang, and was soon catching up. This meant intense competition with the rival Canary Wharf crowd, although thirty years later Cassidy contests the suggestion that it amounted to all-out war between Travelstead's team and the Corporation. Travelstead is not so sure. When the American went to the Guildhall, invited by Cassidy, to explain his plans, there was plenty of scope for cultural confusion, and in trying to convince the councillors who ran the Corporation that Canary Wharf would be a success he may have left them with the impression that the new arrivals thought the City itself was past it, which did not go down well with the audience. Either way, Thatcher and her ministers had got what they wanted, a highly competitive race to build and adapt London to suit the requirements of those operating in global markets. The City – spurred on by threats to its position – had become once again a great, expansive, international centre open to investment, as it had been in the Victorian and Edwardian period. Another figure who was supportive of Travelstead's scheme was the Prince of Wales. The American was invited by an equerry to Kensington Palace for a discreet conversation with the heir to the throne. On his arrival he encountered two children running around naked chased by a nanny. It was William and Harry. Charles said that he was in favour of Canary Wharf, but given his reputation for getting involved in rows about architecture he realised it might not help if he said so publicly. 'Sir,' said Travelstead, fearing a fresh outbreak of hostilities between the Prince and the architect profession, 'it is probably better if you don't say anything.'

Back on the Isle of Dogs in 1986 it was war of a different kind. On the ground, the network of community activists stepped up their campaign when Travelstead's plan was published and models were displayed for investors and residents to examine. The protests by the Association of Island Communities against Canary Wharf itself are captured in the documentary *Hardworking People*, made by the film-maker Woody Morris in 2013. It includes images of the day in July 1986 when the activists decided to storm the ceremony marking the turning of the first sod at Canary Wharf, attended by assorted senior bankers, dignitaries and Reg Ward. Compared to highly policed contemporary events, in which even the most humdrum press conference tends to be patrolled by security guards and a battalion of press officers who fear the sack if so much as the tiniest detail goes wrong, the Canary Wharf protest of 1986 was a thing of wonder.

The artist and activist Peter Dunn was one of those who watched the dignitaries assemble. He told Morris: 'They arrived in their big limousines ... they had their sunglasses on, they looked like a whole series of mafia bosses to be honest. They had models of what Canary Wharf would look like in their marquee.' At the agreed signal, a whistle was blown and banners were unfurled declaring that 'Canary Wharf condemns the community' and demanding on behalf of locals the right to have a better say. Their banners were just the overture. Joining the protests were those in charge of Mudchute Farm, a community farm nearby that feared it would be closed down or threatened as part of the wider redevelopment of Docklands. They hired a lorry and, having filled it with sheep, drove to the ceremony uninvited, approaching from the other end of the dock. The lorry trundled towards the marquee and the podium, where the sheep were duly let loose to the bemusement of the guests and the horror of the organisers. With sheep wandering about, and some eating the flowers around the base of the podium, at one point Ward tried to be conciliatory. He took over some champagne to the protesters, which seemed not to go down very well with the representatives of the banks, who wanted to know why champagne was being handed out to the enemies of progress with the press watching. As it was, the protest received little more than a few passing mentions in the next day's newspapers and would have been lost to history but for the efforts of the activists and local historians.

Even better than the sheep, the team from Mudchute unloaded a beehive in front of the podium and took off the lid as the Governor of the Bank of England attempted to make his speech. But Robin Leigh-Pemberton was unflappable. Not only had he been in the Grenadier Guards, serving in Palestine after the Second World War, but it also emerged that in his spare time he was a beekeeper, so he was untroubled when the bees were released near him. Many in his audience of the great and good, and not so good as the protesters saw it, were less relaxed and fled the bees by moving into the marquee to take shelter and have a drink. With the bees buzzing about him, and with his elite audience gone, Leigh-Pemberton kept going for a while with his speech before good-humouredly giving up.

It was all very British and as the protesters packed up it might have seemed as though any property consortium that presided over such a farcical occasion could not possibly be capable of creating and filling the largest development in Europe. Neither Ward nor Travelstead would complete the project, and von Clemm had already moved on in January 1986, when he suddenly resigned from CSFB. But they had forced the City to respond, to think about how new towers would be built and the Square Mile reshaped. What Travelstead, von Clemm and Ward envisioned and started at Docklands would grow. Out of the desolation, new temples to mammon soon began to rise.

9

BANG

'These theories were based on the hypothesis that all the matter in
the universe was created in one big bang at a particular time in the
remote past. It now turns out that in some respect or other all such
theories are in conflict with the observational requirements.'

Astronomer Fred Hoyle, speaking in 1948

Thatcherism hit its peak in 1986. Within that year were clustered a
series of events that might be considered remarkable enough indi-
vidually. Taken together they amounted to the opening of the final
act, the first intimations of the cavalcade of carnage that closed the
decade and helped define the Tory Party's divisions for several
decades. On 9 January, the Defence Secretary Michael Heseltine
walked out of the cabinet in a row over the Westland helicopter
company, heading to the backbenches from where he waited for an
opportunity to challenge Margaret Thatcher for the Tory leadership
and the premiership. She narrowly avoided ruin over Westland and
Heseltine himself waited more than four years to strike. Although
he was not to know it at the time, he would be aided enormously by
Thatcher's doomed flagship policy, the Community Charge.
Following many months of internal arguments, it first appeared
formally in public in 1986, on 28 January, with the publication of a
'green paper' entitled 'Paying for Local Government'. The replacement of local rates with a charge – quickly dubbed a 'poll tax' by
opponents – was the work of Kenneth Baker, the Environment
Secretary, and William Waldegrave, the Minister of State at
Environment, with Thatcher's enthusiastic backing. They were

assisted by outside 'expert' Lord Rothschild, who had been appointed chairman of N.M. Rothschild, then specialising among other activities in privatisation. Victor, the third Baron Rothschild, had led an extremely eventful life. At Cambridge he was close friends with Philby, Burgess and Blunt, three of the Cambridge spies, an association which later caused him to be accused (wrongly) of being a Soviet spy. During his wartime service with MI5 he won the George Cross, and as a Labour peer and one-time backer of Ted Heath he ended up as an enthusiastic supporter of Thatcher and a trusted advisor. That is how he came in January 1986 to help unintentionally plant a slow-ticking poll-tax-shaped bomb under the government. As Lawson later put it in his memoirs: 'Rothschild prided himself on having no political judgement. He was above that sort of thing. William Waldegrave seemed to regard this as an advantage.'

The following month, the Single European Act was signed by the twelve members of the European Community, to make it easier to scrap physical, technical and fiscal barriers to trade. It led to the single market, in which European Union members agreed to abide by common regulatory standards and traded freely within the boundaries of the EU. This landmark measure in 1986 had been agreed only with some difficulty, and Lord Cockfield – the former Trade Secretary who, with David Walker, behind the scenes just before the 1983 general election had seen the way to a deal with the City and Nicholas Goodison – was one of the driving forces behind a programme designed to increase commerce within Europe, overseeing the White Paper ('Completing the Internal Market') that led to the Act. Thatcher wanted free trade and in return she agreed to an expansion of the European Community's power, only a little later realising the full extent of what she had conceded. Yet even in 1986 Cockfield was deemed by Thatcher to have become too pro-European, meaning he was not given a second term in post in Brussels. That did not matter, one term was enough for him to put a large dent in European history. The Act he helped instigate turned out to have two massive impacts on

Britain and Europe. It ushered in integration that eroded national sovereignty – because there was no longer a requirement for unanimity among the member states – and it eventually riled Conservative Eurosceptics. Rows over Europe helped split Thatcher's administration, contributing to her fall. But the effect on the City would also turn out to be enormous in that the single market helped London accelerate away from other European financial centres to become the undisputed hub in Europe, from where global banks could do business across Europe.

That same year, the Financial Services Act, overhauling regulation of the City and banks, also became law. Thanks to another piece of legalisation enacted that year, humble conservative-minded building societies (British savings and loans companies) were allowed to demutualise and compete with banks. Meanwhile, the government prepared the biggest privatisation of the lot: British Gas.

And all the time the clock ticked down to the day of Big Bang, scheduled for 27 October. At the Stock Exchange, much of the responsibility for preparations rested on George Hayter, the director of technical services. His team were attempting to construct a computer system that could handle the Stock Exchange's switch to an entirely electronic marketplace. Transactions would be expected to happen at high speed and not on the traditional floor face to face, although not all of the elements were new. Since the 1960s there had been a rudimentary electronic system for displaying prices, and in 1978 the more sophisticated Teletext Output of Price Information by Computer (TOPIC) was introduced. The FTSE 100 index of prices of the top 100 British listed companies, developed as a joint project with the *Financial Times* and then owned by the Stock Exchange, had replaced the FT 30 index. It gave anyone needing to get a sense of the direction of the market a good feel for it, with its red and green flashing icons. It was also faster, being updated every minute. The Exchange Price Information Computer (EPIC) held a database of the prices, but it depended on prices being observed physically and reported by staff on the floor of the Exchange. Even small delays meant that prices could have changed in either direction, and what really mattered in the old system was what the brokers and jobbers said to each other as they quoted a price and did a trade. For Big Bang to deliver an improvement, it all had to happen in real time or as close to it as possible, so that the numbers on the screen were not just a reflection of what had been the position very recently. The data seen on the terminal by the new generation trader would be the real price at that moment, based on the most recent trades, not an approximation. This was more than a minor spot of computer modernisation. It was a different way of looking at the world, in which flashing numbers on a screen came alive and the underlying data moved ever faster, way too fast for the human eye to see. The electronic prices would become not just a reflection of reality but the reality itself.

Hayter was unfazed by the practicalities. As he saw it, he had worked on larger projects, particularly the BOAC airline reservation system in the 1970s. Big Bang, though, was more difficult because it was akin to working in a goldfish bowl. Or it was, he told an interviewer, a little like swimming in a heavy sea. 'Every time I thought we had the project under control, we were hit by another roller.'[1] Satisfying every firm – the entire securities industry and every trader in the Square Mile – would prove impossible, but with time tight, Hayter's skill lay in finding a way through the internal politics of the Stock Exchange, and its ruling committees, to create a workable compromise. The ideal option of starting from scratch was not available, and when international shares started to be traded in significant quantities by foreign banks in London away from the Stock Exchange it brought additional pressure. Those firms doing it wanted a price system that suited their needs and if Hayter's team didn't build it, someone else might. Hayter and his team had to construct something quickly that would please sufficient members of the Stock Exchange and firms outside it that the Exchange wanted to attract. The answer was Seaq (Stock Exchange Automated Quotation System), on which all firms selling a particular share listed their prices, so that other firms could pick the best price quickly. The results of those trades, and their prices, then flowed automatically into a version of TOPIC in which a screen displayed the top 100 shares with pulsing red and blue lights, giving the trader a very quick feel for what the market was doing. If it was all red, that was not good. Seaq International also provided a bridge between New York, London and Tokyo, allowing brokers to see prices instantly elsewhere, creating a twenty-four-hour market. The way of conducting business that had existed for centuries was being abolished and in its place the Stock Exchange would become simply an electronic marketplace. Charging for access to the flow of information and controlling the platform on which buyers and sellers traded was what the new Stock Exchange was going to be about.

As Hayter and his programmers grappled with making their computers work, Parliamentary Under-Secretary at the Department of Trade and Industry Michael Howard was locked in early 1986 in a series of meetings with those who represented the firms that would come under the aegis of the proposed regulatory system. The experience was a little jarring for both sides, including for Stani Yassukovich. He was the son of a White Russian and a leading City figure who had arrived via Harvard and the US Marine Corps. He had been at White, Weld from 1961 and had become a Euromarkets pioneer in 1960s London. He was now chairman of Merrill Lynch Europe. When he and his colleagues encountered Howard, the government minister who had been given responsibility for steering the Bill through the House of Commons, they felt that for all his undoubted intelligence he was, as a non-financial person, having some trouble grasping the intricacies of how trading worked. But that sounds like market manipulation, Howard told them, when Yassukovich explained a manoeuvre (called a Greenshoe) by which liquidity was created by market makers. Howard said he might have trouble convincing his colleagues that this was acceptable. From Howard's point of view, he was attempting to educate the City's senior figures in the realities of politics and public perception. If high finance was on the rise then it could expect a good deal more scrutiny and would have to be able to explain itself clearly. They were, he made clear, now going to be accountable .

The role of Howard the lawyerly minister was to turn the competing claims of financiers, the Stock Exchange, the foreign players in the Eurobond market – such as Salomon and Nomura – the Bank of England and the Treasury, into a coherent, workable piece of legislation. The Gower Report had begat a government White Paper, the establishment of a network of self-regulatory bodies under a new Securities and Investment Board (SIB) appointed by the government, and then the bill itself. Labouring, as the *FT* put it, under a portrait of Gladstone and his cabinet, Howard pushed it through in several months, dealing with complaints along the way and trying to get the right amount of regulation with the opposition shouting for more and the City for less.

But the battle fought in 1984 by John Redwood and others against Gower and statutory regulation of one form or another had been lost. The free market Redwood's recommendation of minimal regulation – via reliance on the common law and simple rules imposed by the City's own institutions – ended up being rejected in favour of the creation of a regulatory bureaucracy. The Bank of England's David Walker and the Treasury were convinced that the increasing complexity of the market made this inevitable and desirable. Thatcher herself seems to have understood little of these nuances. In the words of her biographer, Charles Moore, the Prime Minister's involvement in the details of City reform were 'seldom more than marginal'[2] and she was simultaneously deeply involved in foreign affairs, particularly in the thawing Cold War and in arguments over how to deal with the Apartheid regime in South Africa.

Howard had to deal with fresh complaints late in the process in the summer. He was astonished when Britain's clearing banks suddenly woke up and realised that the legislation might have implications for them if they sought to expand their activities out of straightforward banking. The accountants were also unhappy. In August, Derek Boothman, representing their professional body, went to see Howard and said that accountants must have immunity. As the *Financial Times* reported: 'At some point auditors may be expected to "shop" rogue clients to the Bank of England or the SIB, a prospect that is causing considerable heart-searching.' Howard rejected the special pleading. That did end up having an unintended consequence, in that it contributed to the reduction of choice in London. Only the biggest accountancy firms could afford the professional liability insurance that would be needed to audit the accounts of banks and larger financial companies. It was an added spur to the growth and dominance of a small number of giant firms that audited the big banks on rotation. As banks grew in size and diminished in number, the firms auditing them got much bigger too.

The clashes and compromises meant that the Financial Services Act 1986 was no purist piece of Thatcherism. It was pragmatic; it was a fusion. Simplistic talk of 1980s *laissez-faire* financial deregulation, as though Thatcher ordered all controls to be swept away, is daft. That is not what happened. The Thatcherite fondness for the term deregulation, and the way critics used the term with contempt, caused it to be fixed in the public imagination as a period in which ancient, strict rules were swept away in favour of libertine licence. Yet it was not the introduction of a free-for-all. The intention was to formalise regulation while safeguarding enough of the City's independence, with various interested parties pushing all the while for their version of regulation to be adopted. The Governor of the Bank of England pushed for some of the old City culture to survive, particularly the so-called reliance on 'the Governor's eyebrows', the phrase meaning that historically a raised eyebrow from the Bank of England should be enough to compel reckless firms to rein it in. Robin Leigh-Pemberton explained his position:

'I, and others speaking on behalf of the Bank, have stressed that such regulation is seen as a means to the greater end of continuing to attract international business to London as an open but well-regulated financial centre. The City has a long tradition of regulation by consensus and the principle of being bound by the spirit of the rules as much as by their letter. I would like to see this tradition survive the move to a statutory framework and the influx of firms from different cultures.'[3]

This was all very well, and there was much that would go wrong with the importation of more of an American-style system, but at that point (as Bank of England and senior Treasury officials understood) the government was under sustained and justified attack because of excesses in the City. For the most part, compared to what came later, the cases involved were small time. But the steep increase in the amounts involved in cases of financial fraud and the gradual exposure of a web of corruption at Lloyd's, the insurance market, was ammunition for enemies of the City. At Lloyd's, shady underwriting practices – and the failure to make it clear that claims for asbestosis would hit the market hard – left some 'names', investors, exposed. It would get worse. But most of the new wealth elsewhere in the City was legitimately and legally earned. The contrast with the situation in poorer areas of Britain was obvious. While in 1986 parts of the country were only just beginning to recover from decline and degeneration, the populous southeast boomed. And its most visible manifestation was the City, which sucked in talent, provided opportunity, put rocket boosters under house prices and became the source of footage for eager TV journalists needing images that embodied the freewheeling spirit of the Thatcher era.

It was just about possible for defenders of high finance to claim that there was no more fraud or wrongdoing than there had ever been. Perhaps the law was only catching up. But the sums to be made – even by the mid-1980s – were already much bigger, and by such a magnitude that it would be odd if there had not been a commensurate increase in temptation. Indeed, outside the City, the merger mania, pay-outs to partners and the beginnings of higher salaries and bonuses had been noticed by the British voters, MPs and media. Combined with reports of fraud and sharp practice, accusations of greed could be used to make the case against Thatcher. In the Commons it was observed by the opposition parties during the passage of the Financial Services Bill that many Conservative MPs were serving or former stockbrokers and City lawyers, accountants and insurance types, the strong implication being that they wanted to shield their colleagues from full statutory regulation or more stringent scrutiny. This meant that the ethics of the City and risks of greed were back being discussed, as they had been periodically in the eighteenth and nineteenth century on the floor of the House of Commons by the leading politicians of the day. In a debate instigated by Labour in the House of Commons on 12 March 1986, in which the motion called for proper regulation to crack down on City fraud and misbehaviour, the attack was led by Roy Hattersley, who as Labour Minister of Consumer Affairs a decade previously had refused to exempt the City from restrictive practices rules. Hattersley, a skilled polemicist with a gift for a turn of phrase, was coruscating:

> Unemployment now stands at between 3.5 million and 4 million, manufacturing trade is in deficit and real interest rates are at record levels. Each of those individual catastrophes has been intensified by the Government's enthusiasm for economic policies which benefit the City but damage the rest of the economy. We have today a Government of the City for the City and, by far too large an extent, by the City.

Paddy Ashdown, then a young Liberal Democrat MP and future leader of his party, said the City had become far too dominated, although not all of it, by 'the short term, the turn of a quick buck by tomorrow'. Unlike in the UK's competitor nations, he said, it was far too often uninterested in investing in the future, and in industry. He was appalled by the sums being earned:

> Young men, not yet 30, in the City are earning £60,000 or £80,000 a year. I see that the chief executive of Guinness has had his salary raised to £195,000 a year and has received shares worth more than £1 million. As the Big Bang approaches, such frenetic activity to buy people will get even more frenetic.

The Tory MP who attacked most ferociously was Geoffrey Rippon, a former Heathite who disliked Thatcher and was disliked in return.

Nonetheless, his comments about the culture of takeovers and egomania were cogent.

> What is happening in the City today in the sphere of mergers is utter madness . . . No one can stop takeover bids and no one would want to, but the message should go out to the City: 'For heaven's sake cool it.' A distinction must be made between mergers by agreement which stimulate organic growth and hostile bids that are designed to promote egomaniac empire building.[4]

Rippon was not referring to takeovers in the Square Mile itself, of brokers and jobbing firms. His target was the frenzied effort to facilitate and encourage lucrative takeovers of established retailers or manufacturers by the empire-building entrepreneurs, usually acting with borrowed money sourced from the City. The Labour MP Tam Dalyell praised Rippon's contribution and said that there was deep concern about the deals and spiralling salaries: 'There is real worry in the country . . . if there is another scandal, or series of scandals, the top will come off.'

The Cabinet Secretary agreed with enough of those criticisms to send a note five days after that parliamentary debate to the Prime Minister's private secretary Nigel Wicks. 'I do not know whether you are having the same experience but I am finding, among people who work outside the City of London but whose activities bring them into touch in some degree with the City, that there is increasing disquiet about the things that people think are going on in the City', he said.

> I do not just mean the levels of remuneration; a lot of people, including some from inside the City, think that it is a bubble that will be pricked in a year or two. They think more about the way in which corners are being cut and money is being made in ways that are at least bordering on the unscrupulous. It tends to be summed up by the people saying that they doubt whether it really

is good enough any more to leave the policing of the City to self-regulation. I'm afraid that all this is pretty vague and unspecific; but I find it sufficiently prevalent to be concerned.

The tone was strikingly different from that adopted the previous year in memos sent by John Redwood, when he had hailed Big Bang and urged Thatcher to take her share of the credit for what was coming. Redwood then left the Policy Unit to rejoin N.M. Rothschild as a director, responsible for overseas corporate finance and selling expertise on privatisation to governments outside the UK. He was joined there later by another member of the Policy Unit, Oliver Letwin. David Willetts, who stayed on in Downing Street, was notably more cautious than Redwood, and the tenor of discussions about Big Bang inside Number 10 changed with the great day drawing close. While free market theorising was all very well, the cold, hard implications for the government of it potentially backfiring were now considered in detail. At that point Thatcher was still, just, for all her reputation for being unyielding, a canny assessor of political risk. On the afternoon of 5 June 1986, she met to review Big Bang with the Chancellor, Nigel Lawson; the Secretary of State for Trade and Industry, Paul Channon; the Governor of the Bank of England, Robin Leigh-Pemberton; the Treasury's Permanent Secretary, Peter Middleton; John Caines from the DTI; David Walker from the Bank, and Professor Brian Griffiths of the Number 10 Policy Unit. Ahead of their discussion, Griffiths and his colleague David Willetts encapsulated the concerns in a note to the Prime Minister: 'If Big Bang goes off successfully, it will be seen as a showpiece for Government policy on deregulation and increased competition; if it leads to scandals and liquidations, it will be labelled the unacceptable face of unpopular capitalism.' They posed some good questions. Will there be boom and bust? Will there be fraud? Might the Americans and the Japanese dominate London? Is the regulatory regime right? Will the technology be ready?

Lawson opened the meeting by agreeing with Thatcher that there were risks and that inevitably there would be mistakes. Yet change was essential if the City was to remain competitive, he said. In the discussion that followed, the opportunities for fraud were a particular concern. 'The temptation to fraud, or to unethical behaviour, would be increased by the competitive pressures', an official wrote. Those present were encouraged that some financial institutions had hired compliance directors to ensure their colleagues stayed within the new rules that were on their way, although it was also observed that firms were increasing the scale of risks they carried off balance sheet. The new regulators would need to cooperate closely with their counterparts in other leading countries, although it was claimed the regulators were also finding it difficult at that stage to attract top-quality staff. Lloyd's the insurance market got a mention too, thanks to the assorted ongoing investigations into corrupt practices. When it came to Big Bang every effort must be made, it was agreed, to promote the benefits to the wider economy. Otherwise, 'there was a risk that people would only look at the high salaries and the deal-making' (this turned out to have been something of an understatement). Thatcher closed by requesting a further report to be circulated in mid-September, a month or so before D-Day.

There were portents of trouble ahead for British firms that summer, with several of the institutions that had paid large amounts for jobbing and broking firms still struggling to resolve the culture clashes that had resulted from takeovers and mergers. At BZW, the Barclays concoction created by the merger of Barclays merchant bank, de Zoete & Bevan and Wedd Durlacher in the hope that it would become a truly British rival to the major American investment banks, they were still stricken by internal warfare more than a year after the formation of BZW. This was despite the best efforts of chairman Martin Jacomb, formerly of Kleinwort Benson, who used to tell his team that challenging Goldman Sachs and Merrill Lynch 'is within our grasp'. One of the senior executives recalls it being a doomed venture: 'I'm afraid it was the worst type of British disaster. Many good staff and ideas. A lot of amateurishness. And a fair amount of strutting about.' As his colleague, Martin

Vander-Weyer, then a Barclays merchant banker and later a journalist, said: 'This was supposed to be the sexy side of finance, while high-street lending to personal customers and smaller businesses – the area in which Barclays had real expertise in depth – was an unglamorous poor relation.'[5]

Another esteemed British merchant bank was not making good progress either. The efforts by some of the management at Morgan Grenfell in 1986 to inject some dynamism and aggression produced a culture that was robust bordering on the nasty. As in other firms, the recruitment of outsiders caused resentment and some badmouthing of existing staff. Geoffrey Collier, who would be in the headlines very soon, and not in a good way, ran the new securities team in a particularly lively manner. Other British Establishment names dealt with the coming change differently. Barings opted not to partner with an outside investor, thus continuing family control. Hambro went in the other direction, when the family – Jocelyn, and his three sons, Rupert, Richard and James – departed in early 1986. Lazard, the merchant bank that was tied closely to its American and French counterparts of the same name, had stayed out of the securities business entirely. And stockbroker Cazenove would carry on as before, having not bought a jobbing firm or sought to change its business model.

There were further growing pains at the Stock Exchange, where Nicholas Goodison, with the help of Stani Yassukovich, was attempting to deal with a row that had the potential to jeopardise Big Bang, or at least to render it a damp squib over the next few years if it was not resolved soon. The original Gower proposals and the government's proposals for reform had been written almost as though the Eurobond market had not been invented. But this was the largest capital market in the world, so it must come within the scope of any new regulation, surely? Yassukovich, as a leading Eurobond practitioner, had become embroiled in trying to resolve the dispute, so that the regulation of Eurobonds (which were issued and traded beyond the remit of the Exchange) and the regulation of the Exchange itself might be merged. There was much opposition to the Exchange having control, particularly from Ian Steers of Wood Gundy, one of the biggest operators. It was only in September, with the 'Treaty of Throgmorton Street', that a compromise was agreed. The International Securities Regulatory Organisation (ISRO) merged with the Stock Exchange and Yassukovich became deputy chairman of the renamed International Stock Exchange. After almost two and a half decades in which it had attempted to act as though Eurobonds did not exist (the Eurobond market was the much bigger international market), they were now working together.

At the Conservative Party conference that year in Brighton, the Prime Minister was in a highly optimistic mood on the domestic front – not necessarily about Big Bang, but about the wider programme of which it was a part, a mission she termed a 'popular capitalism crusade' to enfranchise the many in the economic life of the nation. 'Millions have already become shareholders. And soon there will be opportunities for millions more, in British Gas, British Airways, British Airports and Rolls-Royce. Who says we've run out of steam? We're in our prime!'[6] The Conservatives under her, she said, were returning power to the people. 'That is the way to one nation, one people.' If she felt that she was now in control of events and in command of the battlefield at home, a jolt was delivered a few days later. At the Reykjavik summit between President Reagan and the Soviet leader Mikhail Gorbachev on the 11th and 12th, the American leader got carried away and proposed scrapping all nuclear weapons within ten years, a suggestion which terrified Thatcher. Persuading Reagan that his idea was impractical, and a threat to Western European security, occupied much of her time from then until her trip to Washington in November, where she succeeded in correcting American policy. Big Bang would not get much attention from Number 10 until after it had happened.

In October 1986, as the day approached, George Hayter continued to have difficulty convincing older London firms that the changes were going to succeed. Some well-established firms simply could not believe that the days of face-to-face trading were going to be over. Will George's computers work? they asked Goodison. They will work, Goodison said repeatedly. Even so, unconvinced market makers also wondered whether computers could entirely replace human contact on the floor of the Exchange. The sceptics had lobbied successfully for the installation of screens above the floor itself, at a cost of £2m, and they demanded increasing amounts of space. Twenty-eight firms declared they wanted to keep a pitch for face-to-face trading. Smith New Court was convinced it would need several dozen traders on the floor itself. It was as though they could not quite compute the disruption that was coming.

The full implications of London's expansion were beginning to be understood abroad, however. In Florence, the week before Big Bang at a conference of analysts from European financial institutions, the theme was 'towards an integrated European financial market', an aspiration that was fashionable in the light of the creation of Europe's single market and the determination of Europe's major governments to push for more trade, in finance as well as in goods.[7] The danger for other European financial centres, it was admitted, was that they were about to be left behind by London. A German analyst, Jochen Neynaber, warned about the impact: 'Frankfurt, Milan and Zurich will be provinces, particularly if we continue to be unable to synchronise our dealing and settlement mechanisms.' Patrick Lanney, a Brussels stockbroker, said that stock exchanges on the European continent must modernise urgently to keep up. From the US giant Morgan Stanley, Archie Cox – who ran its then still relatively small operation in London – made it clear that London would extend its lead. The future was big firms and big banks that would operate as 'global financial supermarkets' in which customers could access all the services they needed in one stop. Those giants would gravitate towards, and put their headquarters in, where most of the action was, he said. The strong implication was that London would be it. To underscore the point, a member of the Stock Exchange Council in London somewhat cheekily urged the members of other European Exchanges to come and play in the City.

There was a little less confidence on the ground as the City prepared for its first full rehearsal. Hayter's team had been testing the systems for months, but it was only on 18 October, nine days before Big Bang, that everyone tried it together for real. There was grumbling from some firms that there had been insufficient support and guidance from the Stock Exchange, although such complaints were dismissed by Goodison and Patrick Mitford-Slade, chairman of the Information and Communications Committee. If the newly merged firms had not invested enough in computer firepower then that was their fault. The Stock Exchange could not do everything.

It had been more than twenty years since the City stopped trading on Saturdays but for the rehearsal that old Victorian custom was resumed on a one-off basis. The *FT*'s reporter recorded the scene as work began early in the tower blocks and offices of the City. 'At 7.30am rows of strip lighting started to come on, shining through the mist and low cloud, as the newly integrated firms . . . prepared to log on for the first time to Seaq.' In the Christopher Street IT office, the computers were ready for early trading at 8am; shortly after that, the first attempts at buying and selling began. At 8.45am seventeen transactions per second were being processed, against a capacity of forty transactions per second, with the market on track to hit a deadline of 30,000 share prices having been accurately updated by 9am. But then problems developed, and not just because of the computers. 'It was very noisy,' recalls one participant. 'There was suddenly a lot of shouting across the desks and people standing up.' In the offices of dual-capacity firms, where former jobbers and brokers were now working together across from each other, within the same operation, it would take time for a smooth working partnership to develop. At the first real test with the market live, there were misunderstandings when cultures clashed. The brokers with clients on the telephone wanted their favoured customers dealt with first and let their colleagues know when they were unhappy or thought the service was too slow. The jobbers were too used to effectively being in charge.

The Bank of England's problems were simpler. A fire in a lift shaft at lunchtime meant the building had to be evacuated, although Eddie George and his team running the gilts operation had some trouble convincing staff that this was not a drill. Only when there was smoke in the corridors did the building empty for half an hour, disrupting the trading of gilts. While the central gilts office, which housed the Bank of England computer that settled all the deals in UK government debt, also went down for ninety minutes, Eddie George and his team were not concerned. Elsewhere the results of computerisation were mixed. Tim Coghlan, the BZW head of equities, said that there had been a 'fair feeling of depression' when the computers seemed to 'clog up'. But it picked up as the day went on, he said. Wood Street Securities suffered worse malfunctions, and there were problems too at Akroyd and Smithers, Kitcat & Aitken, Scrimgeour Vickers, Wood Mackenzie, W. Greenwell and Hoare Govett. The complaints were dismissed at a press conference given by Patrick Mitford-Slade at the Stock Exchange Tower at 5pm on the Saturday evening. He said that most of the problems were caused by the companies themselves and not by Hayter's team. There was even a suggestion that in some firms staff had overloaded the systems earlier in the day because they hoped to get away early, although it is more likely that there was a rush of excitement from those keen to try the new systems. As a result, a few firms declared that they would have to attempt further intensive rehearsals in the week ahead.

The fear of failure and embarrassment in public was accentuated by the sudden increase in interest from the international media, although not all of it was entirely serious in tone. American journalists in particular seemed to relish the concept of British City gents in bowler hats having to make it into the office before 9.30 in the morning. The *New York Times* put Peter Rawlinson, a partner in Schweder, Miller & Company, on its front page, in a photograph in which he was engaged (in a bowler hat, wielding a rolled umbrella) in the apparently remarkable act of going to work early. Phillips & Drew, a London broker, had even taken to providing a full English breakfast of eggs, bacon, sausages, mushrooms, 'the works', now that their staff were in before 8am. There was considerable mockery from Americans on Wall Street, who seemed in contrast so energetic that they might as well have got up before they went to bed, so eager were they to get into the office and begin trading. As usual, behind the headlines, the caricature of sleepy London and dynamic New York was not entirely fair. The smarter Wall Street types understood that the creation of the International Stock Exchange, and its merger with ISRO, was a threat, especially when added to London's exceptional cocktail of advantages: time zone, language, proximity to mainland Europe's markets, global links and centuries of financial innovation.

The reality of London's decades-long return and rise was also captured in the exhaustive pull-out in the *FT* on the morning of Big Bang. Such strong interest from the media resulted in a full house on the morning of Monday 27 October, when Hayter readied himself for launch. The risky notion of making the switch in one go on that morning as the London markets opened for business, and calling it Big Bang, had seemed like a good idea several years before. Now, shortly before 8am as Goodison surveyed the floor of the Exchange crowded with foreign television crews and curious journalists, he was a little apprehensive. After so much hype about the possibilities, and difficult negotiations with Margaret Thatcher's ministers, together with efforts to persuade the more conservative elements in the City that the revolution was really necessary, Goodison and his team were about to find out if the new computing systems would work when real trading started. Had the IT team in which Goodison had put so much faith to deliver the most widely advertised change in the City of London's long history done its job properly?

On the floor of the Exchange that Monday morning, some of the journalists – shepherded by the Stock Exchange's head of press Luke Glass – were waiting to find out the answer while explaining to each other why they were there. Sheila MacVicar of the Canadian Broadcast Corporation told the *Financial Times* that it was obvious

Toronto would be interested in Big Bang because Canadian financiers (living in the long shadow of New York) were keen to plug into the new global market. There was also interest in the implications for class-conscious Britain, she said. Canadians wanted to see 'how bowler-hatted gentlemen with rolled umbrellas who lived stable lives with their dogs in the country' would adapt to the computer era.

A producer for the West German TV station, ARD, explained that he and his crew had almost not made it along to watch Big Bang. The previous day – on Sunday – a British tabloid had exposed the Tory politician and novelist Jeffrey Archer. The order from Germany was that the ARD crew should drop plans to cover the Stock Exchange in London to go after a seemingly bigger bang, namely the story of Archer handing over money to a prostitute in Victoria Station and resigning as deputy chairman of the Conservative Party all the while proclaiming his innocence. Archer pledged to sue for libel. His denial echoed down the years, triggering a chain of events that took him many years later to prison for perjury. The man from ARD decided to ignore the demand from Germany to switch attention to Archer and turned up at the Stock Exchange on the Monday morning regardless. 'Knowing what I do about news editors I decided to go ahead anyway in case they changed their mind and asked for the pictures,' he said. This was to prove a sensible decision, considering what happened next.

As the journalists prattled and poked their noses around the hexagonal trading positions on the Exchange floor they were watched from the sidelines by traders waiting to get on with it, some of them impatient and annoyed at the presence of the media. They did not have long to wait. The computers warmed up, feeding information back to the offices of firms around the City, and at 8am the market opened formally. For almost fifteen minutes all was well. Then it started to go wrong.

John Scannell, the chief engineer, was in one of the operation rooms. He later described the system becoming overloaded with requests from curious firms eager to try it out:

Eight o'clock comes and the systems all come up. And we're looking at the page response request and it goes up to 1.7 million immediately which is a little bit bloody worrying. Then it crept up to sort of two million, three million, and four million. What's going on? This is quarter past eight. Then it got to five million, then everything is going berserk. Bells, and whistling, and ringing, and popping and banging.[8]

At 8.25am the older and more basic TOPIC system, Teletext Output of Prices Information by Computer, was approaching full capacity. At 8.29, more warning lights came on and the much-vaunted Seaq system went down. Seaq, the Stock Exchange Automated Quotation, was the new part of the system that was supposed to supply almost instantaneous, accurate prices to brokers, many positioned in the new, enormous trading floors built in offices across the City and beyond. Sitting in front of computers at new, expensive trading positions, they would do their deals with each other on the telephone, all fed by a continuous perfect stream of information in real time flowing from Hayter's computers. That was the theory and already it wasn't working. It looked to the watching media as though the revolution had gone phut and splat instead of bang. It was all rather embarrassing and very British.

Sir Nicholas Goodison decided that the best approach was not to panic. Far better to deploy some good old-fashioned dry English humour when the journalists gathered around him demanding an explanation for the difficulties. There was too much strain on the system, he told them, because every trader, carried away with the novelty, was trying it out. 'If you put a new monkey or dodo in the zoo,' he said, 'people will queue up to see it.'[9] For the sceptics among the old hands suspicious of the claims made for Big Bang, use of the term dodo – a bird that had been doomed to early extinction because it could not fly – sounded highly appropriate. How could computer screens with flashing lights and bleeping terminals ever be more effective than old-style stockbrokers and jobbers, often acquainted for years, looking each other straight in the eye and drawing on intuition and decades of experience? Here, on day one, was proof that the revolution was a flop. The computers had crashed.

Out in what the *Financial Times* referred to as 'the provinces', where the sister exchanges were hooked up to the mothership in London, confusion reigned among stockbrokers looking at blank screens. In the Stock Exchange Tower, parts of the system would work for a few minutes and then get overloaded again. Hayter and his team battled throughout the day, introducing patches and doing the equivalent of turning off the computer and turning it back on again. There were mocking headlines in the next day's newspapers, inevitably. 'Computer snafu derails London's new Stock system', was how the *Los Angeles Times* put it. The technical problems looked like a classic British balls-up, involving a Heath Robinson contraption resting on little more than the high hopes of gentlemen amateurs.

Such sniggering cynicism was deeply unfair. Hayter and his team were skilled professionals working under pressure who had devised something that stood a good chance of working, once the initial embarrassment faded and the TV crews disappeared. By the close of business on day one they had stabilised the situation. One of the brokers, Martin Pope of Hoare Govett, shrugged off the difficulties and gave the classic City response that could have been uttered for centuries: 'We had a good day, we made money. That's what it's all about.'

By the end of the week the system was functioning with only a few restrictions. Seaq started to work in harmony with TOPIC, and the volume and speed of trading grew rapidly. Like one of the first successful flying machines, bumping along the ground before only slowly gaining a little height and then beginning an ascent, they were up and away. The positions, the old booths on the floor of the Exchange, were not needed either. Goodison went down to look a few days after launch and the place was deserted because the brokers were all back at their offices with their colleagues, using screens and doing business by telephone. The old floor would not be needed. Big Bang had not brought the House down after all. It had cleared

the way for an ambitious new computerised era. The City was ready
for the future.

Margaret Thatcher, whose name is bound irrevocably with Big
Bang, even though she had little to do with the intricacies of the
measures, was not there that day. She did turn out two days later to
another opening that encapsulated the can-do side of Thatcherism
and the possibility-laden spirit that dominated then in the southeast
of England. The completion of the final stretch of the M25 finished
the orbital motorway around the capital that had first been proposed
in 1905 and begun in 1973. Now cars would theoretically be able to
whizz around the capital at high speed, in the motoring equivalent
of the money revolution that had been launched a few days earlier.
On the morning of the opening, 29 October, the Transport Secretary,
John Moore, was taken over the route in a helicopter with officials
to check that all was well before the Prime Minister turned up to cut
the ribbon and make a speech. She was photographed striding out
alone across the empty lanes, clutching her handbag, looking like
Elizabeth I crossed with Elizabeth II. In her speech she said the M25
and the skills of the construction firms that built it symbolised
Britain's 1980s revival. Then she returned to her increasingly weari-
some complaint that criticism was running down the country: 'Now
some people are saying that the road is too small, even that it's a
disaster. I must say I can't *stand* those who carp and criticise when
they ought to be congratulating Britain on a magnificent achievement and beating the drum for Britain all over the world.' The M25,
variously termed 'the most hated road in Britain' and the 'road to
nowhere', soon became so busy and so essential to the economy of
the capital that it was difficult to imagine a time when it had not
been there.[10] It also presented illicit opportunities for those with
sports cars to race at night, as part of a mysterious group termed by
the media the 'M25' club. Police in Enfield said they had uncovered
a dastardly plan for illegal road racing. Sergeant Eric Lock said: 'It is
a rich race, with Ferrari [sic], Porsches and the very high-perfor-
mance cars. We are pretty sure the race will be around the M25 in
the early hours. We shall have extra patrols watching out and of

course we have surveillance cameras dotted around the motorway. As well as all this all the drivers will have to stop at the Dartford Tunnel so we shall be ready for them.' The claims of the existence of a London equivalent of Hollywood's Cannonball Run, with yuppies and traders speeding around the orbital in their Ferraris, were first reported by a young journalist then working for *The Times*. His name was Boris Johnson.

GUINNESS IS GOOD FOR YOU

'If it was just insider dealing, it's not a proper crime like stealing.'
Scilla, in Caryl Churchill's *Serious Money* (1987)

By 30 October 1986 Nicholas Goodison had had more than enough of the press writing cheeky stories mocking the initial misfiring of his Big Bang. In a letter to the editor of *The Times*, the chairman of the Stock Exchange defended the launch and said the problems had been resolved.

> For four days now your columns have carried lurid and emotive words like 'fiasco', 'utter confusion', 'shambles' and 'collapse' – and not a single word about the huge improvements in the operation of the market. Whilst we are aware of our outstanding problems, and are working hard to solve them, I think you should be aware, Sir, that your packaging has been garish and your contents deficient.[1]

Goodison felt that the media saw it all as a tremendous lark in the long-established tradition of good old-fashioned British bungling. And he was right to feel aggrieved, in that the achievement of Hayter and his team was remarkable, especially given the pressures on time and the spotlight under which they were working. Trading had been moved largely successfully off the floor of the Exchange and the computers had worked 97 per cent of the time with £2bn worth of business (a normal amount) transacted each day. Within a few days many of the remaining glitches would be dealt with, the

A pair of 1980s yuppies, of the London variety.

trading floor at the Exchange would be left all but empty, trading volumes would soar, and the execution of Big Bang would be hailed as an achievement, even if the ethical implications would remain a subject of dispute outside the City.

That autumn, the Prime Minister was certainly keen to celebrate what had been achieved. In her annual speech to the City's grandees at the Mansion House on 10 November, she praised Goodison by name, and his colleagues, for their foresight and hard work in the face of 'teething troubles' and 'a good deal of knocking copy'.[2] The carping obscured an injection of youthful energy and dynamism, she said. 'The City's growing confidence and drive owe a good deal to young people. Its vast new dealing rooms are run by the young. People who made it not because of who they know or what school tie they wear, but on sheer merit. That is the kind of society I want to see. Gone are the controls which hampered success.' Once again, the Thatcherites were talking in terms of control being abandoned. Even though Thatcher went on to explain in her speech that the government had established a new legal framework, the greater and more excited emphasis was put on the liberating aspects of technological change and the virility of younger traders. It is little wonder that this rather than the truth about regulation became the dominant narrative. Nevertheless, she added that the City's prosperity depended on its reputation for probity and fair dealing. 'The Stock Exchange has long had an impressive motto: "My Word is My Bond". That principle is not only part of its history, it is the basis of an even more successful future.'

Earlier that day, before Thatcher's speech in the evening at the Mansion House, someone senior who had betrayed that 'My Word is My Bond' motto resigned at Morgan Grenfell. Geoffrey Collier, head of the securities division, had been caught trading on inside information and funnelling the proceeds into an offshore account under another name. Until August 1985, Collier ran the Vickers de Costa operation in New York, before he was poached by Morgan Grenfell ahead of Big Bang. His signing-on fee, buying out his interests in the US, was a tax-free £250,000 and in his first year in his new position he earned £125,000. Even so, he traded on his own account without informing his employer, in breach of the rules, losing £30,000 in October 1986 when a tip he had about Cadbury Schweppes went wrong and the share price dipped unexpectedly. In early November he met with Robert Maxwell who was seeking to purchase an engineering group. Collier tried again and, through a contact in the US, secretly bought himself £144,000 of shares, giving him a profit of £15,000 when the news of the takeover offer became public. The management was alerted quickly by suspicious staff at the broker he had used, Scrimgeour Vickers. Not only was Collier in breach of company rules, which dictated every personal trade had to go through the company's own broker so it could be scrutinised; he had also broken the law. Collier – whose tough talk before Big Bang faded when it became clear he was a quiet family man facing potential ruin – was fired that day and a police investigation was launched. Several days later, Christopher Reeves, the chief executive of Morgan Grenfell, assured the press that such activity was not widespread: 'Mr. Collier clearly breached staff rules. This is something we are not prepared to tolerate, however senior the man.' It was an isolated incident, said a spokesman.

Following this setback, the year which had begun so promisingly at Morgan Grenfell was about to get a good deal worse. Reeves was regarded as one of the best bankers of his generation and after taking over the aged merchant bank in 1980 he had built it into a formidable machine. When it floated some of itself on the Stock Exchange in the same year as the run-up to Big Bang, raising more than £150m, demand was high and the offer was five times oversubscribed. But the aggressive push made by Morgan Grenfell turned out to have come at a cost, as was revealed by the exposure of Collier, and then a few weeks later by the emergence of the much bigger Guinness scandal. Although it had nothing to do directly with Big Bang, and its origins preceded the autumn of 1986, the illicit dealing and share support that were suddenly revealed were an extreme manifestation of the takeover mania consuming British business and finance in the 1980s. Indeed, Morgan Grenfell's testosterone surge that got it into such trouble was rooted in its aggressive expansion in that area. In 1986 it was the leader in London, seeking out, suggesting and advising on 111 takeovers. The revelation that the Guinness deal was suspect came via an investigation by US regulators that exposed a network on Wall Street of insider trading and share ramping by elite investment bankers supplementing their already vast incomes with trading on the side. Ivan Boesky, a tough operator who had used his wife's wealth to found his own stock trading firm, had made a fortune of several hundred million dollars by gambling on company takeovers. In November 1986, with Boesky cooperating with the SEC investigation in the US (he had even turned federal agent) he offered the information, almost as a throwaway, that Guinness in London had invested $100m with him. When news of this connection was passed to investigators at the Department of Trade and Industry in London, it led to an inquiry into the bid for Distillers. On 1 December, with Ernest Saunders, chairman and chief executive of Guinness, at work at his desk in London, two DTI officials turned up unannounced in reception at 9.30am. Their arrival caused panic.

In the US it was a tiny part, incidental even, in the uncovering of the multi-billion dollar racket in which the ringmasters were arbitrageurs such as Boesky. Eventually the much bigger fish – Michael Milken on the US West Coast – would fry too. In the UK, however, Guinness turned into the biggest corporate scandal of the decade. The transatlantic nature of the dealings and the sums involved demonstrated the increasingly interconnected nature of fast-moving markets, which was attributable to the spread of technology and the presence of the Americans in London and Tokyo. Although dynamism brought benefits, it also increased the potential for cultural contagion, not just in terms of market panic if stocks crashed, but also in the manner in which serious sums could be diverted almost instantly and the way in which corruption might spill across continents when borders were blurred. To critics of the City, it looked then as though an American virus had been injected into the British bloodstream, especially when figures such as Boesky were prepared to make the following statements: 'Greed is all right, by the way,' he told the 1986 graduation of UC–Berkeley's business school. 'I think greed is healthy. You can be greedy and still feel good about yourself.' Even if you think that, and you shouldn't, it is unwise to say it in public. There was another plausible interpretation, of course: that it had always gone on and the new generation was just more blatant and less embarrassed.

What was Saunders accused of in December 1986? During the takeover battle for Distillers that began in late 1985, he had organised a share support operation to keep the Guinness share price high and stiff the rival bidders, the Argyll Group run by James Gulliver. Those under investigation protested that this technique was hardly unknown in the City, even if the sums involved this time (as much as £300m) were large. The money invested with Boesky had landed after he bought Guinness and Distillers shares heavily. He was operating alongside a small group of investors and favoured speculators in London and Switzerland who were invited into the secret operation and given payments and an indemnity against any fall in the price of the shares they bought secretly on behalf of Saunders' team. Literally, they could not lose. 'They were greedy but they were caught in between eras, when one era ended and another began,' says a leading banker of the time, referring to the changes in regulation and the government's hardening attitude. 'It was that point when the music stops in musical chairs, and some people are left standing.'

Saunders was not the only person left exposed. Soon it became clear that some of the City's smartest names – including Cazenove – had been involved in arranging these trades, although they protested that they were innocent of wrongdoing. As an advisor to Guinness, Morgan Grenfell was implicated and Reeves – whose friends claimed he had known little directly about what had gone on – came under pressure from appalled officials at the Bank of England. On 30 December, amid a blizzard of revelations in the press, Morgan Grenfell resigned as advisors to Guinness. That day

Roger Seelig, the Morgan Grenfell takeover specialist who had handled the Guinness deal, was sacked. In mid-January, Saunders himself was fired by the board of Guinness, and at Morgan Grenfell on 20 January, Reeves resigned along with Graham Walsh, the corporate finance director. Rarely, since the scandals of the nineteenth century, had there been such a casualty list in a financial scandal, and the investigation had only begun.

Somewhat awkwardly, the City authorities and the government were then caught between hoping that the incidence of white-collar crime and insider trading was extremely low, while also wanting to advertise that the place was being energetically cleaned up. Both could not be true. Says one leading banker of the time on the question of insider dealing: 'It would not be legitimate at all to say that everyone was at it but it was a significant minority I think.' Says a former jobber: 'Some people had thrived for years on that "fill your boots" mentality, running their little sidelines. Most of it was pretty small. You have to remember that before the law changed the City ran anyway on inside information, on price-sensitive information that if you were attentive you picked up on the way to lunch or to the pub. You ran into someone and they said, "I'd take a look at X, very interesting. They've just had some good news that's not public yet; going to be good for the share price." People being what they are, some didn't abuse that. Others did.' One infuriating and baffling aspect, as far outsiders were concerned, was that as the City grew, financiers and traders such as Collier at Morgan Grenfell were already – legally – making large amounts of money. Yet still it seemed not to be enough and some made illicit trades in addition. How much more did they really need? As someone who has spent a lifetime in the City and worked on many of the biggest deals of the period puts it thirty years later: 'I'm sorry, it was greed. Big Bang let a lot of the crooks in. There you have it.'

That may be an exaggeration. George Blakey, in his history of the Stock Market, explained that there was nothing new about encouraging institutions and large individual investors to support a share price during a takeover attempt. It was merely a question of discretion and scale. It had usually been done by a nod or a wink over lunch at the Savoy Grill, or in the evening in clubland in St James's. 'Until this point, no authority would have been expected to question seriously the conduct of the City's leading merchant banks, stockbrokers and their clients. What the Guinness/Morgan Grenfell/Cazenove case did was to shatter the belief that the customary test of legitimacy was who you were, not what you did.'

The government's unease about these events was understandable. In all other respects Margaret Thatcher was extremely well placed ahead of an anticipated election in 1987. The economy under Nigel Lawson was growing strongly – at 3.2 per cent in 1986 and picking up speed – while unemployment had started in January 1986 to fall from stubbornly high levels. On the industrial front, the violent Wapping print dispute rumbled on over that winter, when thousands of activists fought with police outside the print plant that had been built in London east of Tower Hill to end the 'Spanish practices' that bedevilled the newspaper business.[3] After the Miners' Strike of 1984–5, Wapping marked the death of the power of the militant side of trade unionism. Indeed, the Tory leader recorded in her memoirs later that she felt at the end of 1986 as though it was all coming together. The reforms she had put in place were embedded and the privatisation and liberalisation of financial markets would soon be copied abroad. The Thatcherites had won.

The only economic blot, even in the parts of the country well disposed towards Thatcher, was the strong whiff of corruption wafting over from the Square Mile. In mitigation, the Prime Minister could point to the privatisation of British Gas in December 1986, centring on an advertising campaign bearing the catchphrase 'If you see Sid, tell 'im.' Sid was supposed to symbolise the British 'punter' being let in on a valuable secret. Although the tone was jocular and patronising, irritatingly so, the intent was deadly serious. There remained widespread public scepticism about privatisation (a word even Thatcher said in public that she did not much care for) on the grounds that it involved selling what many taxpayers thought they already had collective ownership of through their government. When the advertising agency Dewe Rogerson drew up its initial report planning the sale, it warned that overcoming voter hostility would require a television, radio and press advertising campaign that presented it as a not-to-be-missed opportunity for small investors. It was the creative agency Young & Rubicam that came up with the everyman Sid. It worked. With six weeks to go until the offer, there had been almost two million enquiries made to the telephone hotline, and polling suggested that there was a 74 per cent awareness of Sid among adults. When the final adverts were made, the agency wanted to give Sid a good send-off. He was cast as a climber disappearing into the clouds at the summit, as the final message reminded Britons not to forget to apply for shares in British Gas. In early December 1986, in a buoyant market, more than five million people did just that. 'British Gas', the Energy Secretary, Peter Walker, told the Commons, would have 'the largest number of shareholders of any company in the world'. Some 85,000 employees of British Gas, 99 per cent of the workforce, had applied, he added. A sale raising £5.6bn was used by the government to hymn the success of the concept of 'popular capitalism' and the extension of ownership. The opening up of one-time state monopolies to outside investment could not have been done without the help and expertise of the City.

There was not much time for ministers to celebrate, however, as early in the new year the focus was straight back on the flow of revelations and resignations resulting from the Guinness scandal. On 22 January 1987, Thatcher attempted to make it clear in the Commons that she would not tolerate any nonsense from the City, a line of defence that did not impress Labour MPs. 'I remind the House that this Government is fully committed to rooting out financial wrongdoing wherever it occurs,' she said. 'Because this Government made insider trading a criminal offence and provided that upon conviction it should carry a prison sentence.' On 28

January, Cazenove was cited in the Commons over Guinness. With the protection of parliamentary privilege, Labour's Robin Cook accused the firm of ramping up the share price. Sir Alex Fletcher, a Tory MP who as former Minister of Consumer and Corporate Affairs had enjoyed a small walk-on part in the preparations for Big Bang, spoke of dark deeds, although he was a consultant to Argyll, the rival to Guinness in the Distillers battle. He said that Price Waterhouse, the accountants tasked with examining the accounts of Guinness, 'might find evidence of cash payments for which there are no invoices that were probably made in plain brown envelopes and made to members of the professional criminal classes'. What a combination: 'might find evidence . . . cash payments . . . brown envelopes . . . the criminal classes'. Even Tory business-minded MPs were upping the rhetoric. The government was so concerned by the furore that Norman Tebbit even went as far as to invoke Conservative trade union reforms to illustrate the determination to tackle insider dealing and other illegality: 'We cleaned up the trade union movement and we'll clean up the City,' he said in early 1987.

Here there were a number of difficulties. At the time, the Secretary of State for Trade and Industry was Paul Channon. Being a Guinness he had to recuse himself during the investigation, even though he was not directly linked to the management of the company.[4] The association was unfortunate in the middle of a clean-up, even though he was blameless. Worse, the phrase self-regulation in terms of the City had become fixed in the political media and public imagination as the root of the problem. The Thatcherite emphasis on the term deregulation meant that there was no chance of getting a hearing for the notion that the rules were being tightened or that for the first time there was a statutory, legal framework. Sir Peter Tapsell MP, who had worked in the City, summed up how it looked: 'To the average citizen, defending self-regulation sounds like letting the privileged protect their own. Nobody blames the US Republicans for Boesky because Wall Street is regulated by the SEC. If Britain had a similar body, the Conservatives could no more be blamed for this than for the Great Train Robbery.'⁵ The Labour Party was even more blunt in its pre-election criticism of the government's handling of Guinness. 'The scandal shows how easily the unscrupulous and shameless reward themselves in Mrs Thatcher's Britain,' said John Smith, the party's trade and industry spokesman. This line of attack infuriated government ministers. To Michael Howard, who had steered through the Act mandating re-regulation of the City that became law in November 1986, it made no sense whatsoever. They were cracking down hard, weren't they? The DTI launched another four investigations into insider trading in the weeks after the Boesky and Saunders revelations and there were some signs that the DTI investigations were beginning to have the cooling effect that the government desired, at least ahead of the election. There seemed for a while to be a pause in the take-over boom. Why would aggressive takeover artists risk poor publicity and worse with the government under pressure to show it was not soft on the City? In mid-January, the corporate raiders BTR dropped a bid for Pilkington, the long-established British glass-maker. Amid concern on the government side, and with members of the Labour front bench revving up to attack City greed and corporate vandalism, it was not the ideal moment to attempt a controversial takeover of a prominent British company. The lull was short-lived, however, and contrary to much of the reporting in the early part of that year, 1987 set a new takeover record in the UK.⁶ There were 1,125 such deals to a value of £15.4bn. In 1984 the equivalent figures had been 568 acquisitions to a value of only £5.5bn. Merger mania was not over yet, and it would take something else other than Guinness to reduce the pace and restore a sense of proportion.

First, there was the 1987 general election to prepare for. In Lawson's Budget on 17 March, the Chancellor cut the basic rate of tax (by 2p to 27p) and taxes on small business were reduced in a package that was received warmly by Conservative backbenchers looking to hold their seats. It was popular with those in the market too, and the FTSE continued its rise. The stock market was only the most public manifestation of exuberance and rising confidence in the City's position. London's clout was also demonstrated by the increasing commitment of the American and Japanese houses to the UK capital. Between 1984 and 1986 the American firms – CSFB, Goldman Sachs, Merrill Lynch, Shearson Lehman, Drexel Burnham Lambert and John Gutfreund's Salomon Brothers – had more than doubled their staffing in London, from 2,311 to 5,519. The Japanese staffed up too. This was encouraging, although there was a drawback. As the economist John O'Matthews put it: 'The result was to add capacity to markets with existing overcapacity.' The foreign firms were also there for access to the Eurobond markets, and to make money from the dramatic increase in Euromarket activity. The volume of new issuance increased by almost 400 per cent from 1983 to 1986, in which year it hit $191.7bn. The total turnover of the Eurobond market, three-quarters of which was in London, stood at $2 trillion. Again, this received little attention. It was simpler by far to concentrate on the glamour of takeovers, and the hypnotic graphs on television news programmes that showed share prices for household names rising, and footage of confident young men (and increasing numbers of women) looking serious on the telephone while making millions and then taking the edge off it with a glass of champagne in one of the City's wine bars in the evening.

London's confidence was by no means all chemical-fuelled hubris, however. It was well positioned to prosper from what had begun (in the early 1970s) as a veritable explosion in money, in how it could be moved, traded and imagined. It seemed as though the US was losing its advantage. Japan's securities houses had been growing so rapidly – fuelled by money from booming Japanese industry – that they now dwarfed their American counterparts. Nomura had a market cap of $33.6bn at the end of 1986, against $5.9bn for the aggressive Salomon and $4bn for Merrill Lynch. London, with its historic advantages, was in the process of becoming the global crossroads where all these firms needed to be. In the spring of 1987, in international terms, despite the scandals and disgrace, Britain was back. Thatcher sought a third term looking forward to further reform and innovation, and Lawson made it clear to the Prime Minister that he would be part of it. He wanted to stay on as Chancellor after the election because his ambition was to complete his overhaul of the UK's tax system, and to bring down those taxes substantially.

Later in the same week as the March 1987 pre-election Budget, a play opened at the Royal Court theatre in London that sought to encapsulate London's financial revolution and to capture the essence of Big Bang's afterglow. The playwright Caryl Churchill's *Serious Money* was a satire on trading in which the new City was presented as being simply a cruder version of its ancient predecessor. In the text there are echoes of those plays written in the eighteenth century in the aftermath of the South Sea Bubble, and in particular of William Chetwood's *South-Sea; or the Biters Bit*. ('Plow: A Stock-jobber! Pray, Sir, what Religion may he be of?') Churchill and the cast – which included Gary Oldman, Alfred Molina and Meera Syal – visited the floor of LIFFE to familiarise themselves with the colourful, noisy futures market operating out of the Royal Exchange Building. When the play opened, the theatre critics were, as is usually the case, divided.[7] Martin Hoyle, of the City's own *Financial Times*, hated what had been done by Churchill and the director Max Stafford-Clark, the artistic director of the Royal Court. Stafford-Clark had been, along with David Hare, one of the founders in the 1970s of the socialist alternative theatre company, Joint Stock, which shared a name with the term used to describe early capitalist companies, the joint-stock companies such as the South Sea. An unimpressed Coveney described Churchill's writing in *Serious Money* as witless and facetious, churned out in doggerel, 'neither Restoration couplets nor Victorian panto poesy but a broken-backed jumble of varying rhythms, metre and rhyme that the author shoves into the ragbag from one moment to the next . . . Insiders may well enjoy the play. Outsiders may experience a numbing boredom.'

Some critics had perhaps missed part of the point, in that *Serious Money* was meant to be noisy, bawdy, uneven, cunning, silly, fun and fast-paced, just like the City, mirroring a trading session at LIFFE or a spot of stockjobbing in Change Alley in the eighteenth century. Churchill had produced an era-defining classic. Michael Billington in the *Guardian* rightly judged that she and Stafford-Clark, and the cast, had set out to produce a critique, a 'socialist play about a capitalist pleasure' as the *Listener* magazine called it. Yet they had ended up, in Billington's words, as fascinated by the City's frenzied energy as they were by its moral unscrupulousness. The critic from the *FT* was prescient in one sense, in that it was the insiders who loved *Serious Money* most. Tickets soon became coveted by dealers; indeed, they were that summer a tradable commodity. The City journalist Neil Collins in the *Daily Telegraph* described the excitement: 'Designed by Ms Churchill as a savage attack on the City, the same rough-edged dealers have flocked to see it in their hundreds, organising parties, taking the whole office, and having fun identifying themselves on the stage.' Max Stafford-Clark insisted that he was pleased the traders liked their portrayal: 'If you capture accurately enough the world of the people you are depicting, then it's very flattering and they will come and see it, just as people did in the Restoration.'

The success of the play had demonstrated one of the paradoxes of the period. Those in the vanguard of the financial revolution – the new generation of fast-rising traders who were questioned and increasingly mocked by middle-class journalists for their ethics, their accents, their behaviour or their taste in clothes or cars – were not ashamed. And why should they be in the circumstances? Their heroine, the Prime Minister, presented their ambition as a force for good, banishing memories of national decline. And who were the upper middle classes in particular to call the socially mobile traders vulgar anyway? In the City, as partners, the officer class had taken the money and run away at high speed during the carnival of largesse when old firms were bought up by Americans and other firms pre-Big Bang. Now that the Bang had boomed why shouldn't the troops see some of the action too?

The drama was not over, though. As spring turned into summer, it looked to outsiders as though levels of smugness on pay and status were going through the roof. As far as Thomas Sutcliffe was concerned, writing in the *Independent* that summer on the City dealer fashion for going to the theatre to see Caryl Churchill's play, the enthusiasm had got completely out of hand. The traders flocking to *Serious Money* were spoiling things for the rest of the audience, he wrote. 'It's now a little like going to see *The Resistible Rise of Arturo Ui* with a coach party of SS men.'

HIGH SUMMER

'I don't think we're going to see any more scandals on a very large scale. I think people have learnt their lesson.'

Ian Harwood, Warburg Securities, June 1987

On Friday 12 June 1987, the day after Margaret Thatcher's third general election victory, the BBC sent the presenter Joan Bakewell across to the City in search of jubilant traders at lunchtime. Let's go, said David Dimbleby, the forty-eight-year-old anchor of the Corporation's rolling election coverage, to an aerial shot from the airship the BBC had hired for the day: 'Looking down over the Big Bang . . . those huge towers that have gone up over the last few years . . . where the yuppies live, the people who drive down there between half past four and half past seven in the morning in their Porsches we're told and make a lot of money.' Signalling the relief of traders who did not want a Labour government, the stock market opened up strongly that morning in response to the news that the Conservatives had been re-elected with a majority of 102 seats.

It had been a scratchy contest defined by infighting in the Tory high command over how best to take on Neil Kinnock and see off Labour's slick but ultimately unsuccessful campaign. Once the camera crew with Bakewell had got its pictures of brick-like mobile phones and champagne flutes outside a bar, she asked a group of traders wearing the coloured jackets of those who worked at LIFFE whether they were going to become even richer now the Tories had got back in. They demurred at the idea that they were rich at all. So why were they celebrating? 'Why am I so pleased? Because I'm standing out here drinking champagne, basically,' said one. If Bakewell was looking for triumphalism among Thatcher's children, what she found instead was calm reflection and an eloquent explanation from several of the traders that the result would not make them any better off. Labour's high taxes, they said, would have made both them and the country worse off. But, asked Bakewell, what about the unemployed and the homeless? Unemployment would go down now, hopefully, one of the traders said: 'It's the safest and steadiest the country's been for years. Keep it on an even keel.' 'We've never had it so good, as they say,' said his colleague. 'Yeah,' said the first trader, taking a swig of champagne, 'Harold Macmillan. Where is he?'

The answer was that Harold Macmillan was no longer with us. The former Prime Minister had died in December the previous year at Birch Grove, his country house in Sussex. Macmillan's death represented the passing of a particular kind of patrician twentieth-century Toryism. The old 'actor-manager' was born in the late nineteenth century; he had fought and was wounded five times in the First World War; his career had been rescued and reinvented thanks to his appointment by Churchill in the Second; and as Prime Minister he hosted President Kennedy at Birch Grove in 1963. While he was opposed to Thatcher's approach to economics, it would not be true to say that Macmillan lacked understanding of aspiration. Far from it. He was introduced to an earlier version of social mobility when he lost his northern parliamentary seat, Stockton, in 1945 and switched immediately in a by-election to the safe seat of Bromley in Kent, where the Old Etonian encountered the rising, southern part of the lower middle classes working in new industries and in offices. He was curious about those who came from a different background to him, as he had been in the trenches. 'I am always hearing about the middle classes', he wrote to the director of the Conservative research department in 1957. 'What is it that they really want? Can you put it down on a sheet of notepaper, and then I will see whether we can give it to them?'[1] Thatcher needed no such guidance in discerning what Middle England voters wanted out of life; she was of striving Middle England herself and her instincts accorded perfectly with those voters she needed to reach to win. She was helped to that final electoral victory in the summer of 1987 by the opposition forces remaining divided too.

What had most troubled Macmillan and other so-called 'one nation' Conservatives about thrusting 1980s Thatcherism was that it seemed to have divided the country itself, between south and north and haves and have-nots. Such opinions were hardly unusual in the British Establishment in the 1980s, and indeed they formed the main thrust of the account the *Sunday Times* had already published of the Queen's concerns about the style and policies of the Prime Minister. The Conservatives certainly won a thumping majority in 1987, but in large parts of the country they had few or no seats. In Scotland, they were down to only ten constituencies and unlike in the US, where the Reaganite revolution was far more evenly spread geographically, pro-market Thatcherism was by this point a phenomenon that was in electoral terms largely (although not exclusively) restricted to the populous south centred on London and to parts of the Midlands. This puzzled Thatcher no end, especially in relation to Scotland, from where hailed the eighteenth-century father of market economics, Adam Smith. Her polite attempt to explain all this enraged her opponents when she later made the 'Sermon on the Mound' speech to the General Assembly of the Church of Scotland in Edinburgh in 1988, extolling the virtues of capitalism and giving the Scots credit for originating free market Thatcherism via Smith. The Tory leader's remarks went down that day in much of Scotland about as well as a request for a glass of Pimm's and a copy of *Tatler* in a Glasgow bar.

The other source of Macmillan's concern about the state of mid-1980s Britain in the years before his death was less well advertised, although it was linked to his condemnation of privatisation that was being achieved with the assistance of bankers and brokers. Macmillan had long retained an intense suspicion and dislike of the City, which was rooted in his experience of the late 1920s and the failures of finance that then caused large-scale unemployment. Anti-Semitism may have played a part. In private, Macmillan even used the term 'banksters' to describe bankers, according to Nigel Lawson, who knew him and in 1963 was drafted in to improve Macmillan's speeches. Macmillan had resigned by the time Lawson arrived and he found himself working for his aristocratic successor Alec Douglas-Home instead. In the mid-1980s as Chancellor, Lawson was pivotal in unravelling the Macmillan approach to economic management, rejecting the old Keynesian nostrum of delivering full employment through demand management and government involvement in industry. The Thatcherite programme so hated by opponents at that point and celebrated by its advocates as a British rebirth was not conservative in the usual sense, even if it involved going back to open markets, mobile money and the concept of London as a leading international trading hub as it had been at its Victorian and Edwardian peak. The Thatcherite impulse involved the sudden unleashing of such powerful disruptive forces in terms of class and attitudes to money that it made supporters and opponents alike aware that there was a revolution underway.

In such potentially combustible circumstances, with large parts of Britain unpersuaded and sympathetic to the colourful charges made by Labour that the Thatcherites were empowering spivs who cared only for cash, it would have helped if everyone in the City had behaved themselves that summer of 1987. Unfortunately that was not the case, and with a four-year bull run reaching its culmination, optimism tipped into outright greed and recklessness. Those in the markets pushing up prices on the FTSE 100 – up almost 25 per cent in 1986 and up 46 per cent in the first seven months of 1987 – did not have the benefit of hindsight, although those who cared to look could have found plenty of indications of what might be around the corner if they had examined the history of financial markets during periods of exuberance. There had also been a warning in another part of the market that what goes up can come down. In late 1986 and early 1987, the Floating Rate Note market – in the Eurobond market – experienced extreme turbulence. At Salomon Brothers in

London there was an inquest. Many of those selling in other firms had no experience, it was noted in memos. They were youngsters earning a lot of money with no understanding of the destructive power of a sudden change in conditions for the worse. Bosses were obsessed with getting their firm higher up the league tables, which meant reckless over-expansion. They had collaborated to ramp up the market, and investors who had grown careless had now been driven away when they realised they were being exploited.

Elsewhere, among traders there was comfort in knowing that the rises were replicated and even exceeded in the international centres. It was the Japanese who seemed to have taken complete leave of their senses, and if there was a correction due it would surely be worst there. Tokyo's Nikkei 225 index, bigger by total value than the US stock market for much of the 1980s, rocketed almost 11,000 points in the twelve months before October 1987, and it soon recovered from a tumble that June and July.

There was also a brief dip in the FTSE 100 in July after it hit a peak for the year on the 16th of 2443.4 points. The correction suggested share prices were coming back into line with the reality and that after this sensible adjustment there was no need for anything more dramatic. There were other positive signs too that the British were adjusting to life after Big Bang. After the excitements of the winter, one of the City's biggest names seemed to be in the process of sorting itself out. John Craven – of Phoenix Securities – had been drafted in that spring as chief executive at Morgan Grenfell to clean up after Collier and Guinness. That summer when he joined he reassured the press and investors that although Morgan Grenfell may have been bruised by scandal it was fundamentally sound: 'It's a hell of a good business that happened to have a couple of nasty setbacks recently.'[2]

It was possible to think post-election that all was set fair. Another talking head used by the BBC on election day plus one was Ian Harwood of Warburg Securities, who explained to the interviewer Nick Clarke the prospects for the years ahead. His remarks stand as a pretty good epitaph for the era, as well as being an example of the age-old tendency to excessive optimism in a boom. What, asked Clarke, about all the scandals? 'I don't think we're going to see any more scandals on a very large scale,' said Harwood. 'I think people have learnt their lesson.' That hopeful statement about lessons learnt could have been made in one form or another at pretty much any time since the 1720s and the mopping up after the bursting of the South Sea Bubble.

The denouement of the Geoffrey Collier case on insider dealing came on 1 July, when the former Morgan Grenfell man was sentenced. A media scrum outside the Old Bailey greeted the Oxford-educated Collier and his wife, although inside he got a more considerate reception. Collier had made a terrible mistake and he felt deep remorse, his wife Barbara said. This was echoed by his QC, Sir Robert Alexander, who, by a remarkable coincidence of the kind then not exactly unknown in the City, had recently been appointed chairman of the Takeover Panel, the voluntary body that policed mergers and acquisitions. The large house the Colliers owned in the Kent countryside had been traded in for something much smaller in Sevenoaks and the judge acknowledged that the experience of the trial had been crushing. He spared Collier a jail term, handing down a twelve-month suspended sentence and an order to pay £32,000 of fines and costs. During the trial his QC pointed out that Collier was a talented young man who would now struggle to find employment worthy of his abilities. He and his family subsequently moved to the United States and, based in Connecticut over several decades, he worked his way back legitimately working for a French bank.

With Wall Street enthralled and terrified by the ongoing SEC investigations, and Boesky awaiting sentencing by spending the summer enrolled at the Jewish Theology College in Manhattan studying Hebrew and the Talmud, it seemed as though the American taste for sudden and swift retribution was kicking in. In the UK, where the treatment of financial wrongdoing had traditionally been less robust, or handled with possibly too much discretion, the authorities were getting tougher. The investigation into the Guinness scandal continued, and the Department of

Trade and Industry also finally confronted the reality of fraud in Barlow Clowes, a non-City firm run by Peter Clowes that had promised extraordinary returns to investors while Clowes bought a château in France and private jets. Since Clowes was based outside the City, it was not the DTI's responsibility. He was supposed to be licensed by the DTI, and the rackety bond-buying business he had begun in Manchester was registered in Jersey. In the excitement of 1987 he attracted City attention by trying to go legitimate through buying other firms and attempting to list them on the Stock Exchange.

There was another striking example of peak boom behaviour that summer, although this time it was entirely legal, when the fledgling development at Canary Wharf in London's Docklands changed ownership in July. Michael von Clemm had already left Credit Suisse First Boston the previous year and the other bankers involved in the consortium gradually came to the view, in property developer Gooch Ware Travelstead's words, that they did not want to be developers and builders of the biggest property development in Europe. A buyer would have to be found for the land and the plan. This is not unknown in such projects, as the originators and initial investors decide to sell to a developer with deeper pockets or greater appetite for risk. But publicly it looked for a while as though the sceptics were right and Travelstead's vision of creating a rival or an extension to the City in the east would not be realised.

In early July the banks pulled out and the project was up for sale, prompting considerable press speculation about potential embarrassment for the government. The press did not know that Travelstead had been negotiating with Paul Reichmann, a Toronto-based property tycoon who was expanding his business rapidly. The UK – revived by Thatcherite reform, as he described it – was a place to invest big. Travelstead and Reichmann discussed the potential of Docklands as an international financial centre and on 17 July it was announced that Reichmann's family company – Olympia & York – had bought complete control of the £3bn project. At a drinks reception held a few days later to celebrate the deal, Reichmann forecast that the first phase of five million square feet of Canary Wharf office space would be ready within two years. If the locals remained unconvinced and community activists continued to put up billboards saying Docklands regeneration promised only 'jam for the developers, traffic jams for us', the organised opposition had started to wane after Thatcher's third election victory. Labour councils realised Canary Wharf was going to happen. On 30 July the Docklands Light Railway was opened by the Queen. She was taken by boat from Greenwich across to the Isle of Dogs, and by train to Poplar and then Tower Hill.

The Reichmann deal also meant two visionaries departed the scene. Reg Ward, the unorthodox but brilliant chief executive of the London Docklands Development Corporation, was levered out in murky circumstances. Gooch Ware Travelstead went voluntarily too from his beloved project. In doing so he claims he faced one of those life-changing binary choices, when for his 20 per cent of Canary Wharf Paul Reichmann offered him cash then or a five-year unsecuritised note from Olympia & York potentially paying out far more. Travelstead, to his eternal regret, took the note and only a little cash up front. In a decade of deals, the Reichmann trade turned out to be not as good as it seemed at the time, although in mid-1987 the atmosphere was so relentlessly go-go that the prospect of an imminent market crash or a serious reversal in the property market seemed distant enough to take the chance.

The atmosphere was most exuberant in the area of pay, as a survey of earnings published by *The Times* in 1987 demonstrated.[3] With firms competing to recruit the best, an investment dealer could expect £102,613, made up of £65,984 in basic pay and £36,629 in bonus. A chief Eurobond dealer earned a total of £84,133; a director of corporate finance £62,402; and a manager of forex dealing £42,719. These were averages for specific tasks and it was possible to gain the wrong impression from such surveys when the overwhelming majority of staff were not earning large salaries. As had long been the case, the City functioned thanks to the hard work of an army of staff who did not attract high pay or publicity. Even so, the rates of pay at the upper and middle end were rising fast, along with bonuses across firms that all staff benefited from. This was at a time when the average wage in the UK was a little over £11,000 and pay rises in parts of the public sector were held to a minimum after years of freezes. In the years before the television deals that transformed the English game, a footballer playing in the top English division in 1987 earned on average £62,400, although large bonuses could be earned on top of that.[4]

The London Banks Personnel Management Group also kept score in the City. In one of its regular surveys in 1987 it noted that typical pay outside finance had risen 45 per cent between the end of 1981 and late 1986. Meanwhile, general banking staff in London had enjoyed an average increase of 57 per cent in the same period; pay for foreign exchange dealers and Treasury specialists had increased 74 per cent and for management in investment banking and the capital markets the rise was 176 per cent in just five years. Simultaneously, interest rates fell from 14 per cent in 1985 to 9 per cent by 1987 and house prices climbed correspondingly when it became easier to borrow and confidence rose. A typical London property bought in 1983 for £50,000 was worth £95,559 by 1987. Although the average figures in the rest of the UK were lower, the rate of increase was similar. It was clear that if you were in work in the UK, your financial position was improving. If you were in work in the City and had serious responsibilities you were doing very well indeed.

Philippa Rose's City headhunting business was booming in mid-1987, and what she had started on her own aged twenty-one was now in such demand that clients were competing to persuade her to work for them. It was a glamorous and exciting time, in which she darted around Europe, staying in the best hotels and never having to worry about expenses, working direct for chief executives or other senior bankers, finding them the best, brightest young talent as business grew. There was a reason some people in the City were now earning loads more money, of course. London had long been underpaying for senior roles compared to Wall Street, and in the new dispensation the gap was suddenly transparent and unsustainable. As the *Guardian*'s Maggie Pagano, surveying the City employment market, described it: 'It was clear that employers would eventually have to pay the guy dealing in equities in London, earning perhaps £20,000 five years ago, the quadrupled salary level his equal in New York would be earning.' That being the case, no wonder ambitious youngsters wanted in.

By mid-1987 the City and finance more broadly had acquired an increased allure. In the US, Wall Street firms and management consultancies had increased their efforts from the early 1980s to recruit top graduates from the leading colleges, spending money on dominating recruitment fairs and marketing themselves to elite undergraduates. This was mirrored in the UK, where the share of new graduates in the UK going into banking, finance and insurance rose from 13.8 per cent in 1983 to 17.7 per cent in 1987. A skills shortage pushed up starting pay for gifted graduates, and the profusion of increasingly complex forms of trading and computer-based work meant that mathematicians and computer wizards were suddenly in demand. Modelling became the fashion and firms that had previously relied exclusively on the instincts and experience of their partners and senior staff, quite often working with inside information, now hired a new kind of financier.

'Peter, aged 27, is a classic example', wrote Pagano. 'He finished his PhD in nuclear physics about two years ago. He is now writing computer programs for the options trading desk and working on new products for one of the US's biggest investment banks based in London.' It could cause tensions and the infusion of technology did not always produce positive results. One trainee – being taught how to recommend stocks on the strength of minimal analysis, lunch and gut instinct – remembers his superiors mocking the nasal, mockney tones in which their new programmer, who had been hired from British Telecommunications, talked about his 'model'. 'How's yer model?' they asked him repeatedly. The 'model' and the recommendations it made turned out to be completely unsuited to stockbroking and worse than useless. Not every initiative worked, although a large part of the future belonged to those who understood numbers and computers.

Just as there had been on Wall Street earlier, there was a boom in demand for skilled analysts, who had long researched and compiled reports on individual companies and market trends for their broking firms or fund managers. Increasingly their work would become fused with the sales force that existed to sell to clients. Theoretically, there was supposed to be no blurring of the line between what analysts recommended to customers and what suited the company for which the analyst worked. Yet there was an obvious risk of the customer being ill served by businesses that were becoming more cutthroat and driven according to targets. The old, clear division between brokers placing orders on behalf of the client and jobbers in separate firms no longer existed. In many post-Big bang firms it all came together under one roof with bigger potential rewards.

Loyalty to an employer and colleagues suddenly counted for a lot less in 1987, which was not simply down to the prospect of higher pay. When the partners sold their firms, only a few firms adequately shared the largesse with those in the executive tranche below – the so-called marzipan layer – who were not partners but often did a great deal of the work. 'We in the old guard were pretty selfish, yes,' says one of them now. 'I regret that too late.' Why should an ambitious employee commit to one of the new conglomerations for life when the older generation of partners had enriched themselves and shown no loyalty to the heritage of their own firms? It all combined to make employees much more willing to move jobs for the right package, which imported something of Wall Street's ruthlessness and its hire-and-fire culture, pay by results, big bonuses and macho posturing.

Language coarsened too. There had always been a certain amount of colourful talk in the City; now it acquired a cutting edge. In this language you hadn't been ripped off or treated poorly by a rival in a deal, you had been 'raped'. In London, the mingling of Wall Street-style bond trader bragging, upper-middle-class uber-confidence and

Essex-boy-and-girl market-stall-trader straight talking produced a strange fusion, rich with possibility for satirists.

There was also an explosion of colour and sartorial extravagance in the hitherto buttoned-up City. Braces (suspenders in the US) had long been a City staple, or certainly among partners and senior management, but the dress code had always stipulated muted colours, along with plain white shirts and regulation suits. Now there was an eruption of colour on trading floors, in the form of brightly coloured braces, and the striped shirt, which would once have been considered a vulgar non-starter in the better firms, now became ubiquitous. The increasing number of young women being hired by banks and broking firms also had available a new palette of style choices thanks to the emphasis on power dressing. It blended aspects of the extravagant New Romantic fashions favoured by young clubbers in the capital earlier in the decade; the shoulder-padded sheen of American soaps such as *Dallas* glamorising ruthless businesses practices; and the increasing popularity of Italian designers such as Giorgio Armani. That burst of fresh colour in London and Wall Street did not extend to skin colour, however, other than in Japanese banks that employed Japanese staff sent to London. On trading floors, in backroom settlement operations and in banks, the staff remained almost exclusively white. There was an alteration in the balance of the classes, although so rapid was the cross pollination that it was sometimes hard for outsiders to work out where the street smart types – the barrow boys – ended and where the alleged 'Hooray Henrys' recruited from universities or the army began.

What everyone involved agreed on was that time itself was now a precious commodity, which was a remarkable change in a country which had little more than a decade earlier taken such a lax approach to industrial relations and productivity that power shortages led the government to introduce a three-day working week. The attitude was self-consciously American; with longer working days and so many deals to be done there was no time to waste. Time or the lack of it was the new signifier of status; the less you had of it the more important you were. This is where the Filofax came in. The Filofax was – and is – a personal organiser, a small leather cover containing neat removable sheaves of notes, diary and addresses. The concept had actually been launched in the US in 1910 and the UK in the 1920s, but like so many elements of 1980s fashion it was an old favourite updated and adapted for a brasher age. It became so popular in Britain that by 1987 it, and the inserts filled with useful information (making it the smart phone app of its day), were stocked in 1250 stores across the UK. The company had a turnover of £12m and was floated on the USM, the Unlisted Securities Market.

The Filofax was *de rigueur* for the 1987 go-getter who wanted to emit the signal that he or she was so incredibly busy planning take-overs and making reservations – or calling their PA to request reservations – at fashionable restaurants such as Le Caprice or Terence Conran's Bibendum. The latter opened in 1987, as did the River Café and Harvey's starring Marco Pierre White. If you were well-paid enough, your Filofax could sit on the passenger seat of your Porsche 911 turbo, or your BMW 5 Series, as you drove to one of those restaurants or back into the City at dawn. Indeed, fast cars, and foreign-produced cars particularly, were part of the package. Even if a sports car was out of reach, manufacturers such as Volkswagen used the advertising techniques and stylistic signifiers of the period to pitch to the mass market well beyond London. In a reflection of the changing balance of consumer power, the advertising for cars also started to be aimed directly at women for the first time. In David Bailey's 'Changes' television advert for the VW Golf in 1987 the model Paula Hamilton was dressed as an immaculately coiffed and tailored Princess of Wales character, walking away from a mews house and an unreliable man to find solace and happiness in her VW Golf. In fashion, too, the yuppie style revolution was packaged for millions of consumers, particularly by the chain Next, where an affordable version of the 1980s dream – including City chic – was sold to millions of consumers. Inevitably, the style revolution was repeatedly parodied on shows such as *Spitting Image*, perhaps best of all in a spoof of the Dire Straits song 'Money for Nothing', complete with references to Filofaxes, Laura Ashley blinds and GTi's (the latter supposedly a favourite of Fergie and Lady Di's).

There was something distinctively British and class-fixated about this mockery, though. As the historian Graham Stewart put it, in the US the aspirational yuppie was sometimes mocked a little but in films such as *Trading Places* – a riches to rags to riches tale starring Dan Aykroyd and Eddie Murphy – the accumulation of money on the commodity markets was celebrated as representing a victory of the young over the old, and in the case of Murphy's character of the bright ghetto hustler, over entitled Establishment snobs. In large parts of the British media, particularly in the BBC, in which liberal arts graduates predominated, there was little sympathy for the Thatcher experiment and there were very few positive expressions in British popular culture or the arts of the benefits of markets.

This tension was highlighted when Caryl Churchill's *Serious Money*, which had been such a hit with City traders, transferred to Broadway later that year. The theatre critic of the *New Yorker* thought the work was a success in Britain because it appealed to the prejudices of the liberal-Left members of the audience even more than it appealed to traders. 'It's easy to see why this play was such a big hit in London', Mimi Kramer wrote.[5] Not only did it involve actors swearing, pulling down trousers and pretending to vomit, which was always going to appeal to the Brits, it combined all that with 'a confirmation of many of the British intelligentsia's most dearly held beliefs: that privatisation and free enterprise are bad things, the "the British Empire was a cartel", that foreigners buy Burberrys, that money is somehow something that one is better off yearning for than having'. In Britain, open ambition was unpleasant and impolite, she said. The play was simply an attempt to cash in on 1980s ethics and yuppie fashion. The Americans would be unimpressed, she thought. That is not to say that in New York there was no fun poked at the super-rich of Wall Street, especially in a city with such noisy tabloid newspapers. John Gutfreund of Salomon Brothers and his much younger wife Susan, a former Pan Am air hostess turned interior designer, made themselves targets. 'It's so expensive being rich,' she is reputed to have said. Infamously they had a crane hoist a twenty-two-foot Christmas tree into their Manhattan apartment. But the underlying assumption in America, in contrast to the UK, remained that, joking aside, it was better to make a lot of money than not.

By the late summer and early autumn of 1987 in the UK some City veterans had a nervous feeling that it was all running too fast. Ben Wrey was by then the boss at Henderson Global, a money manager that had expanded too quickly, going from 146 employees in 1983 and £1.1bn under management to 525 employees and £9.75bn by September 1987. He said later that he kicked himself for sensing that autumn what was wrong but failing to realise the full extent and not ordering a different course. David Mayhew of Cazenove, who had been dragged into the Saunders scandal and was backed all the way by the senior partners in protesting his innocence, felt a shudder of premonition but had Guinness hanging over him: 'Everything was flying. It was a rip-roaring bull-market.' Numerous others speak decades later of the sense that the numbers were so large that they no longer made any sense. Wanting so badly to be wrong, few of those involved changed their behaviour in time.

How wrong could it go? The answer came from the US that autumn, where Ronald Reagan's joke that the US budget deficit (the gap between income in tax receipts and government spending) was 'big enough to take care of itself' was no longer funny. Nigel Lawson and some economists had been warning for several years that the US was storing up problems. A falling dollar prompted fears of an international economic slowdown. There was also concern that Wall Street's reliance on electronic trading systems had introduced an extra layer of risk. The software had never been tested in a crash. On Monday 12 October the *Wall Street Journal* reported fears that a problem could 'snowball into a stunning rout for stocks'. Then, on

Wednesday the 14th, there were two pieces of news that sounded ominous to traders fearing higher interest rates. The news wires revealed that the US Congress was seeking to crack down on take-overs by tightening tax loopholes and the Department of Commerce posted trade figures that were worse than anticipated. This caused a judder on the markets. And then the bubble really burst.

PART THREE
COMBUSTION

12

GREAT STORM

'Earlier on today, apparently, a woman rang the BBC and said she heard there was a hurricane on the way . . . well, if you're watching, don't worry, there isn't.'

Michael Fish, BBC weatherman, October 1987

Hurricanes hardly ever happen in the Home Counties. Yet at 2am on 16 October 1987 hurricane-force winds were exactly what hit southern England. Nineteen people lost their lives in the carnage, a wind speed of 149kmph was recorded at Heathrow Airport, much damage was done to the foliage at the Kent estate of the Governor of the Bank of England Robin Leigh-Pemberton, and the town of Sevenoaks lost six of its famous trees. During the clear-up operation, BBC weatherman Michael Fish was widely ridiculed for his television broadcast made the previous evening as the storm wheeled its way towards the British coastline. Ever since, Fish has said that he had been misunderstood, and that his dismissal of a hurricane being on the way referred to the question of whether one was due in the Caribbean. He had warned of high winds in the southeast of England in the expectation that the worst would pass through the English Channel and subside. The Met Office was operating with rudimentary satellite technology and only one weather ship thanks to government and EC cuts.[1] Something as awkward as the truth was not going to prevent the misleadingly edited clip of Fish's hurricane comment being re-run in countless documentaries and news reports ever since.

Blow me away: the value of your investments can go down as well as up.
A US trader contemplates the chaos during the October 1987 crash.

That Friday morning the storm caused chaos in commuter land, and with train services cancelled, and roads blocked, very few staff in the City made it to their desks. Some battled through, among them Brian Winterflood, who was one of the proud few who kept trading. The Stock Exchange was open for business, although the Seaq computer system was not working and after a few hours the FTSE was suspended for the day because so little was being done. The timing of this day of disruption could hardly have been worse. Entirely unrelated to the chaos in England, Wall Street's falls on Wednesday and Thursday were followed by further volatility on Friday. It was exacerbated by traders in a hurry to get out of stocks and swamping the market for futures options. By the time the markets closed it meant that the S&P 500 had lost 9 per cent of its value in a week, making it one of the worst results in more than a decade. This timing mattered because in Tokyo and London executives, analysts and traders now had all weekend to call each other and worry about how bad it might be on Monday morning. The weekend newspapers also carried appropriately gloomy commentary about the prospects, and many of those making decisions finished their weekends knowing they would have to get in sharp the next morning and begin selling right from the start. Even so, the force of what followed came as a shock. In the words of Ben Wrey at Henderson Global, when it hit the City that Monday it hit 'like a hurricane'.

In their offices, with the screens running red, traders did their best to hold on tight. There was shock, awe and panic all around. Many of the younger traders who were earning comparatively large salaries had known little but rising share prices and optimism since they signed up a few years previously. Some were witnessed crying. The Eurobond specialists might have had an apprenticeship in market chaos the previous winter, but those who dealt in shares had enjoyed, with a few deviations, one of the great bull markets in history. Now prices were collapsing in a terrifying orgy of selling. Indeed, prices fell so much for the simple reason that it was all but impossible to find buyers.

The situation deteriorated when the US opened, and again the attempts of arbitrageurs to profit from the volatility caused confusion. At 10am in New York, some specialist firms did not trade for the first hour. Many of the top stocks – eleven out of thirty on the Dow Jones Industrial Average – opened late, causing traders to rush into the futures market to buy options.[2] Then the stocks opened lower than the arbitrageurs had anticipated. The result was chaos and wild selling, at which point the chairman of the Securities and Exchange Commission, the US regulator, proceeded to unintentionally make it much worse. Speaking at the Mayflower Hotel in Washington, David S. Ruder, relatively new to the post, said: 'There is some point, and I don't know what point that is, that I would be interested in talking to the New York Stock Exchange about a temporary, very temporary, halt in trading'. This was a logical development of the position he had outlined earlier that month, in his speech to the Bond Club of Chicago. There he mused on the risks from volatility in derivatives markets, of products based on options, or baskets of options linked to indexes, increasing the potential for confusion among traders and regulators. It might make sense to introduce a system to halt the market temporarily for thirty minutes or so to allow the restoration of order during an emergency, he had suggested in Chicago. Such rational concerns made sense in a quasi-academic speech. Those views, repeated initially without the full quotes, in a garbled fashion, a few weeks later on the day of a real live stock market crash, only intensified the panic. At 11.41 a wire report flashed up: SEC HAS DISCUSSED TRADING HALT. NOT NOW. Thirteen minutes later, there was an update: RUDER ON HALT. ANYTHING POSSIBLE.[3] 'Anything possible' are not words financial speculators like to hear during a panic. Rumours spread that the New York Stock Exchange (NYSE) would close completely for the day, worrying traders who feared they were about to be stuck with stock they didn't want that would be marked right down if the markets closed for a pause and then reopened later. Selling increased as traders raced to offload whatever they could. At 1.04pm the Dow Jones News Service published the full Ruder quote from a few hours earlier. In the confusion it looked as though this was Ruder's second comment within two hours, when it merely repeated his earlier remarks. The Dow Jones report was the trigger for more hysteria. It rippled right out across the US, as smaller stockbrokers tried to explain to their small investor clients what was happening. The next day, the *Wall Street Journal* reported a stockbroker in Pittsburgh answering the phone as 'John End-of-the-world-Posterato', telling a client: 'Oh no! Shut up and listen to me . . . You're in bad shape. I told you guys to get out, but you don't listen. What should you do now? Pray a lot.'[4]

For the young Christopher Tomkinson at his trading desk at Fulton Prebon in London, the drama gave him his first lesson in the power of panic and markets going berserk. His early trades in London left him exposed when the US market fell. The market in London went (twice) into what was termed 'fast market' status.

That meant that prices were not held. He had committed to the trade but the outcome depended on where the prices ended up later. It was, he told *Financial News*, too late to extract his orders. 'I could only watch and wait. We smoked a lot . . . I dared not trade anything else. I felt like an amateur juggler faced with eight flaming torches.'[5] An hour after the US markets shut he discovered that, thanks to that day's volatility, what should have turned in a $900,000 profit was actually a $122,000 loss. When London closed on Monday, the FTSE had fallen 11 per cent, or a record fall of 183 points. All manner of big companies were now worth a lot less than they had been twenty-four hours previously, not least of which was Rupert Murdoch's media business, down $1bn in value.

In the chaos, worsening news sometimes took a while to filter through. Before the age of the smart phone, it was possible (incredible as it might seem) for even senior people to be out of touch for an hour or two when they made the commute home. Ben Wrey knew it had been bad that evening, but when he got home and turned on the *Nine O'Clock News* he saw it was even worse than he feared. The Dow had fallen more than 500 points. In response he almost fell off his armchair. It had been a day of records, and not in a good way. In New York, the Dow fell 508 points in the end, closing at 1738.74, a 22.6 per cent slide and worse than any single day of the crash of 1929. More than 600 million shares were traded, which was a huge surge in volume. It was, wrote Chris Huhne, then the economics editor of the *Guardian*, 'a brutal reminder of how elemental and untamed economic forces still are. As in 1929, the financial tempest was unheralded.' The speed of the collapse also meant that a central weakness of the system was exposed when a multi-billion-dollar chain broke down. Part of the problem was that investors buying a futures contract lodged a sum as security with the broker. The broker lodged a portion of that with the exchange. In normal conditions this worked to create liquidity and to encourage trading. If the contract deteriorated, they had to post more security before the market opened for business the next day. When the market fell as fast as it did on Black Monday, the margin calls

– the calls to post ever more security on contracts that were losing value – were ten times the normal level and many firms looked as though they would have to cease trading. Phelan at the NYSE had to contact the Federal Reserve to plead for assistance in encouraging the biggest banks to extend large lines of credit to investors and brokers. According to the Fed's investigation, Citigroup's lending to securities firms that day was reported to have hit $1.4 trillion as against $200m to $400m on a normal day. The Federal Reserve, keen to avoid a repeat of 1929, let it be known that it would do whatever it took to help the banks and the markets. When the markets closed, the ex-Marine chairman of the New York Stock Exchange, John Phelan, held a press conference in which he was frank: 'I call it the nearest thing to meltdown I'm ever likely to see . . . If it wasn't a meltdown it was certainly as hot as I want it to be.' Phelan had warned trading firms for a while about their over-reliance on electronic trading and derivatives such as stock index futures. He believed these had the potential to exacerbate the panic, since only a handful of traders understood the concepts and technology well enough to use them safely in a crisis. In an emergency, many others were just guessing.

In London terms this crash amounted to the worst experience since the secondary banking crisis of the early 1970s and this was much more concentrated, fast paced (thanks to technology) and high profile because of media attention. Suddenly London's geographical position seemed not to be such a boon either. What had been perceived as an advantage around Big Bang, in good times, of the glamorous market that never sleeps running on an almost continuous global loop, with Tokyo and other markets in the East leading off, London following and then New York and Chicago kicking in five hours after that, now seemed a year later like a carousel out of control. A bad session in one time zone influenced behaviour in the next, and round and round it went. How could you stop the world's markets and say I want to get off? The answer was that you could not. At the close of Black Monday, the Chancellor of the Exchequer watched developments with some trepidation. Nigel

Lawson's first concern was to prevent a complete collapse in confidence in Britain's boardrooms. He felt it was his job to project confidence, certainly much more confidence than he felt, in the hope that a crash in the markets was not followed by a dip or worse in the wider economy. 'Privately, I wasn't sure which way it was going to go,' says Lawson thirty years later.

There was little clear guidance from senior figures in the Reagan administration, with splits at the top of the government over how to respond, and the Treasury Secretary, James Baker, indicating that he was relaxed and did not think US interest rates should have to rise to deal with the dollar problem. It fell to America's central bank, and governor Alan Greenspan, to offer reassurance to the markets. 'The Federal Reserve, consistent with its responsibilities as the nation's central bank, affirmed today its readiness to serve as a source of liquidity to support the economic and financial system,' Greenspan said on Tuesday the 20th. In essence, he pushed banks to keep on lending and to extend lines of credit, assuring them that the government would stand behind them if needed. This reassurance came at a price, it would transpire much later. Greenspan's spraying of liquidity during any emergency came to be expected by those who operated in the markets. Might the confident assumption that they and the system would always be saved make them a little friskier when it came to risk and willing to take bigger gambles? The answer with the benefit of experience of the aftermath of the sub-prime crisis of the mid- to late 2000s seems to be 'yes'.

Black Monday and the following week was not a disaster for everyone. Ross Jones and the team at Gerrard & National, the discount house, were transfixed by the turmoil and then retreated on the evening of the 19th to a Lord's Taverners dinner at the Savoy Hotel where they had booked a table. One of their colleagues – Roger Gibbs – arrived late with the news that 'Wall Street's down seven hundred points.' Gerrard & National were less exposed than many others, because they traded in fixed incomes – bonds – although the following day they pondered nervously what to do, until a member of their board phoned in to point out that they were in an extremely good position. There would now be a 'flight to quality' and the relative security of bonds. 'The 1987 crash was terrific for us,' says Jones. They made a lot of money that week. Elsewhere, almost immediately, the crash had produced a change in atmosphere and outlook. The young head-hunter Philippa Rose noticed first the quietness and seriousness that descended on the City in the days following Black Monday. And that the phone rang only with banks saying that all hiring was suspended.

What the merchant banks and securities houses wanted suspended most of all was the British Petroleum privatisation, which by unfortunate timing was underway right in the middle of the market emergency. The British government's attempted £7.2bn sale of its remaining 31.5 per cent share in BP was, as Lawson said, 'the largest share sale the world had ever seen'. On the morning of 15 October, when those initial tremors were hitting the global markets, Norman Lamont (the government minister dealing with the privatisation programme and reporting to Lawson) and the chairman of BP, Peter Walters, announced the price of the sell-off (330p per share). By the morning after Black Monday, those who had agreed to underwrite the BP deal for a fee decided to ask the government to cancel, which Lawson and Lamont refused to do. The scrapping of the sale would not only have punched a hole in the government's accounts for the year, it would have suggested that institutions that had done very nicely out of privatisation wanted to be bailed out when market conditions were not in their favour. Lawson did, though, order the suspension of advertising, as in a falling market the government did not want to encourage any small investors to put their money into BP.

At that point, the chief smoothie from N.M. Rothschild, Michael Richardson, attempted to persuade Lawson to pull out. Richardson was an arch-networker – a City grandee and Freemason – who was used to being able to talk his way out of trouble, although this time he would have only limited success. On Friday 23rd he told Lawson that the seventeen British banks leading the underwriting were meeting to examine invoking a clause in the contract enabling them to withdraw and not purchase any unsold shares. Incredibly, and to the fury of Lawson and Thatcher, the Bank of England then took the side of the merchant banks. Lawson decided not to concede, and while he and the government offered to put a temporary floor under the price – buying back shares below an agreed level – the issue went ahead.

While these awkward discussions over BP continued, history played one of its tricks on the architects of Big Bang. The week after Black Monday, the Stock Exchange had arranged an anniversary conference on Monday 26 October 1987 to celebrate the success of their venture. At a press conference Goodison and other prominent figures made presentations on Big Bang before being questioned about the crash. Goodison acknowledged that the circumstances were not ideal, although he defended London and accused Washington policy makers of incompetence. 'The cause of the fall has not been the markets,' he said. 'It has been the decisions taken, or not taken, by world governments, particularly the United States of America . . . My view, and the European view, is that something needs to be done with the US fiscal deficit. One of the sad things about the present scene is that the U.K. is an outstanding country at the moment economically.' And the reformed London Stock Exchange was holding up during the crisis, he said. The next day's *Washington Post* summarised Goodison's explanation as follows: 'The computers didn't crash, the exchange did not close, and no one jumped out of a window.'

That day in the House of Commons, on Monday 26th, Labour MPs were far less sanguine. There was uproar as news of further falls on the markets filtered through from the City. The Shadow Chancellor John Smith, who had been appointed a few months earlier, demanded an urgent statement from Lawson and offered to scrap a debate on education to accommodate a full discussion of the market turmoil and the BP row. Lawson, it was explained to MPs by a Tory frontbencher, could not be in the Commons because he had to fulfil 'an existing engagement in the City'. That involved him speaking at Goodison's conference on what a brilliant success the previous year's Big Bang had been. Labour MPs went quite wild at this explanation and Brian Sedgemore MP described Lawson in such unparliamentary language – 'the arrogant bastard' – that the Speaker who presides in the Commons forced him to withdraw. The sharp-dressed cockney wit Tony Banks, another Labour MP, got further when he said that the 'fat bounder' of a Chancellor should be dragged to the Commons in a tumbril to explain himself. The Speaker, Bernard Weatherill, objected to the term 'fat bounder'. A vintage Commons exchange followed.

> Speaker: 'I dislike that expression.'
> Banks: 'Right. Corpulent gentleman.'
> Speaker: 'Almost as bad.'
> Banks: 'All right. Rt Hon corpulent gentleman.'

For John Smith and Labour, the crash was the first good news they had had in a while in their battle against a Tory government with a large majority. It was not that the Opposition wanted the value of Briton's pensions and investments to fall, but here was some evidence that the value of free market reforms, much like a share price, could go down as well as up. Labour spokesmen had used the City scandals of recent years to suggest that what had been unleashed was inherently corrupt, with the Conservatives creating a suspect set-up to suit their rich friends. Now the modernised City and global capitalism had delivered a crisis.

The press reaction to these events revealed contrasting perspectives. The *FT*, its journalists presumably mindful that there had been crashes throughout history and would be crashes again, dialled down on the hysteria and a week after Black Monday was almost relaxed in its analysis. The *Daily Mail*, a newspaper that had, and has, such an instinctive feel for the hopes and fears of southern England, was much more direct. The further falls a week after Black Monday caused the paper to get stuck into the authorities. Over two pages on Tuesday 27th the headline ran: 'It was relentless . . . down, down, down . . .' Another item mocked Goodison's Big Bang anniversary conference, declaring that there had been 'smoked salmon' but 'no signs of suicide'. The front page was even more to the point, taking up Lawson's theme about failure by the Reagan administration and urging action by the Americans. The waspish splash headline – 'Don't just sit there . . . do something!' – was a clever play on Reagan's famous non-interventionist small-government dictum that it was often better for government to just sit there (don't do something) rather than making matters worse.

Few had seen the October crash coming. The father of Zac Goldsmith, Jimmy Goldsmith, the swashbuckling businessman and corporate raider with a complicated private life straight from the pages of a thriller, was one of those who did. Ahead of the crash he sold every share he had. Only a few others did likewise and the usual recriminations, and calls for inquiries, observable in most crashes down the ages, then played out. In Washington the Reagan administration urgently wanted answers and turned to Nicholas F. Brady, an experienced financier, Yale athlete, WASP and friend of George H. Bush, then Vice President. On 8 November 1987, President Reagan issued an executive order establishing a task force led by Brady to report within sixty days on why the crash had happened and what might be done to prevent a repeat.

Brady stands out as one of the most fascinating Wall Street and political players of his generation. He was largely responsible for an improvement in the fortunes of the investment bank Dillon, Reid & Co. in the 1980s, although he was solidly unfashionable. He was sceptical about the takeover boom, spent some time in the US Senate, and later, under Bush, became Treasury Secretary. Brady bonds, the ingenious invention which allowed the restructuring and reduction of debt in developing countries in the late 1980s and early 1990s, carried his name. Contrary to expectation, the Brady Report on October 1987 when it landed the following January was an impressive piece of clear-sighted work. The assorted markets that had developed – in stocks, in futures, in swaps – were not set up to operate as 'one market' and, on the day, confusion had been the defining feature. The clearing systems – by which trades were logged and transacted – were not good enough and computerised programme trading introduced risks that should be mitigated, it said. Brady's team suggested the introduction of so-called 'circuit breaks' that could be used to pause trading and prevent a repeat of overly drastic falls in prices. Some of these conclusions were contested, particularly by more free market types who feared that the response would require greater bureaucracy, rather than allowing the Exchanges in New York and Chicago to adapt and find their own solutions.

Regardless of such concerns, the report formed the basis of reforms made in the US, and it and other reports encouraged regulators and policy makers to cooperate more closely with their counterparts in other major countries. Indeed, the crash had shown how quickly developments in markets in the Far East could work their way to London and then New York and back again. The transmission speed of a shock could now be measured in seconds rather than hours, days and weeks. That being the case, there was a need for much closer cooperation and international standards in markets that had become far more global. Later, Brady attributed the events of October 1987 in large part to the increased clout of the Japanese. Their traders had started the crash, over fears about the US economy and the dollar, and the powerful Japanese finance ministry and biggest firms had halted it. It was a seeming testament to the erosion of American power and to the increasingly interconnected nature of markets, or rather the speed at which shocks and corrections were transmitted between trading centres. 'The real trigger', said Brady,

was that the Japanese came in for their own reasons and sold an enormous amount of U.S. government bonds and drove the 30-year government [bond] up through 10 per cent. And when it got through 10 per cent, that got a lot of people thinking, 'Gee, that's four times the return you can get on equity. Here we go, inflation again.' That, to me, is what really started the 19th—a worry by the Japanese about the U.S. currency.[6]

When the markets crashed, the Japanese government encouraged the country's biggest securities houses – Nomura, Daiwa, Nikko, and Yamaichi – to prop up the market, which halted the slide in Tokyo and produced (for a few days at least) a relative respite in the US and in the UK.

The comprehensive nature of Brady's response in the US was in contrast to what happened in the UK. The Governor of the Bank of England, Robin Leigh-Pemberton, acknowledged in a speech in February that the British had been criticised for not having much to say about the causes of the crisis. Leigh-Pemberton did then make a stab at offering a cogent analysis of the crash. He explained just how big the bubble had been: 'In London, prices began to rise in a sustained way in early 1982, when the FT 30 share index stood at around 550. Over the succeeding five years or so, to the middle of 1987, the index moved up, to about 1850, an increase of almost three and half times.' Allowing for inflation, the real terms increase in prices was still in the region of 170 per cent. That had inflated profits and pay at securities houses and they would now feel the strain. It was not complacency, however, to claim that in difficult circumstances the trading systems in London had worked, he said. They had functioned relatively well under extreme pressure. And no amount of technology could ensure that everyone who wanted to get out of a market in an emergency could do so without suffering ill effects. 'So far, at least, the financial system seems to have weathered the storm passably well.'

These were lame Establishment excuses according to those who had expressed scepticism about the City revolution, the rising salaries of traders and the concept of increased share ownership. Wasn't Black Monday and its aftermath evidence that the hyped global financial revolution had encouraged greed and brought destruction? Those who thought so could get a dose of righteousness, and a hugely entertaining ride through boom-time Manhattan, by reading Tom Wolfe's *The Bonfire of the Vanities*, which was published in October 1987. Wolfe's central character, Sherman McCoy, was a greedy bond trader who crashed in his Mercedes and was propelled into a race row that landed him in the tabloids and the dock.

Alternatively, concerned citizens on both sides of the Atlantic could go to the cinema at the end of 1987 to see a film that had been made with the Boesky insider-trading investigation in mind but which now looked like a perfectly timed indictment of an entire era. On 11 December, Oliver Stone's morality tale *Wall Street* was released. The lead character was the corporate raider Gordon Gekko, a new-generation Wall Street titan with slicked-back hair, braces and a beach house full of modern art. He and his protégé Bud Fox, a hungry young trader who sells out his heritage in search of wealth, were from different angles archetypes of the age. In the film, Fox is so greedy for 1980s success that he is drawn into insider dealing and persuades Gekko to purchase the airline for which works Fox's blue-collar father, played by Martin Sheen. Stone presents the resulting scandal as a collision between honest toil and rampant greed. In the most famous scene, Gekko explains his philosophy to the shareholders of a paper company that is struggling. He explains how he can unlock value and make the discontented shareholders money. Hidden value, squandered or overlooked by corporate bureaucrats and managers, can be liberated and put into the pockets of the owners. At a mass meeting of hundreds of shareholders of Teldar Paper, his Michael Milken-esque polemic is a popular message. Greed should be embraced, Gekko tells the audience. It is nothing to be ashamed of, he says – Greed is good, Greed is right, Greed works; indeed man's fundamental progress as a species is down to Greed.

A week after the release of *Wall Street*, Ivan Boesky was sentenced to three years in prison for his part in the insider-trading scandal, for conspiring to file false stock-trading records. He admitted buying inside information from Dennis Levine, an investment banker. Levine was already in prison. Marty Siegel, formerly one of the leading corporate merger specialists on Wall Street, had taken $700,000 from Boesky for illicit information on deals. Siegel also pleaded guilty to criminal charges. The greed of Boesky and his accomplices made it seem that the cinematic representation of Wall Street was a fair reflection of real life in investment banking and on trading floors. Here Oliver Stone cleverly pushed some extremely old buttons too. The G-word – greed – was transgressive, an old testament taboo, a deadly sin, that all but the most extreme capitalists and coked-up traders would recoil from. While wealth creation and ambition are one thing, and rampant greed is another, the extravagant behaviour in the years leading up to October 1987 and the way in which it was portrayed by a novelist and a film director helped blur the distinction in the public imagination.

In Britain, rather typically, as has been the case for centuries, the artistic response to a crash and the forces that created it was primarily satirical and amusingly silly. In early 1988, the comedian Harry Enfield unveiled the character 'Loadsamoney', a brash plasterer waving about his wad of 'dosh' on Channel 4's 'alternative' comedy show *Saturday Live*. It was much more effective to satirise Thatcherism and condemn an obsession with acquisition by using a plasterer as opposed to a pension fund manager. But mortifyingly for the satirists, the vulgar Loadsamoney promptly became extremely popular and even had a hit single that took him onto *Top of the Pops*. The joke for a while was on Enfield, although the royalties may have eased any embarrassment. Indeed, there was something a little rich about alternative comedians – many from privileged and extremely affluent backgrounds – being so snooty about others, from places such as Essex, getting a shot at rapid advancement. Enfield had to kill off his creation when he became concerned that too many viewers relished his boasting and rudeness towards the poorer regions of England, although not before Labour leader Neil Kinnock deployed Loadsamoney as an example of all that his party asserted was wrong with Thatcher's Britain and the City.

Was that fair on those who had enjoyed such rapid accumulation of wealth? The rewards and the excitement had produced a surge of excessive confidence that this would not end. Like many other practitioners of his generation, Ben Wrey felt that the youngsters who had flooded Wall Street and the City were too optimistic and had become intoxicated by the market climbing ever higher. 'My view of markets was a different one, that they were tough . . . I mean they just make you look like a fool so often.' Such criticism was understandable and Wrey's was an astute observation born of experience, but who had allowed them to act like that? It was the elders of high finance on Wall Street and the City who had sanctioned the construction of the post-Big Bang machine, with its aggressive assumptions about the power of technology and the possibilities of rocketing pay. It was hardly surprising that some of those who had been recruited to man the machine were naive about its defects and blasé about the potential for disaster. But then the crash of 1987 wasn't a sustained disaster, or at least not one that seemed to endure in the couple of years immediately after the Great Storm, either in the City or on Wall Street. What was remarkable after such an intense episode was how quickly the markets recovered. The falls were reversed within months, so that Lawson could later describe October 1987 as an economic non-event. It seemed not to spread much into what the media referred to as 'the real economy' and it would not create a repeat of 1929. Growth was strong in 1987 and 1988.

There was a lot more to it than that though. There had been what amounted to an explosion of money in the decades since the 1960s, a revolution that facilitated bigger debt markets, new forms of trading, new products, changed markets, and computerisation that shrank the Western world and increased transaction speeds dramatically. At home, the Reaganites and Thatcherites had also enabled easier access to credit and the creation of a property bubble that would eventually result in overheating and the recession of the early 1990s. The seemingly inexorable rise of Japan would soon be halted, and in the UK and the US politics was about to transformed by leaders who accepted the framework of expanded markets and nascent globalisation. Simultaneously, the aftermath of the crash caused considerable carnage in the City, when it exposed how unprepared for competition were the firms that had been bashed together ahead of Big Bang. More scandals and explosions were on the way too. The City's trajectory was up and up, again, but not in a straight line.

CLEANING UP

'Go for the jugular.'

George Soros, Black Wednesday, 1992

Nicholas Goodison had more than done his time as chairman of the Stock Exchange. In November 1988 he went off to spend more time with his clocks and barometers, but he also constructed a portfolio of City directorships to go alongside his membership of boards in the art world. If during his busy tenure Goodison had failed to please everyone in the City – an impossible task, akin to herding cats – he and his team of technologists had brought the institution through the most extraordinarily intense and rapid period of change in the Square Mile for centuries, although there was more upheaval and innovation on the way. The London Stock Exchange was one of the institutions that would at points struggle to cope.

Nonetheless, the view of Ranald Michie, a leading financial historian, was that what had been achieved in London by the late 1980s in the creation of a new securities market was remarkable. It was not very British to boast about success, but London was once again a global marketplace, where big banks from around the world, in the right time zone, in their offices, traded by telephone based on current prices that were displayed on a computer screen. All of this was now done under a regulator and stamped with the brand of the London Stock Exchange. 'The New York Exchange had failed to achieve this in the 1970s,' pointed out Michie, and indeed there had been little innovation on the NYSE itself since 1975.[1] The change there had come from new, rival electronic platforms outside the traditional exchange, such as NASDAQ. Not a single one of the exchanges on the continent, neither Frankfurt nor Paris, could rival London's scope. Throughout the decade the increasingly open flows of capital across borders and the transformation wrought by technology produced a surge in volume in major markets, but the increase was most staggering in London. Over the course of the 1980s, trading volumes on the New York Stock Exchange increased fourfold. In Tokyo, volumes increased nine times. In London the figure was seventeen times.

Competition intensified, which meant that established City names and some habits – decent claret in the boardroom at lunchtime, family connections at all levels throughout organisations, knowledge of market history and personalities, the lustre of tradition and order – that had only a few years earlier equated to elite status, now counted for a good deal less. In the case of some stockbroking and jobbing firms from the Old World, those supposed advantages were now all but worthless. The partners who had left with the cash, to fill their cellars in the small country houses and rectories of England with even better claret and good burgundy, had made a smart move in leaving just as life in the City became tougher, faster and less congenial. In that respect, Big Bang in 1986 was the pre-ignition moment. What followed the crash of 1987 was accelerated creative destruction.

The main impact in the years immediately following Black Monday was that it helped expose and destroy many, not all, of the British merchant banks and brokers in a manner that was humiliating for the City. Although share prices in London recovered to their early October 1987 level by August 1989, many established, experienced British firms in the City never recovered, either as standalone entities or under their new owners who had paid so much for them during the bull market. It had been clear to the observant even before Black Monday that there was excessive capacity, and too many people on high salaries chasing business on which the spreads – the difference between the sell and the buy price – had narrowed, as the bigger participants moved to drive out smaller firms. Everyone had to fight harder to get critical mass and they were all under pressure to chase recognition on the league tables that clients referred to when choosing which firm to use. There was no hiding in the event of failure or poor performance and the new owners were ruthless in closing down or stripping back the old City firms they had paid premium prices for just a few years earlier.

The historian David Kynaston estimated that a total of £4bn had been spent on buying established operations large and small, and equipping them with new technology and higher-paid staff in preparation for the revolution, only for their names to be retired or closed down a few years later. Messels was destroyed by Shearson Lehman; the brokers Laurie Millbank and Simon & Coates were butchered by Chase Manhattan. Security Pacific killed Hoare Govett. Vickers da Costa and Kitcat & Aitken also disappeared in the carnage. Even some of the super-confident American incomers suffered problems. Had the vast spaces the size of football pitches accommodating the recently enlarged operations been leased to accommodate an expanding staff and their egos, or had the staff been hired to fill the vast new spaces? It was difficult to tell sometimes.

As Valerie Thompson and some of her colleagues at Salomon had seen during the Floating Rate Note emergency in late 1986, too many of the new, younger staff had never experienced one market reverse, let alone two or three. Elsewhere after the 1987 crash, as volumes fell temporarily and weaker outfits became vulnerable, some of the new generation discovered just how tough the business environment they had entered could be. Layoffs began across the City and for a while hirings were on hold. An estimated 12,000 jobs were lost in the following year. One British bank that struggled was the high-street Midland, which had bought the broker Greenwell and bolted it together with its merchant bank, Samuel Montagu. It closed its equities unit in early 1989 and Midland was eventually taken over by HSBC.

The clearest evidence yet that the Brits were struggling badly in the face of competition came at Morgan Grenfell. Its reputation as one of the premier British merchant banks had been damaged by scandal and it was a business experiencing acute culture shock. Not that long previously, it had been an archetypal last-generation institution, populated at the upper echelons by well-heeled City archetypes who would have been recognisable figures at any point in the preceding century. As *Financial News* recorded, the old joke was that a clerk at Morgan Grenfell famously asked for a pay rise because he could not live on his salary. His superior was astonished: 'You live on your salary?'[2] In an attempt to modernise in the 1980s it had grown staff and its spending much too quickly, in an understandable effort to achieve parity with the Americans and become a global force. In 1980 Morgan Grenfell had in the region of a thousand members of staff. By 1987 it had around two thousand, seven hundred employees. The overheads had quadrupled since Goodison and the government did their deal in 1983. And it had expanded most aggressively of all in the securities business, in the belief that it could become an all-rounder, one of those global financial supermarkets that it was predicted would force out smaller banks and brokers in the years ahead.

By 1988 the acquisitions – of the jobbing firm Pinchin Denny and the brokers Pember & Boyle – that had been made during the pre-Big Bang buying spree were not working, and the Morgan Grenfell people, an employee remembers, didn't like the new people: 'We thought they lacked the right experience and were not sophisticated enough. We weren't very nice about it.' Morgan Grenfell managers were put in to manage the new unit and while all seemed as though it might be fine during the final run of the bull market, the October 1987 crash revealed that it was not. Soon the securities division that had been billed to investors as a great new source of world-beating profit was losing close to £1m per week. John Craven took the decision to close it down and concentrate on banking and corporate finance. This revelation was promptly leaked to the *Daily Telegraph* and published on 6 December 1988. Craven got in at 7am and shortly afterwards unofficially confirmed the bad news to staff, speaking over the loudspeaker and apologising for the distress. The decision to close the securities business within Morgan Grenfell with immediate effect was formally confirmed at a board meeting at 9am. More than four hundred and fifty people lost their jobs that day, and while media attention was fixed on those who earned hundreds of thousands of pounds, and had sports cars thrown in as part of their packages when they joined, along with them went many who earned a lot less doing the support work.

In City terms the Morgan Grenfell reverse was profoundly shocking and humiliating. One of the most esteemed British banks, with a 150-year history, had tried to take on the world and lost. It was then left in that most dangerous position in the City of being a medium-sized operator in a business that was increasingly dominated by large players. For a while it had seemed Morgan Grenfell might be sold to the French bank Indosuez – sold to a French bank, imagine – before Craven talked to Alfred Herrhausen, the chairman of Deutsche Bank. The German banker flew to London and secret discussions began between the Morgan Grenfell team and one of the most alluring figures in the West German Establishment.

A long-time advocate of German reunification, Herrhausen had another merger on his mind that autumn. On 9 November 1989, the crossings between East and West Berlin were opened, thousands flooded westwards and the fall of the Wall and Communism began. That month, Herrhausen was in regular contact with political leaders, including the Soviet leader Mikhail Gorbachev. The more mundane matter of Deutsche Bank's purchase of Morgan Grenfell was also resolved that month when it was announced on the 27th that the Germans would pay £950m for Morgan Grenfell. It was stated that London would retain operational autonomy – this is often claimed in press releases about takeovers, and the promise held for five years – and Craven was given the great honour of being invited to be the first non-German to join the board of Deutsche Bank.

There was a chilling postscript, however. Three days after the deal was announced, Herrhausen left his home outside Frankfurt for work at around 8.30am, in a three-car convoy which took a route he had not taken in several weeks. In the late 1980s, German bankers and industrialists still had to take their security seriously, with communist terrorist cells remaining active. Yet somehow, someone knew the route and on a bicycle parked by the roadside was a bag full of armour-piercing explosives. The detonation was triggered when the infrared beam was broken by the car carrying Herrhausen.

The Red Army Faction, a West German terrorist group, was initially believed to be behind it, but did they have the expertise in their depleted state? Then it was rumoured that the Stasi, the East German secret police, had organised the attack or at least assisted. Some pointed to Herrhausen's attendance at the secretive Bilderberg conference and his enthusiasm for debt forgiveness for developing countries, which apparently angered some American banks and the US government. The case was a conspiracy theorist's dream: the Stasi, allegedly irate Bilderbergers, mysterious American bankers, the CIA or a combination of all of them must have done it. Herrhausen's murder remains unsolved. It is a reminder that as recently as 1989 Germany was divided and a leading European financier could be blown up on his way to work in Frankfurt while statesmen and leaders grappled with the fall of Communism.[3]

Back in London that November, the question at Morgan Grenfell was more down to earth. Was the deal of which Herrhausen had been the architect still on? Craven sent a note to staff on the day of the murder assuring them that the other managers at Deutsche Bank wanted to press ahead in spite of the shocking news. 'I have conveyed my sympathies to the Board of Managing Directors,' wrote Craven, 'and we shall all have to work that little bit harder to ensure the relationship is as successful as I know it will be.'

The future these European institutions were chasing seemed to belong to institutions such as the American Merrill Lynch, Morgan Stanley or Goldman Sachs, or the Japanese at Nomura – the banks and securities houses that had the scale to cope even when they hit serious trading losses. Their recently graduated youngsters putting together deals, overseen by their elders who had survived the mid-1980s, needed quite particular skills, different from those of their trader colleagues who worked on a different floor. They had to be able to conceptualise what might work for their clients if it was bolted together, acquired or sold, then structure the deal in a clever way and marshal City lawyers and tax specialists to assist, taking as fees a percentage based on the final price. More and bigger deals meant bigger bonuses. The notion that the big American banks, particularly, operated according to their own allegedly reptilian code, ruthlessly rejecting sentimentality, sacking at will and focusing on the interests of the firm, is a complaint heard a lot from some older City types. Yet the City, and the government, had invited these people in and created the marketplace in which they could do their thing. It was a bit rich to act surprised when American investment bankers smashed the competition and behaved like American investment bankers.

For the young head-hunter Philippa Rose, running her own firm and finding talent for big banks in London, the complaints were nonsense. After a brief dip following the 1987 crash she was soon prospering again. Her approach involved refusing to deal with human resources departments, and she broke every HR rule in the book, believing that what mattered was finding brilliant people rather than merely 'ticking boxes'. She was in demand and the banks fought over her services. 'As the business grew we had a lot of people phoning up trying to get me and that made me a bit smug about life,' she recalls. Her greatest triumph was her company winning the business of Goldman Sachs when it decided in the early 1990s to make a major commitment to Europe and London, and to make the UK capital the centre of its operations outside the US. Assorted head-hunters sat an exam, testing their knowledge of finance and the identities of senior figures and fast-rising stars in the City. Rose's habit of quizzing clients to learn more about all areas of finance – 'what the fuck is a Eurobond?' – produced its dividend when she came top with 82 per cent. Goldman consumed as much as 40 per cent of her time as the bank filled its new international headquarters on Fleet Street, in the Peterborough Court building vacated by the *Daily Telegraph*, whose poor journalists were moved to the Canary Wharf development where there were as yet no pubs. And then Rose tried to leave, explaining that Morgan Stanley had hired her company. She went to see the chief executive of Goldman Sachs International and was told: you can't resign. She was driven home immediately to pack a bag and then to the airport for a first-class flight to New York, where Goldman Sachs installed her in the presidential suite of the Plaza hotel. Dinners and meetings ensued with the most senior people, who all but brainwashed her out of the notion of working for Morgan Stanley. She came back to London, told Morgan Stanley the bad news and was blacklisted by them for the best part of two decades.

The leader who had helped unleash those market forces – the ambition, the transatlantic deal making, the wooing of young executives for ever-larger sums, the ruthless hiring and firing – got the sack herself in November 1990 when the Conservative Party ejected her from Number 10. Thatcher's departure was no ordinary vacating of office, because she had been no ordinary leader. Most leaders being booted out are not usually treated to adulatory statements from the US President; the Japanese Prime Minister; former French President Valéry Giscard d'Estaing; Czech anti-Communist freedom fighter turned President Vaclav Havel; and members of the tottering Soviet leadership that she had done much to defeat. Among Britain's allies, only the German government – perhaps understandably, considering Thatcher's opposition to German reunification – did not join in. A spokesman asked for a statement said: 'We would find it rather difficult to do that.'

In Britain, there was even less unanimity. Labour's Tony Benn was coruscating: 'Mrs Thatcher did more damage to democracy, equality, internationalism, civil liberties, freedom in this country than any other Prime Minister this century.' A furious Ann Widdecombe MP disagreed and said the removal of her heroine would make the rest of the world think the UK had gone completely mad, while Keith Joseph, Thatcher's intellectual mentor, wrote to the departing Tory leader describing her as 'a giant – a beautiful giant'. Former cabinet minister John Biffen MP said generously of the leader who had cast him aside: 'She was a tigress surrounded by hamsters.' Outside Westminster, the tigress's opponents celebrated and her stunned supporters swore vengeance against the successors who had the temerity not to be her. The hotelier Rocco Forte waxed lyrical about the triple election winner: 'She was a lady sent to us on wings from heaven.' The entertainer Max Bygraves even composed a tribute song – 'So Long Maggie' – and went on LBC, the London radio station, to perform it to put-upon listeners:

They say a week in politics
Can be a long wait,
But you stayed on eleven years
And made Great Britain Great.

In contrast, the City was as unsentimental as ever. Business is business, after all. Share prices actually rose. Over the course of the week in which she was removed, the FTSE 100 went from 2068.30 to 2170.50. The market rose in 1991, 1992 and 1993, providing more evidence of the disconnect between the increasingly international City and distress when it occurred in the domestic economy. Out in the country, the 1990s began with the 1980s boom turning to a brutal bust, causing a property crash and a surge of repossessions.

It even took down the owner of the development at Canary Wharf Thatcher had championed as Prime Minister. Paul Reichmann's Olympia & York had spent in the region of £7bn on the development, but with the tube link that Thatcher had promised being delayed for a decade, and her gone, it was difficult to attract sufficient high-paying tenants to the newly opened tower and surrounding buildings. There was the light railway that took an age from the City, and river taxis. But who really had any appetite to sit on a boat from central London, getting seasick going down the Thames on a freezing cold February morning at 7am? Loaded with loans, in 1991 Reichmann's property empire went into meltdown; by spring 1992 it was bust. A new company was formed and Paul Reichmann eventually bought his way back in. The private, deeply religious man who had taken Travelstead and von Clemm's idea and made it manifest in concrete and steel lived to see it become a success. It was later sold – at too high a price – to another consortium before it was rescued by the China Investment Corporation in 2009 during the next property crash. If anyone in the mid-1980s had suggested this chain of events, pre-Tiananmen Square when China was not yet a market economy and Canary Wharf was a wasteland, it would have sounded insane. Or it might have been thought someone had got Japan and China mixed up. In the intervening years

Japan had become stuck in its debt-addled slough and China has risen to challenge Western dominance.

For the property developer whose vision on the dockside in 1985 had started the Canary Wharf adventure, the collapse of Olympia & York in 1992 represented a personal financial disaster. The unsecuritised five-year note Gooch Ware Travelstead had taken from Reichmann had been due to pay out later in 1992, but with Reichmann's empire bust he got almost nothing. It did not make Travelstead bitter and when he looks today at Canary Wharf he is proud: 'I was routinely taken to task by the press as a crazy American. In twenty years, I said, that's the way it's going to be. I'm incredibly proud of it. It became what we said it would become.' The Canary Wharf experience also led to other interesting work opportunities. The Mayor of Barcelona, who had visited Travelstead's Mayfair offices to view the model of Canary Wharf, got in touch and asked him to help with the redevelopment of the Barcelona waterfront. There he built the Hotel Arts, working with the architect Frank Gehry. The Thatchers – out of office – stayed as Travelstead's guest in Barcelona after the hotel opened.

In London, the hangover from the late 1980s was played out in a series of trials and travails. Of course, the most sensational of these court cases related to Guinness, in which Ernest Saunders, Anthony Parnes, Gerald Ronson and Jack Lyons each went on trial for theft and false accounting in relation to the share-price-ramping operation run during the takeover battle with Argyll for Distillers. All four were convicted in 1990. In the courtroom Saunders made what turned out to be a calamitous decision, by choosing to go into the witness box to give evidence in his defence. As the *FT* explained the day after his conviction, a trial that had not necessarily been going well for the prosecution was transformed by his spell under cross-examination. 'Unemployed and with nothing to distract him from his troubles, he had become obsessed with the need to vindicate himself.' His version of events stretched plausibility. 'He alleged a vast conspiracy that included the government.' Everyone but him was a liar, he seemed to suggest.

A subsequent trial of Roger Seelig, former head of corporate finance at Morgan Grenfell, and Lord Spens, another banker, collapsed. The case against David Mayhew, who had been backed throughout by Cazenove, was also scrapped, and he became senior partner at Caz. Saunders then infamously won early release from open prison, when it was claimed that he displayed the early symptoms of Alzheimer's. Gerald Ronson – who had been dragged into the share support operation by Saunders – was in the same prison as Saunders and had to endure regular visits to his cell by his nemesis. Ronson later claimed he was the first to think of the ruse that got Saunders out of jail. 'I joked, "Make out that you're mentally ill. It wouldn't be difficult for you because besides being a psychotic liar, you are mentally deranged . . . If you made out you've got Alzheimer's, nobody could ever prove it, because if they looked inside your head, what are they going to find?" '[4] That revelation confirmed the suspicions of those who thought that Saunders' 'recovery' was an act rather than a medical miracle. Friends and supporters of the convicted tycoons maintain they had only been caught doing what was commonplace in pre-Big Bang London, and furthermore they were targeted unfairly. Certainly, three of the Guinness Four were Jewish, and it seemed as though they had been pursued when non-Jews were not. The episode hardly reduced the City's reputation for anti-Semitism.

Next up was Robert Maxwell, although he cheated justice. The City had had plenty of warnings about the ebullient Maxwell, publisher, owner of the *Daily Mirror*, decorated war hero and a serial shyster. The satirical magazine *Private Eye* had battled him for years and his fellow tycoons knew he was deeply untrustworthy and corrupt. His credentials as a former Labour MP, and ownership of the Labour-supporting *Mirror*, meant that he was part of the Labour family, however. Given way too much licence by his board, he looted the pension fund of Mirror Group to the tune of £440m. Before this was revealed, but with it being reported that Maxwell was struggling to repay debts to banks including Goldman Sachs, on 5 November 1991 he fell, or more likely jumped, off the back of his yacht, the *Lady Ghislaine*.

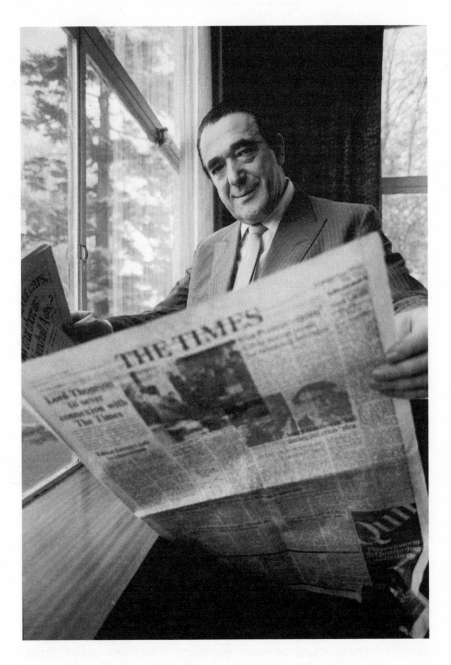

Mirror, mirror: crooked Robert Maxwell could not have got away with it for so long without the help of some of the City's finest firms.

'Bob was always squeaky clean to me', was the much-mocked verdict of Sir Michael Richardson at N.M. Rothschild. Indeed, the City was up to its neck in Maxwell's activities, along with smart legal firms who cranked out libel writ after libel writ. Even Geoffrey Collier's undoing at Morgan Grenfell was down to intelligence picked up in talks with Maxwell. For a period, N.M. Rothschild's US operation – Rothschild Inc. – had had a close relationship with Maxwell, making $17m in fees from his battle to win control of the publisher Macmillan. Sensibly, the bank's owners then put some distance between themselves and the tycoon, with his closest advisor, Robert Pirie, pushed out. After Maxwell's death, Rothschild in London was summoned to help pick through the wreckage of Maxwell's companies.

The budget version of Maxwell was Asil Nadir, a charlatan puffed up and sold to the public with the assistance of a selection of eager politicians, investment bankers, brokers, lawyers and accountants. Nadir's company made no rational sense. It was a rackety creation. It had begun as a textile firm, moved into fruit packaging, more textiles, Japanese electronics and household appliances. The main purpose it seemed was to build Nadir into an international tycoon, and create a suitable impression by offering lavish hospitality and wooing politicians.[5] For a while Polly Peck was taken very seriously, and Nadir's acquisitions were funded and his deals trumpeted as the efforts of a man of vision, until the early 1990s recession exposed the Tory donor's looting of the company to the tune of £29m. Nadir was a crook but he was also just the latest incarnation of Trollope's Melmotte, the mysterious man on the make, welcomed and used by Establishment figures looking for entertainment and easy money, and then dumped in a hurry. Nadir fled the UK for Northern Cyprus, returning seventeen years later to attempt to clear his name. In 2012 he was sentenced to ten years in prison.

The culmination of the Blue Arrow affair was also messy. County NatWest, the investment bank operation of NatWest, had botched the sale of a recruitment agency in 1987. County NatWest had said more shares had been sold than had been, and unbeknown to investors it held on to 19 per cent and stashed the shares in a variety of accounts, hoping to sell them gradually and on the quiet. The deceit might have worked, but for the intervention of the October 1987 crash, which revealed what had gone on. The scandal damaged NatWest badly and inquiries dragged on for years. In 1993 the former chief executive Tom Frost was exonerated of leading a cover-up, and the fraud trial of three directors of NatWest who had resigned became a £40m shambles. They were later cleared by the Court of Appeal. Those in the City who wonder why their good, entirely legal work was often overlooked, should consider it from the point of view of the public, which became accustomed in those years to seeing on their screens news footage of a steady procession of prosperous men walking in and out of court.

The serial corruption by some at Lloyd's, the insurance market, at times made the rest of it look tame. Since the early 1980s the leadership at Lloyd's had been aware that claims for asbestosis were highly likely to cause large losses for insurers, although it was only almost a decade later that the Lloyd's Names, those who were invited to invest in pursuit of high returns, found this out. Being a Lloyd's Name had once been a badge denoting Establishment status, although in the search for funds agents had widened the search. The financial advantage was supposed to be that a Name did not hand over any money – he or she only undertook to write a cheque for their share in a year in which there were any losses – and they could simultaneously use their money to invest elsewhere outside Lloyd's, perhaps doubling it or making it work twice. There would not be any losses, would there? Lloyd's was as safe as the Bank of England. It knew what it was doing with money, surely; if it did not, who did? It turned out to be an extremely risky way to invest because the Names had unlimited liability, and in the early 1990s thousands of them were promptly ruined. Houses were sold and they had to appeal to the Lloyd's Hardship Fund, administered by Mary Archer, for living costs. Their stories were contemporary versions of the woes experienced by the upper middle classes ruined in the South Sea Bubble.

The court cases involving the Gooda Walker syndicates that had run up losses of £1bn revealed the full shabbiness of the affair, with staff testifying that the Names were being treated in a cavalier fashion and even fleeced. Meanwhile, Anthony Gooda and Derek Walker had prospered while piling their Names into appropriately named 'catastrophe syndicates'.[6] A run of disasters, including Piper Alpha in the North Sea in 1988 and the Lockerbie air disaster in 1989, increased claims and made the losses in the early 1990s worse. The striking exterior of the post-modernist Richard Rogers building from which Lloyd's operated might give the impression that the work inside embodied efficiency, mysterious power and the British financial inheritance updated for a new era. Inside, some of the underwriters had behaved with about as much decorum and good sense as Del Boy Trotter. As Julian Barnes explained it to American readers in a letter from London in the *New Yorker* in September 1993 – 'The Deficit Millionaires' – it had been revealed that one of the pillars of the Establishment was made out of Styrofoam.

Did this carnival of sleaze confirm that the Tories had unleashed corruption? Or had their reforms simply amplified what was already there and made its exposure possible? Certainly the roots of the Lloyd's scandal stretched way back before Thatcher's spell in office, and it was a product of a badly run cartel of the kind she detested. Maxwell was a crooked tycoon given houseroom by the Left. But there was no doubt that many of the other scandals involved miscreants being monstrously greedy, playing on a pitch that had been rolled by the Tories.

Thatcher herself was struggling in the early 1990s to adjust to life out of power, travelling the world making speeches, searching for a role, seeking validation, and becoming increasingly agitated by the ambitions of the nascent European Union. The aftershocks from the reinvigoration of markets that she had helped instigate kept on reverberating. One in particular knocked Thatcher's own party off its feet, even more than the scandals, in the process creating an opportunity for a Labour revival.

On 16 September 1992, her successor as Prime Minister, John Major, got a piquant lesson in the power of free-flowing international markets, when the UK was humiliatingly evicted from the ERM (the European Exchange Rate Mechanism). The ERM had been designed to lock in member currencies within agreed bands and to reduce instability. Thatcher's reluctance to join (she relented a year before she lost office) caused tensions with cabinet ministers who were concerned by her growing Euroscepticism. Meanwhile, Germany, France and others saw the ERM as a step towards a European single currency, which she feared. As Chancellor, then Prime Minister, John Major saw the ERM as a tool for reducing inflation, which had surged again. He invested all of his authority in keeping the UK in the ERM.

On the other side of the Atlantic, an international speculator called George Soros became convinced over the course of the summer that this would not work, and by the autumn had placed a series of big bets against the Bank of England. He and several other major investors gambled that governments would not be able to maintain exchange rates at their then levels, and that pressure from the markets would force ministers and central bankers to abandon their policy, leaving those who had bought and sold anticipating that outcome big profits.

Britain crashing out of the ERM on Black Wednesday turned out to be a great boon for the British economy, in that it enabled a devaluation, lower interest rates and a recovery, although all that many voters remembered was the Chancellor, Norman Lamont – who was not an enthusiast for the ERM, unlike his boss John Major – pushing interest rates up briefly to 15 per cent in a doomed attempt to convince those in the markets that they were prepared to do anything to stay in. The resulting farce was highly symbolic, and close to being the economic equivalent of the Suez crisis, in which the limits of British post-war power were demonstrated humiliatingly.

The government had been bested by Soros, who won $1.5bn over the course of September, and the Tory tribe that had spent many years telling its critics that you cannot buck the market had just had the adage proven. When an advisor to Soros said with the denouement approaching that he should build up their position gradually, Soros said no: 'Go for the jugular.'

That the eventual end result of the crisis was the bolstering of the UK's economic recovery initially seemed almost beside the point, with the television news full of footage of very highly paid young people in braces shouting at each other. The Liberal Democrat leader Paddy Ashdown for once caught the mood with a succinct observation on Black Wednesday about the government: 'They have lost control of the economic situation.' That was it. The Conservatives since 1979 had often suffered periods of extreme unpopularity between general elections, but they always came through on the assumption of enough southern voters that, broadly, they had the economy covered and heading in the right direction. As that trader interviewed by Joan Bakewell on the BBC the day after the 1987 election had said: 'It's the safest and steadiest the country's been for years. Keep it on an even keel.' Even keel and steady were certainly not words that came to mind in late 1992. The Republican Party also suffered a reputational collapse in the US election in November, and Bill Clinton became President. Soros, who was presented in the press as part Bond villain and part seer, was, it turned out, definitely not what he termed 'a free market fundamentalist'. Markets worked, he said, but the idea that they were perfection and needed no supervision was a fantasy.

All this had another impact at Westminster. The gusto with which hitherto Tory-supporting newspapers devoured Major and other ministers in the wake of the shambles taught the next generation of Labour leaders what seemed to be the central truths of the 1990s: those in markets wield the power, be nice to them in all but the most exceptional circumstances; and the media is a monster that can eat a government alive if the leading figures in it are insufficiently skilled at manipulating journalists, editors and proprietors.

Despite it being a moment of triumph for the power of the markets, this was not a happy period in the City. At the Stock

Exchange itself there was a technological cock-up, several years after the departure of George Hayter, steward of Big Bang, that brought humiliation. The advances made in computerisation and reorganisation during Big Bang were not followed up successfully, and the attempt to create a faster computer system – TAURUS, the Transfer and Automated Registration of Uncertified Stocks – was an embarrassing failure. In March 1993 the management cancelled the project, at a cost of £75m to the Exchange and £320m spent by member firms. The chief executive, Peter Rawlins, resigned and the Bank of England had to step in to help construct a replacement computer system.

The harm done by the IRA in the same period was much worse. The Irish Republican campaign against the UK had been relentless, with bombs set off in the capital and beyond for decades, targeted at shoppers, the transport network, the armed forces, police, politicians and the Royal Family. The City had received relatively little attention during the Troubles, but now that it had a much higher profile it was the ideal location for terrorist spectaculars and murder. Shortly before 10:30am on 10 April 1992, the day after a general election, the IRA parked a lorry containing a fertiliser bomb outside the Baltic Exchange, killing three people and all but demolishing the building where the market in shipping contracts was based.

Little more than a year later the Bishopsgate bomb was exploded on the morning of Saturday 24 April 1993, killing a photographer, injuring more than forty people and causing £1bn of damage. The scene that greeted staff and managers on their arrival as they rushed to their offices was dystopian. The facilities staff at Henderson, along with Ben Wrey, discovered that their building had had a lucky escape but climbed onto the roof to take a look. Wrey recalled looking across the skyline at buildings including the NatWest Tower and the Hongkong and Shanghai Bank: 'It was just astounding. There wasn't a single window left in place in those buildings. Everything was hanging out, falling out.' The curtains billowed and some of the millions of pieces of paper blown from the buildings, later shredded by the police, were found as far as two miles away. A so-called 'ring of steel' had to be constructed, with roads leading into the City narrowed and armed guards posted.

The impact of these attacks was more than monetary; the damage done to the City's historical fabric was significant too. The Bishopsgate blast almost destroyed Gresham's tomb in St Helen's, and demolished the medieval St Ethelburga's Bishopsgate, which had survived both the Great Fire of 1666 and the Blitz. It had to be rebuilt and reopened later as a centre for peace and reconciliation. The City had recovered from attacks before; of course it had. This time it would take a few more knocks to its prestige and then, via Europe, it would rise to new heights.

EURO VISION

'Frankfurt is not in the same league as London.'

Henrietta Royle, 2002

Siegmund Warburg had been, for a while, a great enthusiast for European political integration. Having experienced pre-war Berlin and the Nazis before he escaped to London – once there, helping fellow refugees recover what they could – it would be a surprise if he had taken any view other than to advocate greater European cooperation, trade and friendship. His Eurobond innovation in the 1960s, which was so enthusiastically adopted by the Americans and others, remaking London, was one of the most effective pieces of cooperation in the post-war period, providing capital and aiding investment. But the firm the great innovator built in London did not survive much more than a decade after he died. Warburg the merchant bank was taken over and integrated out of existence after his successors took a series of missteps.

It began when Warburg's attempted to do a deal with Morgan Stanley in 1994. David Scholey, the Warburg chairman, hoped that the combination would turn Warburg's bank into an operation with global clout. For their part, the Americans wanted to get their hands on Mercury Asset Management, the £100bn of assets, managed by Warburg's parent company. On 15 December 1994 a short statement revealed that the deal was off. One of the most curious aspects of finance is the way in which a failed takeover or merger attempt exposes the smaller party, because those in the market know that it tried to sell itself but something went wrong. It amounts to an admission that the firm cannot prosper on its own. Warburg had approached the Morgan Stanley deal with expansive confidence; now, having been jilted, it found itself vulnerable to the predations of outsiders. It withdrew from the Eurobond market and started to leak senior staff, who moved to rivals. In May 1995, Warburg was sold to Swiss Bank Corp for $1.37bn.

It was a sorry end for the business that had been built by Warburg, and the even more publicity-shy Henry Grunfeld. It is fortunate that Warburg himself – perceptive student of human foibles and the leading merchant banker of his generation – did not live to see it. His successors had conducted themselves precisely as Warburg had feared they would, pushing for scale and ignoring his view that what mattered were relationships and not just money alone. And for all the talk that he was a pragmatist who understood that eventually his bank would have to find a partner, this was a forced sale of one of the most innovative financial institutions of the modern period to a rather boring Swiss institution. Peter Spira, who had been the youngest member of the original Eurobond team in 1963, spoke for many when he said he was appalled at the outcome. Spira had left many years earlier and, following an unpleasant experience as finance director at Sotheby's, where he found the auction house business even less honourable than the City, he joined Goldman Sachs as vice-chairman. When Warburg's went, he could scarcely believe it. 'All my contemporaries who left, we all felt exactly the same: shame, sadness,' he told an interviewer.[1] He and his former colleagues felt as though it was like a club or regiment that they had helped to build up, and now it was gone.

But between the collapse of the Morgan Stanley deal and the Warburg's sale to the Swiss, there occurred a spectacular disaster that eclipsed all the reverses for the Brits and combined several of the themes of the City revolution. The historic British merchant bank Barings had, in trying to compete, moved into areas its owners and management did not understand. Barings was trying to make its own transition from the era of merchant bank to the whizzier world of securities trading, using the bank's own balance sheet to play the markets. Initially it had considerable success, particularly when Christopher Heath ran Barings Securities. In 1989 he was described by the press as Britain's best-paid man, earning more than £3m, a figure which caused resentment in the other parts of family-owned Barings. He was forced out in early 1993 and an attempt was made to bring the securities division under greater control. The new controls turned out to be worse than rudimentary and the bank's owners became ever more hooked on the seemingly magical profits that had started to flow in from its trading operation in the Far East. A young trader, not yet thirty years old, had been put in charge of a new futures operation in Singapore. His name was Nick Leeson.

Giving Leeson, who was enormously keen to become wealthy but not smart enough to do it legitimately, so much control and money stands as one of the most stupid decisions in the history of the City. How it was ever allowed to happen still baffles some of those involved when the collapse was revealed. A Bank of England veteran who was there that weekend says: 'I have thought about it ever since. Why did they keep sending the money to Leeson in Singapore? Greed for the returns is the only explanation I can ever come up with.' In Singapore Leeson had been allowed to control both the trading operation and the settlement operation. That meant that normal controls – where backroom staff would ask questions about his trades – simply did not apply this time. He employed a secret account (88888) to hide his losses. Even when questions were asked it resulted in no action. By February 1995 the losses totalled £832m and Leeson wrote a resignation letter and boarded a flight out of Singapore.

In London, Peter Baring went round to the Bank of England to break the news that Barings had been defrauded and was as a result somewhat awkwardly completely bust. An attempted rescue did not get very far. Salomon and others were contacted, but with little clarity on how much Leeson had really lost it was impossible for them to step in and buy it. Elsewhere in London Ben Wrey was one of many who got a call, in his case from one of his non-executive directors who had just heard the news: 'Ben, overnight your banker has gone out of business and I just wondered what you were doing about it?' Like many senior people in firms across the City that day, he rushed to the office along with IT people to work out how exposed they were, and which clients had money that might be locked in the collapsing Barings.

That weekend, there was a summit of the City Establishment at the Bank of England, at which the performance of the Barings team was quite extraordinary. Attempts to stick to the family line that they had been defrauded were weakened when the team explained that they had sent £800m to Leeson in the months before the losses were revealed. There were gasps around the table when this emerged. Barings was done for. The Bank of England concluded that its failure would not endanger the market, which turned out to be right, and in Tokyo and New York it got little attention. But the end of Barings provided the quintessential example of Britons grown greedy and flattened by forces they could barely comprehend. The Bank of England and regulators were also criticised for their failure to spot how lax Barings had become.

Warburg and Barings had each gone, joining the myriad brokers and jobbers that a decade before had seemingly been fixed landmarks on the City scene. Not all British firms did badly, however. Far from it. Out of the remaining British merchant banks Cazenove prospered, and Lazard stood apart. It was possible to make a new success out of an old business in London if it adapted, although in the case of Smith New Court even it ended up sold to the Americans eventually. The firm was run by Michael Marks, who had started straight out of school as a runner – delivering stocks and collecting cheques when it was still done by hand – at the stockjobber Smith Brothers; then he became a blue button at the Stock Exchange and in 1975 a partner and boss at Smith Brothers. When Smith New Court was created in 1985, part owned by N.M. Rothschild and chaired by Sir Michael Richardson, Marks was one of the pivotal figures that those needing to buy substantial chunks of companies could call on.

In 1995, when Smith New Court was bought for £526m by the Americans at Merrill Lynch, Marks became a leading figure in the company, continuing a career trajectory that proved that, for all Thatcherism had busted open cartels, there existed a much older London tradition manifest in the rise of Michael Marks. The City had only become so stratified along class grounds from the late Victorian period, whereafter merchant bankers looked down at brokers, who looked down at jobbers, who were the ones with the best understanding of personal risk because they had taken most of it, holding shares for sale on their books. Even when the place was more hierarchical, some people burst through, such as Marks, and the City would not have worked half as well without German immigrants. It had been an engine of social mobility and advancement for bright boys such as Marks – always boys – to varying degrees from its earliest days. It is just that Thatcherism and Big Bang made social mobility, for a while, an even bigger component of the City's personality.

In that respect, London in the mid-1990s was a land of opportunity, and the flood of money flowing through it meant you had to try quite hard in the City, or be unlucky or too greedy, to lose everything more than once. If a trader and his or her colleagues knew enough; if they were a certain type who enjoyed risk, had a feel for markets and did not get over-extended; they could become extremely affluent by working themselves into the right place, putting in long hours, trading intelligently and skimming (legitimately) a little of the billions, trillions, that surged through the fibre-optic cables running beneath London's streets and flowed into their offices onto computer screens and back out again. Those little slices of a large sum, taken repeatedly as money sped through the system, soon added up to big numbers. In each area the profits on individual transactions might look small to those who benefited, because the turnover numbers they dealt with for their firms on a daily basis were so large. Bigger numbers, and bigger bonuses, might easily distort one's sense of self-worth.

The resentment at being asked to listen to these increasingly assertive City folk as though they had access to a superior form of insight and intelligence was expressed well by Neal Ascherson in the *Independent on Sunday*. The coverage on television news of almost any major event since Big Bang must it seemed, he said, be accompanied by interviews with rows of 'cream-faced young men' called analysts being asked for their opinions.

> They know a bit about money, in the sense of short-term speculation prospects. But their views on politics, so readily offered, are amateurish. Any of us, given a couple of whiskies and a read of that morning's *Independent*, could do as well. But they come from the City of London, and the City knows about money, and money is what politics is really about.

Trading – in shares, derivatives, foreign exchange or commodities – attracted most of the attention when the press or television examined the City at moments of crisis, perhaps because it was so telegenic and reminded the audience of what they had seen in films such as *Wall Street*. The loudest of the breed, the young working-class men out to make quick fortunes, were dubbed 'barrow boys' who after work in the City's newly busy bars consumed 'shampoo' (champagne) by the cellar-full. LIFFE was searched for drugs by police sniffer dogs, although somehow nothing was found. But there was a lot more to the new City besides aggressive trading. The decisions increasingly were guided by research analysts who studied the market and assessed the state of companies and wrote reports for their colleagues and clients recommending what should be bought and sold.

What had been a pretty rudimentary and unfashionable aspect of finance now became more glamorous, and listed companies had to undergo being grilled by research analysts from big banks and investment houses. The focus started to be on quarterly reporting by companies, meaning that not long after major manufacturers, supermarkets, retailers, airlines and high-street banks themselves had got through one explanation of how they were performing their team had to start preparing the next. The risk there was that while it brought a degree of increased professionalism, it could encourage short-termism and the cult of the leader inside the companies themselves and among some investors. It also required companies and big banks to build large internal bureaucracies dedicated to protecting the scrutinised chief executive, with the help of public relations experts and marketing people. Of course the share price had always mattered and the returns to shareholders too, but it and the CEO, chairman and finance director were now assessed with more regularity and in a less forgiving manner. There still existed plenty of investors, analysts and fund managers who wanted to take a longer-term view and who were genuinely motivated by the excitement of finding far-flung companies worthy of investment; however, there was no doubt that the pressure for short-term returns had increased.

One spot where the Brits really prospered in the 1990s was in building businesses that operated in the space between traditional well-known institutions struggling to cope with the competition and the ruthless foreign arrivals. Often best suited to the new dispensation were the entrepreneurial Brits who had first turned up for work in the 1980s. They had intellectually processed the explosion of money, landed in the City at the right moment and married their insight with a ruthless eye for the main chance. New firms such as ICAP (founded in 1986 as Intercapital by Michael Spencer) placed themselves at the international crossroads of finance, as inter-dealer brokers matching clients such as big banks with pools of shares and interest rate products, foreign exchange, commodities, emerging markets and credit, and trading for themselves too. In asset management, a company such as Aberdeen Asset Management, established by Martin Gilbert after a buy-out of an investment trust in 1983, could fill the need for investment opportunities and advice that came stripped of City insider condescension.

These businesses were tiny at first, and Aberdeen was one of the firms that later ran into severe difficulties for selling 'split-cap' investments to consumers as low-risk when they were anything but (Aberdeen was subsequently rebuilt by Gilbert and his team). But the swashbuckling tenor of the times suited the insurgents, who were unimpeded by having to reconcile themselves to accommodating traditions or form. They would grow quickly. Terry Smith was another such outsider who blossomed in a climate that suited the irreverent and the intelligent. Smith was a grammar-school boy from the East End, who after university became one of the leading research analysts. His approach rested on the extraordinary idea of telling investors the truth. Could this ever catch on? His frankness got him fired as head of UK company research at UBS Phillips & Drew in 1992 when he published *Accounting for Growth*. That incendiary document questioned the assorted ruses and creative accountancy that were employed by advisors and accountants to make some businesses appear more successful to investors than they were. The book sold well and Smith went on to make a fortune as a fund manager with a predilection for punchy comments about politics.

All this put the next generation of political leaders on the centre-Left in an odd position. The new leader of the Labour Party, Tony Blair, and the Shadow Chancellor, Gordon Brown, realised that they had to reconcile their party to many of the Thatcherite market reforms to win, and that meant stepping up what had started under their predecessors as a 'prawn cocktail offensive', wooing City types and convincing them that Labour had changed and was not about to nationalise the banks. The Blair–Brown view had been bolstered by visits to Washington to see Bill Clinton, who had won the Presidency in 1992 by not trying to refight the battles of the 1980s.

Standing in the way of success in the City or in business would only reinforce the old stereotypes that did not appeal to swing voters, it seemed. Some people were going to be paid a lot of money. But who? And what constituted proper reward or grounds for populist complaint? The criteria were unclear. Was the benchmark simply what you could get? The City pay boom in the mid-1980s, which accelerated again in the 1990s, had set an example, and ambitious executives in industry and commerce could see that some of the people advising them on deals, or moving around their company's reserves of foreign exchange, or trading corporate bonds, were being paid much more than the chief executives of major companies that were theoretically their clients. The phrase 'paying the market rate' became fashionable, and remuneration committees found themselves inundated by inflated evidence – from head-hunters and the like – that only by paying what was on offer in comparable jobs would they land or keep the best person.

This ostensibly had a certain logic, but the implications of this self-serving racket first became fully apparent during the infamous case of the chief executive of British Gas – Cedric Brown – who became in the mid-1990s the media's most unpopular person in Britain, hunted by the tabloids and branded 'Cedric the pig'. The Labour leadership proved itself adept at castigating him, to please the voters, while being nice more broadly to business and the City.

Yet Cedric Brown's story, like that of John King who had successfully privatised British Airways and taken a 116 per cent pay increase, might in another context have been considered an admirable tale of hard work and social mobility. When Brown became chief executive of the privatised monopoly, the American chairman of the company, used to US corporate largesse, approved a salary of £475,000, a £600,000 incentive deal, almost £1m worth of share options and a guaranteed £180,000 annual pension on his retirement five years hence. It represented a 900 per cent increase for that role over the course of a decade.

All of the contemporary resentments and accusations – about corporate pay, greed, privatisation, the property crash – came pouring down on poor (or not so poor) Cedric Brown's head.[2] He was accused by the press of a transgression deemed to be even worse in British terms than greed, however. His house was judged to be petty bourgeois and 'neo-Georgian'. In contrast, the chairman of British Gas, who was paid more than £400,000 for a three-day week at British Gas, got a lot less attention than his chief executive. He was self-made too but treated more leniently, having acquired the good taste to live in a flat in Cadogan Square, Chelsea, and own a nice property on the US east coast in the exclusive Martha's Vineyard.

In the US, on Wall Street, the equation tended to be much simpler. You secured high pay? Well done, good luck to you. Although it should not be forgotten that this had not always been the case. The original J.P. Morgan stipulated that no manager should be paid a salary more than twenty times the salary of the lowest-paid worker. Try getting that principle readopted by an American investment bank today. But in the UK it was more complex, partly because of the quirks of the class system and partly because significant changes that came with Thatcherism received inadequate attention at the time and produced effects that were only understood later. It was connected to the argument over financial regulation and the importation of an American approach (if it is legal, it is fine or right).

Combine the two – get paid what you can, it is the market rate; and it is all entirely legal – and you have created the conditions for the row that took place in 2016 about the offshore investments of David Cameron's late father. A partner at Panmure Gordon, he had established a vehicle in Panama through which family investments were routed, perfectly legally. But in 2012 Ian Cameron's son had condemned entertainers who avoided tax (rather than evaded it, which is illegal). Cameron Junior was accused of hypocrisy and the affair illustrated that one of the main contradictions of the Thatcher experiment remains unresolved. Imagine asking Harold Macmillan, or Gladstone or Disraeli, whether the law is all that matters in such circumstances. They would probably answer that while the rule of law is important, and without it we are sunk, there should be more to it than that. What of duty, restraint and setting an example to others? Cameron knew it too, which is why he later withdrew his comments about the immorality of comedians minimising their tax bills. And what of Thatcher, the Methodist? Whether one disagrees with her or approves of her record, she was clear that a moral and ethical impulse – reward for work, and without wealth there is nothing to help the weak – defined her approach to politics.

The New Labour leadership when it swept away the Conservatives had its own unique answer to these problems. Part of the skill of those who restored the party to power in May 1997 was that they initially so cleverly accommodated themselves to Thatcherism, on both sides of the Blair–Brown divide, and adapted it. They rarely attacked her in name because it was recognised that she had won three general elections and remained popular – as a promoter of aspiration – in much of the south where Labour needed to win seats. Peter Mandelson's quote, often used out of context with the second half lopped off, in which he said that he was 'intensely *relaxed* about people getting *filthy rich* as long as they pay their taxes', is much more revealing than the bowdlerised version, for it reveals the essence of the New Labour compact. The leadership now welcomed Thatcherite markets and unashamed wealth creation, and would use the proceeds to pay for progressive policies and higher spending on public services.

In such circumstances who, other than cranks or old-fashioned types who remembered that booms end, could object to the example of the City as a great British success story? It had spread out to Canary Wharf, where banks such as Morgan Stanley, J.P. Morgan and a resurgent Barclays occupied towers. Barclays was again building an investment bank, after selling the struggling BZW and launching Barclays Capital, led from 1996 by Bob Diamond. In the City itself, the remodelling instigated by Michael Cassidy and Peter Rees from the Corporation altered the skyline, and in 2004 the Richard Rogers building, christened the Gherkin, opened. The competition from Canary Wharf had after all compelled the Corporation to approve even bigger office blocks that could rival what was on offer a few miles away.

Another outpost of finance had also sprung up in London's West End, in Mayfair, where on Dover Street and in streets nearby emerged Hedge Fund Alley. Its firms were often boutique in scale, promising superior returns, owned privately with a relatively small number of staff investing borrowed capital. Private equity and venture capital firms abounded, injecting money into undervalued firms and sometimes loading them with debt while sucking out proceeds to invest elsewhere. In such inventive, expansive times some surveys in the mid-2000s showed that London pay and performance had overtaken New York. More than ever, the Americans had to be over here. The investment banking operation of Schroders was sold in 2000 to Citigroup; Robert Fleming went to Chase Manhattan; and even Cazenove under the leadership of David Mayhew was sold to J.P. Morgan in 2004.

It seemed at the time that the simultaneous expansion of Britain's high-street banks, several of which had tooled up to compete at global investment banking, made a kind of sense. These were starting to be talked of, usually by themselves, as potential world-beaters worthy of government endorsement. RBS became, briefly, the biggest bank in the world by balance sheet in late 2007, and a former building society called Northern Rock grew by borrowing money on the markets and repackaging – securitising – the loans, which was a terrific model as long as they could access sufficient credit on a daily basis. The denizens of the City sometimes deny any culpability for this madness. RBS was a Scottish Bank, HBOS was technically headquartered in Edinburgh, and Northern Rock was based in Newcastle. The truth is that the analysts pronouncing on banks'

Clever old Caz: David Mayhew in 2004 when the bluechip City firm Cazenove was one of the last to sell to an American giant, in its case J.P. Morgan.

prospects were based in the City, and they had a mixed record in spotting trouble. The asset managers who bought and sold shares in these and other banks loaded up with other people's money. Many of the accountants and lawyers who assisted the expanding banks were in London. And the securitisation employed by Northern Rock and so many others was merely a version of what investment banks had, they thought, perfected in the field of repackaging sub-prime US mortgages. The British banking boom of the 2000s was in part a creation of the Square Mile.

The media was hardly blameless in talking up all this activity and expansion in banking and other industries. The business sections of Sunday newspapers had long enjoyed the 'Friday night drop', in which companies or their public relations agencies 'dropped' stories to financial journalists. As the journalist Chris Blackhurst put it shortly afterwards:

> Stories that were being hailed as major scoops of journalistic endeavour were often nothing of the sort, involving little more than a phone call from a PR to a friendly, trusted reporter. The drop has all manner of uses. Poor results will be leaked to Sunday journalists in advance to soften the blow. In takeovers, agencies will dish the dirt on the opposition in a way they could not do in any official document. Speculation about next year's figures, even the private lives of the directors, will all be handed to a favoured journalist. The Sunday papers will be used to smoke out possible bidders, to trash business rivals, to bring about votes of confidence by putting pressure on recalcitrant boards.[3]

Were financial journalists breaking any rules? Jeff Randall, a leading observer of the Square Mile, a former City Editor of the *Sunday Times*, was convinced they were not. All they were doing was getting stories: 'In order to be guilty of insider dealing you have to deal,' Randall said. 'Knowing or having access to price sensitive information is not a crime. It is what you do with the information that counts. We are in the business of revealing to our readers price sensitive information. That is why they buy the paper.'[4]

It was a good point. Journalism in London or New York was hardly pure, far from it, before the financial revolution of the 1980s, but what had been created thanks to the increased reader interest in the markets, in the rise of the financial PR firm attempting to better control stories to the advantage of clients, was a bigger and more valuable market in information. Many of those practices in politics that are commonly attributed to the rise of so-called 'spin-doctors' in the 1990s, inflated press officers trying to mould their clients image and control the story, often in vain, were prefigured in the interplay between City PRs, large companies, investment banks and financial hacks that reached a zenith in the 1980s and 90s.

In Britain it had another effect, in TV news. As the scale and importance of the financial markets increased, and access to sophis-ticated insight and gossip about them became a more valuable commodity, so the stock of City journalists rose. In 2000, Randall was appointed as the first business editor of the BBC when its new director general, Greg Dyke, decided that the Beeb had taken far too lofty an attitude to moneymakers. The Corporation had tradi-tionally preferred to have an economics editor, who covered busi-ness too when necessary. This was no longer good enough, Dyke told the Confederation of British Industry in a speech in early November 2000: 'Up to now we thought it was good enough to have the economics editor also being responsible for business cover-age on the side. It was wrong.'[5]

The then economics editor was Peter Jay, who as Britain's ambas-sador to Washington in the late 1970s had been an early convert to monetarism and the concept of squeezing inflation out of the econ-omy by getting the money supply under control. In the early 1980s Jay was one of the founders of TV-am, presiding over programmes informed by a 'mission to explain'. The ratings were dire, and Dyke was drafted in to rescue the situation in the spring of 1983. He promptly ripped up the formula, opted for ratings-friendly excite-ment and introduced a 'rapping' rat – Roland Rat, accompanied by a sidekick called Kevin – who is credited with helping to save the company. Much later, when Dyke hired Randall in 2000 at the BBC, he was implementing his own 'mission to explain', arguing that the BBC had to become much better at explaining markets and companies to its large audiences in terms they could understand. Dyke and Randall were defining media products of the Thatcherite 1980s, and even if Dyke was a Labour supporter, he shared with Randall distinctly meritocratic, anti-Establishment instincts. Their appointments at the end of the 1990s would have been unimaginable in the BBC of twenty years earlier, before the rise to fresh prominence of the City and the elevated position business was now accorded.

It did seem for a while as though there was a lot to celebrate. On 25 October 2006, two days before the twentieth anniversary of Big Bang, the guest speaker at the annual City of London Corporation dinner was someone from the anti-Blair side of the New Labour civil war. Ed Balls, the government's City Minister, had been Gordon Brown's closest aide and a major combatant in the fight to keep the UK out of the single currency.

Big Bang in October 1986 had been a tremendous success and decisive moment in the history of the City, he told the audience of financiers and politicians that evening: 'It confirmed that in financial services Britain would choose global integration and openness over protectionism and national ownership, competition and market discipline over discrimination and cartels.' He also disagreed, he said, with those who criticised the 'light touch' approach to regulation. 'To revert to more heavy-handed, detailed or mechanistic regulation which put process before substance would divert us from proper risk-assessment and stifle innovation. We do not intend to fall into that trap.'[6]

The following day there was a celebration at the Mansion House, with Nicholas Goodison acknowledging in a speech that he was surprised that so many of the old City firms had disappeared following the reforms. It was widely agreed that Big Bang had been a roaring success, though. In the intervening two decades, the value of traded shares in London had increased from £161bn in 1986 to

£2,496bn in 2006. The banking sector had boomed, with total assets up seven times to £5.5 trillion. The Treasury pulled in 26 per cent of its corporate tax receipts annually from the financial services industry. In the *FT*, John Kay eschewed boosterism and offered a more nuanced verdict. The greatest beneficiaries of Big Bang had been the partners of the firms that sold out when brokers and jobbers were bought at absurd prices by large banks in deals that almost all failed, he said. 'The partners retired to expensive yachts and exclusive villas: the marzipan layer of employees below resented the alien culture of their new masters.' And for all the celebration of success, Kay warned that the evolution of competitive markets always has unpredictable consequences. How right he was became apparent only a few years later.

This is not an account of the financial crisis of 2007–9 that followed. There is no shortage of volumes available already on that episode. An earlier book of mine charted the rise and fall of the Royal Bank of Scotland and its chief executive Fred Goodwin. Suffice it to say that on both sides of the Atlantic a lending surge, a mania for excessive scale, too much bad leadership, ineffective regulation, consumer hunger for goods and houses and a willingness to borrow to pay for it, all came together to produce a new version of an old story. The disaster was followed by a rescue operation and then a sustained campaign of ultra-cheap money, creating more lending and in the UK another property bubble in the south of England. Add to that QE, or money printing. A bubble was blown to get us over the bursting of the previous bubble.

But something else extremely significant and positive had happened in the City between 1986, that pivotal year, and the aftermath of the financial crisis. The launch of the European single currency, completed on 1 January 2002, turned out to be the making of the modern City when no one outside the City was looking, and even though the Eurozone suffered its own crisis. The success of the euro in London might be thought odd when one considers the successful campaign waged to prevent the UK joining what Germany and France created out of the ERM. At the time it was claimed by advocates of British entry that Frankfurt, which boasted the European Central Bank, would eclipse London as Europe's new financial centre. To anyone who had ever been there, this seemed unlikely.

As Henrietta Royle, deputy chief executive of British Invisibles, a body promoting the UK's financial services industry, told the BBC in 2002: 'It [Frankfurt] is not in the same league as London.' Michael Lewis (not the author, another Michael Lewis) had worked in Frankfurt and was unimpressed too. He told an interviewer: 'It is about the size of Reading but not as interesting.' London in the early 2000s simply had too many accumulated advantages, and too much had been invested there by American banks. The introduction of the EU single market, and 'passporting', which allowed banks to operate anywhere in the EU if they were adequately regulated in one country, meant that the UK was free to become the centre for trading of all types in euros. By 2013 its lead was enormous. Centred on London, the UK had 78 per cent of all foreign exchange trading in the EU; 85 per cent of all hedge fund assets; 50 per cent of fund management; 74 per cent of OTC (over the counter) derivatives trading; 31 per cent of equity market capitalisation; 19 per cent of all bank lending in the EU; 23 per cent of insurance premiums ; and 18 per cent of total EU financial services GDP.

The irony is that the Thatcher-era reforms had led to London dominating trade in the European currency the UK had decided not to join[7], ending a sixty-year shutdown in global securities markets that dated to 1914, and which had partially been reopened with the Eurobond in 1963. Even if Thatcher did not plan it – and it started before her, with technological innovation making it feasible – it was hardly pure accident. Key decisions were taken by her and her leading ministers which dramatically sped up a European and global financial revolution.

It turned out that the British abolition of exchange rate controls in 1979, allowing money to flow across borders seeking investment opportunity, had been a transformative act that became internationally highly influential. It was copied four years later by Australia and then by New Zealand. It eventually became standard in much of the world. Ten years after Geoffrey Howe, urged on by Nigel Lawson, removed the UK's exchange controls, even France followed. On 12 December 1989 the French finance minister, Pierre Bérégovoy, made the announcement confirming it. The previous weekend, at a summit in Strasbourg, the move had been urged by Mrs Thatcher. The European Community (the forerunner of the European Union) set a series of countries deadlines, and within a few years Italy, Spain, Portugal and Greece had complied.

That cross-border flow had another side effect on the British, who had once taken such pride in national ownership of their industry and commerce. It had not been uncommon for politicians and newspapers to talk of national champions and to oppose foreign firms buying up British assets, even when British companies were buying up so much themselves in other countries. The Royal Bank of Scotland was protected from foreign takeover by Margaret Thatcher's ministers in the early 1980s. But even if there was public disquiet when British brands went into foreign ownership – as in 1988 when the confectionery firm Rowntree was bought by Switzerland's Nestlé for £2.5bn – it started to become the norm and to attract a lot less comment. Some voices were raised asking if it made sense for water companies or electricity providers to be owned by French companies, but complaints rarely lasted long.

The English even accepted the principle – if not the reality, when it did not produce victory for their own team – of football clubs such as Chelsea, Manchester United, Manchester City, Liverpool and Leicester being owned by rich foreigners. The London Stock Exchange itself ceased to be a membership organisation in 2000 and it is now owned by a variety of international shareholders that in recent years have included the Qatar Investment Authority and the American investment giant Blackrock. Money follows money, and just about anything British – apart from the Queen – is for sale for the right price.

The Thatcherite privatisation programme, which could not have been carried out without the assistance of the City, was also exported and adopted widely. In India, Chile, Singapore, Brazil, France, Germany, Israel, South Korea, Norway, and many other countries, telecommunications, banking, airports, airlines, water, electricity, property, and much more besides were auctioned. Big Bang-style reforms were also implemented in stock markets across the world. In Tel-Aviv in 1986 the old exchange was rudimentary until Esther Levanon arrived from more than a decade working in computers for the Shin Bet, Israel's internal security service. 'At the time there were several dozen traders delivering orders,' she said, 'With battalions of typists inputting the data.'[8] She computerised the operation in a model that owed much to London. In the Paris Bourse and in the Amsterdam Stock Exchange open outcry was faded out. At the Frankfurt Stock Exchange, which eventually became Deutsche Borse, computerised pricing like London's was introduced from September 1987. Eventually, Amsterdam, Brussels and Paris grouped together, were sold to the Americans (NYSE) and then ICE, the Intercontinental Exchange.

But they did not – for now – rival London. How could they? With the rich and aspirational from America, Russia, France, the Gulf and beyond flocking to London – rocketing houses prices and creating a luxury goods boom – it attracted money, some of which was invested in changing the face of the place well beyond the Square Mile. The wealth disparities became ever more obvious, but the drabness and a lot of the grime was wiped away. None of it would have happened without the City and its pull. London was a magnet again, a global hub, voraciously sucking in talent, much-welcome investors, shady playboys, oligarchs laundering dirty money, luxury-obsessed layabouts, and the greedy and the needy. Its re-emergence was down to a most peculiar array of advantages, along with a dose of luck, and reforms that between the invention of the Eurobond and 1986 restored London. The City was back. Was this a good idea?

1986 AND ALL THAT

'I maintain it was not a good idea. I question whether it was necessary.'

Stani Yassukovich

Making my way across a large garden in central London, trying not to drop a tray bearing a pot of Earl Grey and two scones, I approach Sir Nicholas Goodison sitting on a bench in the shade. His remark that I would make a good butler may be a joke, but I am not entirely sure. Despite Goodison's physical frailty – he was born in 1934 – his sense of humour and powers of recall are fully intact. 'Why was it called Big Bang? Because everything changed.' We talk for several hours in the summer sun about the City and how quickly it changed in the 1980s. What is remarkable is that, aside from the cars and some of the architecture, those horrible office blocks put up in the decades immediately after the Second World War, the City of the early 1980s would have been essentially recognisable to a time-travelling worker flown in from the 1930s, or even from the 1880s. Many of the big names on brass plates were still the same towards the end of the 1970s when Goodison became chairman of the Stock Exchange. It had been that way for what seemed like forever. The Stock Exchange functioned largely as it had for decades; the Bank of England was the embodiment of financial power; the City of London Corporation ran the Square Mile (it still does) as a self-governing entity; the railways funnelled in commuters at roughly the same time each day as had been the case a century before; business was conducted face to face; and the sober modes of dress and

'Voracious London': the City's Royal Exchange, the Bank of England, the
Stock Exchange, and Thomas Gresham's old neighbourhood Bishopsgate,
now sit in the shadow of a new generation of temples to mammon.

less sober codes of behaviour were pretty constant. Within ten years of Big Bang, the City looked quite different. Behind old facades new bars opened serving the City new generation, some of them modest and others unafraid to proclaim their genius, which was often simply rooted in luck. Most of all the modern City became about what went on in offices of big banks and investment firms in the Square Mile and at Canary Wharf, in equities, forex, interest rates, debt, derivatives, corporate finance, where during a much longer day London was hooked live to markets around the world moving money, trading, hustling based on information that blinked red and green on a computer screen. Trading and doing deals there had always required foreigners in the City. Now there are more Americans, still some Japanese, and lots of the French. Bonuses have boomed. If anyone played a leading role in creating this festival of moneymaking, it was Goodison. Thirty years after Big Bang, does he think it worked?

'We achieved making London the leading international centre. It is a more competitive market, but the Stock Exchange is simply one market among many and I didn't expect that. Things moved in ways I didn't foresee.' What does he think was lost? 'I thought the Stock Exchange was a brilliant informal regulator . . . tough. Now it has all become a matter of law and if something is a matter of law it is open to challenge.' It is now, he says, an international market in people. He simply cannot understand why such enormous fees are paid and he recommends more openness. 'Total disclosure on salaries and how they are made is where I would start.'

The Stock Exchange has changed considerably in the decades since he left. It demutualised in 2000, and is now owned by institutional investors around the world rather than members. It is based in nondescript offices near St Paul's Cathedral that could, really, be anywhere on earth where financiers do business, from New York to Singapore to Frankfurt. In the spring of 2016, the latest attempt to arrange a merger between the London Stock Exchange and Deutsche Bourse in Frankfurt began.

After hours talking through the late 1970s to the mid-1980s I worry that Goodison may be exhausted. Not a bit of it. It is time for a drink. Goodison sends me off to collect a Cinzano and soda and I return with the drinks, handing him his while sipping a glass of white wine as afternoon turns into early evening. 'I mean,' he says, 'supposing that the Stock Exchange had stayed as it was. It would have died.'

Since the 1980s, Lord Lawson has had to endure becoming almost as famous for his diet (he lost five stone after leaving office) and for his daughter being Britain's leading television cook[1] as he is for being a highly significant reforming Chancellor of the Exchequer from 1983 to 1989. He lives in France and commutes to the House of Lords, where we sit one morning discussing the financial revolution. Lawson liked the City from the start and made friends there when he began his career as a journalist in the 1950s. He was the *FT*'s Lex columnist for a while. 'The City was one of the better parts of the British economy, which doesn't say very much for the other parts of the UK economy. It was good at commodities and good at foreign exchange.' When he became Chancellor after the 1983 election, the Trade Secretary Cecil Parkinson was distracted by the Sara Keays affair and Lawson got involved in the discussions with Goodison. Thatcher was in favour of more competition but she took some persuading about the wisdom of a deal with Goodison. It was the united front presented by Parkinson and Lawson that he thinks convinced the Prime Minister to proceed in the face of doubts from her deputy, Willie Whitelaw. 'Her concern was how it would be interpreted politically. She was always in favour of more competition but she was not instinctively pro-City,' Lawson says. Although Lawson thinks thirty years later that Big Bang was entirely necessary for the City to become the global hub it is today, with hindsight he thinks it should have been accompanied by more safeguards. 'We should have had a Glass-Steagall,' he says, referring to the US legislation from the 1930s that used to prohibit high-street banks getting involved in trading. 'Look at the banking malpractices of 2008. A large part of that was the high-risk culture of the investment banks polluting the traditionally cautious culture of the joint stock banks.' But the City should not be derided, he says. 'As we have seen, the bankers certainly have feet of clay and we don't have to listen to them. But look, there are very few industries in which this country is undoubtedly world class. Banking and finance is one of them.'

Sir David Walker has seen it from inside government, the Bank of England and the boardroom. There are not many people who have had a better seat from which to view the financial revolution of the last fifty years. He was there as a young Treasury official when Denis Healey turned back at Heathrow Airport during the IMF crisis in 1976, before Walker played a critical role at the Bank of England preparing the ground for Big Bang. He was chairman of Morgan Stanley International, author of the government-commissioned review on corporate governance after the financial crisis of 2008 and then chairman of Barclays when it was struggling to recover from a wave of scandals. We meet at his office, where the seventy-six-year-old is non-executive chairman at Winton Capital. Did he think Big Bang was a success? 'Oh yes, absolutely. It was essential. I find it hard to see how the City would have survived as a major international centre without it.' He regards the claims of those who say that it was all better, and more gentlemanly, before 1986 as a 'rose-tinted' view that overlooks how much sharp practice there was. Insider dealing was not illegal at all until 1980 and then only definitively with fresh legislation in the mid-1980s. Before that the practices of 'front-running' shares (using inside information or analysts' reports to trade before letting clients in on the action) and exploiting nefariously obtained tip-offs were widespread in the old City. 'These weren't bad people. They were good people, but the barriers to entry were very high with an ancient set of restrictions. The original City coffee houses were designed to keep people out.'

There were drawbacks to the changes in the City, on Wall Street, and beyond, he says. Part of the problem was that as companies and banks became bigger and vastly more complex, relying on technology that had only recently been unavailable, operating across borders, they needed all manner of products, for foreign exchange, hedging to mitigate risk, and for swaps and ways of parcelling up debt. 'The pace of change accelerated alongside the globalisation of trade and the freeing up of capital flows. This explosion in the markets outstripped the ability of regulators to understand it. They found it very hard to keep up. Simultaneously, the fact it was possible to make a lot more money reduced discipline.' Walker became a regulator for a while, chairing the Securities and Investment Board (SIB) from 1988 and trying to disentangle the work of his predecessor Sir Kenneth Berrill, who had created a jumble of rules that could have filled several large rooms if piled up. Walker tried to return to some simpler 'principles-based' regulation that could be understood by those supposed to be obeying the rules. Several years later, after he had moved on, the incoming Labour government in 1997 introduced a tripartite system under Gordon Brown, in which, fatally, the Bank of England lost day-to-day control of supervision of the banking system. Regulatory failure may have contributed to the 2008 banking crisis, but there was not a shortage of regulation. Insufficient attention was paid to the potential instability of large financial institutions, and the perils of big banks being unable to access funding in an emergency. That credit crisis – triggered by concerns about who held sub-prime derivatives – mutated into a financial crisis and a run on the American and British banking systems, which had, once again urged on by politicians, lent too much on property.

As I prepare to take my leave of Sir David we discuss colourful figures now long gone – Michael von Clemm and Baron Swaythling, horse-mad David Montagu, the man who at Merrill Lynch had Don Regan to dinner and then got a note from Geoffrey Howe saying the Western world was doomed if Regan ever became US Treasury Secretary, which he did. All thirty years ago or more but really, underneath it all, are the people and issues involved now any different? Have ethics changed? Walker pauses to think. It is a very big question, he finally says, before acknowledging he doesn't have a definitive answer. Much of what happens in respect of credit and market risk, he says, isn't really new. It is all there, observable in one form or another, in the history of finance. The key differences now are the huge scale and complex global links of financial market activity which have greatly increased the vulnerability of the whole system to shocks.

The history can be downright wrong or misleading though. One sees it written into the record that the deal that ushered in Big Bang is the Goodison–Parkinson deal. But while Goodison persevered patiently to find a solution year after year, Parkinson inherited the idea, gave it a shove in 1983 with the help of officials and Lawson, and then departed shortly afterwards. But ground-breaking work done by the Bank of England was critical in advocacy of a deal. It was Walker who put the game-changing paper by the Bank of England's Andrew Threadgold on the table in Downing Street advocating a deal to reform the Stock Exchange, at the meeting held days before the 1983 election. Geoffrey Howe saw the sense of it and it was the soon to be ex-Secretary of State for Trade, Arthur Cockfield, who really grasped the scale of the opportunity, says Walker. Cockfield turns out to have been one of the most important figures of the Thatcherite era. Yet his name three decades later is unfairly all but forgotten. It was Cockfield as an EU Commissioner who worked on preparations for the Single European Act of 1986, producing a tariff-free EU which along with myriad directives that followed made it possible for the City to become Europe's undisputed financial capital. Major roles in Big Bang and the Single European Act constitute quite a record.

Michael Howard – now Lord Howard, then the minister who steered the Financial Services Act through the Commons – who became Home Secretary in 1993, then Conservative Party leader in 2003, played a significant role in the developments of 1986 too. He says that history has the regulation story quite wrong: 'I get quite cross when people say it was all about untrammelled free markets with no constraints. It was the first attempt to put financial regulation on a statutory footing, albeit on a self-regulatory basis.' The accompanying Big Bang that happened simultaneously, but which had been planned several years before, was an achievement, he says. 'Without it we would not have the world-leading financial services we have today.' But didn't it associate his party with wrongdoing and excess in the City? 'I suspect the Conservative

Party was associated with the City well before Big Bang.' The Guinness scandal was dealt with pretty robustly, he points out: 'No one can accuse us of being soft on the City.' For all the talk that the 1980s was a period of deregulation, the rise in costs demonstrates that the reduction of regulation is largely a myth. In 1986, the direct cost of UK financial regulation was estimated to be £20m; this rose to around £90m by 1992 and £673m in 2014.

What of the practitioners in the marketplace who lived it? To see David Mayhew of Cazenove, the most blue-chip firm of all that is now no longer independent and is embedded in J.P. Morgan, I go to the US bank's Thameside offices near Blackfriars. The look is clinical modern financial chic – I mean the offices, not Mayhew, who is terrifically entertaining and sharp as a knife. J.P. Morgan also has a tower at Canary Wharf and assorted operations elsewhere in the City and he remains involved part time having 'retired' in 2011. 'I don't think Big Bang, one day, properly describes what was happening. Until the abolition of exchange controls we were a little island, then we re-joined the financial world. That combined with the political push and technology were what drove it.' In contrast, according to Mayhew, the 1960s managed to be dull with short working days, punctuated with moments of great drama during takeovers over which there were no rules of combat and no protections for investors. The caricature of alcoholic excess is overdone, he says: 'They weren't all completely pissed.' If the changes had not been made in the 1980s he thinks London would not have had an international capital market, which he says has provided a very efficient provision of capital to Europe and the world. 'Downsides? Loss of morality? Too much money? There is a question as to whether the system has got it right.' Back in the 1950s there was not such an obsession with shareholder value alone. 'I don't want to pretend we're going to have Victorian values but the Americans are very good at giving money away as well as making it.' The whole capitalist system need defending, he says. 'Ain't any other systems that have done so well.' Mayhew is certainly correct that Americans give more once they make it. Giving is regarded as a duty. Even allowing for the difference in the size of population, the money given to churches, and the tax breaks that are built in to the US system, the gap is enormous. In 2014, total US giving by individuals, foundations, corporations and bequests amounted to $358.4bn (£248.3bn) against £10.6bn in the UK.[2]

Ben Wrey visits the City only rarely but at his home in Kensington we discuss the strange beauty and power of the historic corners of the place that have not been rebuilt in recent decades, such as in Austin Friars where Gresham's house stood in the sixteenth century. Ahead of Big Bang Wrey had seen the impact in the US of May 1975, when travelling for Henderson he glimpsed the way in which small brokers were wiped out by competition from big Wall Street firms because minimum commissions had been scrapped, reducing their income: 'There was this feeling in London that it wouldn't be that brutal here because we don't do things like that. They had underestimated the arrival of the big American banks. It was a pretty shocking experience but it was needed. It brought London right up.' The City now, he suspects, is not quite as much fun as it was but it had to change: 'I don't think it's sensible to be sentimental about the changes or the people. The old world was terribly inefficient.'

Philippa d'Arcy (née Rose) is no longer a head-hunter and left her firm to run a business outside London, opening her rather lovely home, which has its own church, for conferences and weddings. She thinks moaning about the downsides of what happened with rising salaries misses the point. The country was in a hole before the 1980s; the world was changing; it was free markets. 'One has to suck it up and move on.'

Sir Henry Angest, the Swiss immigrant who built up Arbuthnot Latham and became a major donor to the Conservative Party and to Eurosceptic causes, claims that regulation is now much too intrusive and that it advantages the biggest banks, the mega-banks, over the smaller institutions such as his. Big Bang and associated developments were worth it though, he says: 'There was huge activity with building, with cranes everywhere. Foreign restaurants and new chefs opened up. Celebrities came back. Life came back to London.' His Chief Operating Officer, Andrew Salmon, son of a stockbroker, joins the conversation in the Arbuthnot boardroom and says that the 1980s were overwhelmingly positive because the markets were opened up. It brought prosperity to the City. There was a flaw, however. 'For my generation it lured one in. The city is what has really boomed. It has sucked talent out of other parts of the UK. For a while the City became deified and the people became heroes.'

Others go much further in their criticism. Charles McVeigh III, formerly of Salomon, which was swallowed by Travellers, and then Citigroup, the Salomon brand disappearing down the plughole of financial history, is senior Advisor to Citi Private Bank and Vice Chairman of their European Advisory Board. He also chairs Rubicon, a successful London-based hedge fund. He is convinced that capitalism as currently constituted is in serious trouble. It is the capitalists who risk blowing up capitalism if they carry on as they are, he says. Part of the problem is that attitudes have changed and those coming into finance are too often not interested in the lessons of history. 'I'm an old fart. I'm asked regularly at Citigroup to meet with trainees, which I love to do. I look at the audience and they don't give a damn. They're bored. What matters to them is what's happening now and what's in it for me.' This is a disaster, he says, because they need to learn and everyone will suffer if they do not. 'I think capitalism in its current form is broken. The trillions of wealth created between 2008 and 2015', by cheap money and in asset bubbles, 'has gone to 4 or 5 per cent of the population. The companies hide behind the idea their job in life is to enhance shareholder value. Fine. But if we cannot take a long-term perspective we're in trouble. Capitalism is not too big to fail.'

Valerie Thompson, who loved working with Charlie McVeigh and Salomon in the 1980s and left to spend more time raising her daughters, agrees and thinks that the markets have become a toxic debt-laden soup. She enjoyed the intellectual challenge at the time and was extremely good at it, although she disliked the sexism of some of her other colleagues. She recalls the boss Gutfreund visiting London, and smoking a fat cigar, ordering her as she walked past, 'young lady, do a twirl'. It was a low point, and another was when she was jumped on by a man from corporate finance. At one point only one in ten of her colleagues on the sales side were women. Parts of Salomon were a get-rich-quick machine run on testosterone.

Stani Yassukovich is the most blunt of all about the shortcomings of Big Bang. He was Goodison's deputy chairman at the Stock Exchange, a childhood friend of the now departed Michael von Clemm, and a leading figure in the Eurobond revolution at White, Weld. He lives in the South of France, where he indulges his interest in the theatre. What happened, he says, was a tragedy, particularly when the best firms were snapped up pre-1986: 'The worst result of Big Bang was that most of the partners took the money and ran to buy estates in Gloucestershire, which meant a huge exodus of talent and experience. That changed the ethos and culture of the City for the worse. We saw the departure of people who had worried about the reputation of their firm rather than whether bonuses will be paid. It created a movement towards acquisition and to consolidation, which led to too big to manage and too big to fail.' Previously, he claims, the financial community provided an agency function serving other businesses. 'When finance became a business on its own it changed. The all-singing all-dancing financial services institution is a nonsense.'

That does not mean that what was achieved lacked worth. Sometimes members of one pre-Big Bang gang still get together and remind themselves that is the case. In September 2013, Yassukovich and some of the other original pioneers of the market instigated by Siegmund Warburg gathered in black tie at the Savoy Hotel in London to celebrate the fiftieth anniversary of the first Eurobond. Peter Spira spoke and Rupert Hambro said in his remarks that for all the talk of innovation in the 1960s the bonds that London had arranged for foreign markets in the nineteenth century surely counted as an earlier innovation. Gene Rotberg, the former Treasurer of the World Bank, told the audience that what had been achieved was socially extremely useful. It had funded and facilitated corporate expansion and trade from the 1960s onwards. It was an essential part of globalisation, which had brought developing countries such as India into the global economy and changed lives. 'You created access, you were the catalyst for globalisation and while you did not invent cross-border financing – you honed it, polished it, adjusted it, made it fit the circumstances and the demands of investors.' The result he said, had been a transformation in economic development and human prospects across the world. Said Rotberg that evening: 'No, it is not likely you will be remembered by name in a hundred years – that kind of immortality – but a little girl from Bangladesh, as yet unborn, one day will have dinner here returning from her studies at Cambridge or Oxford and she will one day do wondrous things. That will bring you a different kind of immortality.'

As someone who is pro-market, I endorse that statement, of course. Open capital markets are a boon to humanity, matching capital with ideas for business expansion, innovation or infrastructure. The attempt to live without them to varying extents, from the First World War until the abolition of exchange controls by Geoffrey Howe and Nigel Lawson, were a disaster. When successive governments combined closed markets with control of industry and excessive trade union power it turned Britain into a madhouse. In narrow terms, the Stock Exchange could not have been rebuilt if it remained a closed cartel either. Shamefully, women were largely shunned until the 1970s (although this was standard in many areas of industry and finance across the West) and the City operated too often according to connections rather than merit. Opening the Stock Exchange to outside capital and foreign ownership were simply a recognition of the economic reality that this was the way the world was headed. But it is no good me giving a Panglossian pro-market pitch and pretending that the financial revolution did not have some serious, deleterious effects for Britain. As Charlie McVeigh, who joined Salomon Brothers in 1971, the year I was born, correctly put it: capitalism is *not* too big to fail. Those – like me – who believe that open markets and trade hold the key to prosperity would be fools to pretend problems were not created.

The side effects of Big Bang were deeply damaging, so I will list them:

1) It eroded the vital idea of loyalty between the generations. When too many of the partners in long-established City firms took millions in the mid-1980s and cleared off, they sent a signal to those in less senior positions they left behind that what matters is what you can get and bugger the institution or your colleagues.

2) In the decades that followed, it encouraged corporate greed and discredited restraint. It is the morality of the modern football club. Of course most of us try to get paid what we can get paid, but the monomania that it induced and the way corporate larceny was discussed as though it was evidence of dynamism, usually in institutions when it was shareholders' money being taken, and other people's money and leverage being used, would have had those involved horsewhipped just about any time before 1970. One hears it said (approvingly) in certain sections of London society: 'Oh, X took £25m out of Barclays', or 'Y took £50m out of Goldman.' Take, take, take.

3) An American concept of law and compliance was imported, in which the sole question was often legality. In financial services in terms of dud products sold to customers this destroyed trust that will take many years to rebuild. The 1990s and 2000s revenue-raisers (Payment Protection Insurance and so on) that British banks have so far paid out more than £30bn of compensation for selling to customers were legal. Does that mean they should still have been sold, so that executives could take bonuses and depart, and now shareholders are fleeced to pay the bill? Does legality always make such behaviour acceptable? Of course not. There must surely be room for adults running companies to add a caveat at times – is it right? – to the legal test.

4) It encouraged merger mania and an obsession with scale in British banking, in which banks copied each other and City firms in bolting themselves together and becoming ever

bigger (and closer to government too) until they became wards of state in a manner that continues to distort the economy, warp incentives and keep the focus on pumping out consumer credit rather than finding and financing business innovation.

There is no point re-regulating the 1980s thirty years on, however. What makes more sense is to look at what is about to happen – is already happening – in finance and to ask how the lessons of London's extraordinary past can be applied to maximise future gain and minimise the pain. Even before the UK voted in the summer of 2016 to leave the European Union, the City was going to face serious challenges coping with the latest high-speed revolution tearing through global finance. That revolution is driven again by technology, innovation and creative destruction, and it seems likely to have consequences as far-reaching as the changes that took place between 1963 and 1986. Now, on top of that, the City has to cope with the destruction of the very settlement (out of the euro, but open and operating as the EU's unchallenged financial centre) that has brought such prosperity to the Square Mile in the first decades of the twenty-first century. Can the City do what it has done so often in the past and reinvent itself again for a new era?

AFTERWORD: THE FATE OF THE CITY AND THE FUTURE OF MONEY

Twenty-four hours after David Cameron announced that he intended to step down as the UK's Prime Minister, someone else resigned. Of the many momentous developments that took place in the hours, days and weeks after Britain voted in June 2016 to leave the European Union, the departure of Lord Hill (Jonathan Hill, Baron Hill of Oareford) as Britain's European Commissioner in Brussels was deemed particularly unexciting. Other than in the financial press it was reported as one resignation among many, seemingly a minor diplomatic curiosity destined to become a historical footnote when the whole, dramatic story of Brexit is written.

In part that is because Hill, a Conservative Peer, is neither bombastic nor well known. That obscurity is entirely deliberate on his part as he hates publicity, which is a highly unusual characteristic in a politician. When I once travelled to interview him in his Berlaymont office shortly after his appointment in 2014, he and his advisors were most pleased that he managed in the resulting conversation about financial services regulation to say nothing newsworthy, other than taking a mild-mannered pop at the UKIP members of the European Parliament he had seen tearing up the bars of Brussels.

Unfairly, Hill had even been dubbed 'Lord Who?' by his critics at home and abroad when he was appointed by Cameron to Britain's post in the EU Commission. The mockery was unjustified because although Hill had kept a low profile, he was an experienced operator who had been a key figure behind the scenes in John Major's Number 10 in the 1990s, and a veteran of the Conservative Party's collective nervous breakdown over the Maastricht Treaty in that period. Much later, as a successful schools minister and then Leader of the House of Lords under Cameron, he had a reputation in government for quietly getting business done, which is why he was sent to Brussels in the first place. When he landed that post of EU Commissioner for Financial Services, he had of course to represent the interests of the Commission, the powerful civil service of the EU, and the interests of all the other member states. Nonetheless, the financial Establishment back in London, in the Bank of England and the Treasury, and in banks and large institutions, knew it had an ally who wanted to protect the City's peculiar and unique deal in the EU, in which it is outside the euro while transacting the bulk of euro business for the rest of the continent.

When Hill resigned immediately it was the diplomatic equivalent of a bucket of cold water in the face for the British financial Establishment. Rather than attempting to remain in post and speak up while the UK negotiated its difficult exit from the EU, Hill left without ceremony, observing sadly that the City had lost its voice in Brussels. This was an understatement from an understated individual, but represented a dramatic shift that many in the City found troubling. As he headed for the last Eurostar out of Brussels-Midi station, he was instantly replaced by a Latvian who had previously had responsibility for dealing with the euro. The City had lost out within days of the UK voting. The consequences of the Brexit vote that much of the City had failed to anticipate started to unfold.

Even someone sceptical about the EU (as I am) should acknowledge that Europe, and the euro, played a part in successfully remaking the City to an extent that was not widely understood outside the Square Mile. With Big Bang providing a further springboard, on top of the benefits of history, language, time zone and attractiveness to American and Japanese financiers, the launch of the single currency propelled the City to new heights. Even the crisis of 2008, which took down banks and caused widespread economic distress in countries such as the UK, and the Eurozone crisis that followed three years later, only dented what had been built in London. The mechanisms for handling the epic amounts of debt that needed issuing and trading in euros, and for arranging the currency hedges and other manoeuvres that needed to take place, survived, even if the post-crisis tightening of regulation reduced trading profits and slashed bonuses. If you were an international bank or institution that wanted to be a proper player, you still needed to be located in London, sitting at the crossroads between the dollar and the euro.

Do these firms need to be in London for much longer? During Britain's bitterly fought EU referendum campaign, the City and its supporters certainly issued warnings about the potential impact of a change in the UK's status. The *Financial Times* estimated in June 2016 that fifteen global banks between them employed just shy of 70,000 staff in the investment bank divisions in their London offices, including 8,000 each at Barclays and JP Morgan, 5,500 at Goldman Sachs and 7,000 at Deutsche Bank.[1]. That is a lot of jobs and a lot of people paying tax. In total, the City of London estimates that financial services contribute £66.5 billion in taxes to the Treasury annually. That amounts to 11 per cent of the national total. The 2.1m working across the UK in banking, and other services such as accountancy, constitute 7.2 per cent of workers. The British may dislike banks, but the City is the powerhouse of a globally significant industry that the UK can ill afford to see damaged.

International rivals have long eyed London's dominance, the jobs it has created, and the tax revenue that flows from employees and corporate taxes. There has emerged again the prospect of the rise of alternative venues such as Frankfurt (home of the European Central Bank and a city sometimes sneered at in London), and politicians in Paris, Dublin and pro-EU Edinburgh in the summer of

2016 took the opportunity to woo banks and others that want to trade inside the EU. In a period of uncertainty, while the UK's trading arrangements with the EU were being sorted out, Parisian civic leaders attempted to rebrand their city as the new London. Even if the evidence is that American bankers would rather live and educate their children in London rather than move to Frankfurt and learn German, and even if France's labour laws make hiring problematic, the risks of a longer-term drift away of activity and personnel to Germany and France are impossible to ignore. Some of those large employers – including J.P. Morgan – committed to keeping a large presence in London, but they have legal entities in place in other countries that allow them to assess the options and then move positions at will.

Fundamental to the City's dominance has been the UK's so-called passport, which has allowed global financial institutions to base themselves in London, the great hub, and from there to do business in countries across the European Union. The efforts of the European Central Bank to insist that institutions should be sited within the Eurozone, rather than simply the wider EU, to settle and clear trillions' worth of transactions in euros, were blocked by a ruling of the Luxembourg-based General Court. It is possible – and a few analysts warned of this before the referendum – that even if the UK had opted to stay in the EU, the ECB and politicians in the Eurozone would have tried again and removed London's privileges anyway; we will never know. The UK chose to leave the EU, and for finance there will be consequences.

Complicating the British dilemma is the deep distrust that has long been felt elsewhere in the continent for the City and its way of doing business. Efforts have been made to regulate finance more aggressively since the last crisis. Hill and other British-born officials spent considerable time attempting to persuade officials and politicians from other parts of Europe that the super-charged Anglo-Saxon model of financial capitalism, as embodied by the modern City, is not the anti-Christ, or at least not quite as bad as they think it is. According to leading bankers, and the Bank of England, this produced a valuable dividend, in terms of measures that Hill and his team managed to mitigate or shelve by the use of quiet diplomacy.

That matters because a lot of modern finance – particularly since the crisis of 2008 – is about the game of managing the profusion of regulations, rules and licences – a boon to lawyers and expanded compliance departments. There is national regulation, and a country such as the US takes the primacy of its law in relation to anything that touches on the US, even if transacted abroad, extremely seriously. Any British or French traders facing investigations on market manipulation find that out pretty quickly.

Other markets such as Britain have their own national codes and rulebooks, and the UK's has been radically overhauled in recent years with two new regulatory bodies in place. There is an effort at coordinating international standards – via the Basel rules, produced by the Bank of International Settlements – and the post-crisis regulation was designed to shock-proof banks against bank runs in a future crisis. Basel III is not implemented across the board, though. As well as that, the European Union and the European Banking Authority has also pushed its own standardisation. The danger is that the UK will now be excluded from discussions and European rule-making that ends up having an impact on British banks attempting to do business abroad. There may even be a degree of retribution from those who have long wanted to nail the Anglo-Saxon financial model and were previously constrained.

Before the referendum, Hill had also been working on the EU's big idea, which sounds dull but which has the potential to power growth and create jobs in the decades ahead. The aim is to create what is termed a capital markets union (CMU). In essence, it will be an EU-wide scheme that will make it easier for companies to access capital. A company now too reliant on bank loans to fund its expansion, to build a new plant or purchase a technology platform, would be able with greater ease to issue shares right across Europe and attract investors. Moving money around Europe at high speed, often passing through London, is easy thanks to the changes of the last three decades, but tapping patient long-term funds for investment across borders could be made much easier. In addition, the over-reliance on debt, as opposed to attracting investors in return for equity, has arguably skewed the European economy, encouraging the creation of a model in which companies in countries such as Britain are criticised for relying too much on borrowing big. The CMU is meant to give companies and entrepreneurs access to cheaper finance from more reliable sources. The project will still go ahead post-Brexit, although the danger for London must be that it is no longer in a position to benefit as much as it might have done. In the worst-case scenario it is left locked out entirely in the final years of this decade.

This is all looking pretty grim for the City, then. As an exit from the EU approaches, the place is entering one of its periodic existential crises when for a few years its leaders wonder what is to become of them and their staff. As a shock to the system Brexit might not supersede David Kynaston's assessment that the First World War was the worst thing that ever happened to the City, because the outbreak of war in 1914 destroyed open capital markets and flows of investment and trade. But for pessimists it is possible to see what is coming with Britain's departure from the EU in the next few years in a similar context. Although it is a development not as bad as a war, it may produce a partial pulling down of the shutters, with a consequent impact on growth. London as a financial centre has thrived when it is free trading and open to outside influence, and now its status and the precise nature of its access to important markets is going to be at least in doubt for what is left of the decade.

There is another more positive way of looking at what comes next, however. Not just because for all the gloom-laden prognosis London is Europe's financial capital too. Europe relies on it and to damage it too much in the years ahead would be an act of self-harm by other European economies. Sensible voices may eventually prevail and a deal may be done to continue cooperation. If we look beyond Brexit too, the waves of digital disruption and innovation are already lapping around the ankles of the world's leading financiers, and the UK is in a good position potentially to benefit. Indeed, there are few areas of economic activity more ripe for being disrupted than banking and finance in the West, with its long-established institutions, powerful central banks, vast internal bureaucracies and closed networks of licensed operators gaming regulation and nursing political links. And it may already be happening.

In the City, and in New York, when it comes to assessing the impact of innovation, a great deal of attention a few years ago focused on the speed of specialist trades in High Frequency Trading (HFT), the way in which big banks and insurgent operators utilise ever-faster internet access, or microwave links, to gain minuscule advantages over each other that when scaled in a blizzard of trades adds up to profit. The automated nature of much of that trading is the logical evolution of the programmatic trading that helped cause difficulties in New York on Black Monday in 1987. Since then the technology on the trading side has changed the dynamics of Wall Street and the City. Where the high-speed infrastructure is most useful is in allowing investment banks to use the platforms of the London Stock Exchange and others to execute complex financial manoeuvres quickly and safely. That means a big investment bank in New York that wants to offset a large exposure – say $10bn of a particular financial instrument – by dispersing it to other banks, or swapping it for exposures which other banks have, can do it with the Exchange acting as the clearance and settlement house that both parties, and the regulator, can trust. Less than half of what the London Stock Exchange does now is about buying and selling individual shares. It is far removed from the days of the old Stock Exchange with its trading floor and noisy capitalist carnival. This is about providing a computerised platform for others to use.

In the US, in New Jersey where space is much cheaper than Manhattan, sit the data warehouses where investment banks store their orders and matches for such trades. The fibre-optic link with Chicago, and the derivatives and futures market of the Mercantile Exchange, is one of the key trading routes in the global economy. In the UK, the London Stock Exchange has its own facility and at Docklands, where goods used to be unloaded having taken weeks to cross the oceans, is the facility that handles foreign exchange trading. In Essex, in Basildon, the US Intercontinental Exchange (ICE) has its data operation, which handles the order matching for many of the trades. Slough, outside London, contains more such operations.

That aspect of high finance – the secretive high-frequency trading for trading's sake – obviously prompts ethical and practical questions. Is it any more than superfast, automated gambling, like a computerised equivalent of the transactions that took place in 'Change Alley in the City of the 1720s? No, not really, but the aim is to identify value and make profit that can then be recycled, reinvested and consumed.

Equally as interesting for the future of the City is the wider revolution that threatens to end the dominance of some existing retail institutions, and to change the way in which those of us outside finance experience and think about finance as consumers. Jonathan Hill, when he was in post, was astonished on a platform at Davos – the gathering of the global elite – to find himself taking part in a discussion sponsored by a major institution on whether or not the digital economy represents a threat or provides an opportunity for banks. It is here, now, he thought. Can't these people see what is happening to them? Traditional banking, or the part of it that does not adapt quickly, could be about to be eaten alive by fast-moving start-ups.

Think about how much has changed in the music industry, or how we watch television or order a taxi or a cab in London, New York or many other major cities. Our expectations of what we can do with an app have developed so quickly, since the arrival of smart

phones. The UK has a great advantage in turning these digital appetites into growth because it has embraced internet commerce more
enthusiastically than any other country. By 2016 the internet economy had almost doubled in the UK since 2010. It is expected to
provide 12.4 per cent of the UK's GDP (total economic output). In
South Korea it is 8 per cent; in China 6.9 per cent; in the US 5.4 per
cent; and in Germany 4 per cent. The British are making the transition to the internet economy fast.

Despite this, in Britain and across Europe many banks and other
financial services providers still function in terms of customer
service and technology not much better than they did a decade
ago. Having been built in the era when consolidation and scale
were fashionable, they have vast overlapping computer networks
that are sometimes ageing and difficult to manage. They have to
spend a lot – and use a lot of technical expertise – just to get simple
apps and online operations to work smoothly across the bank's
systems.

The contrast with those other fast-changing sectors is marked.
Forty-three per cent of Britons do some or all of their supermarket
shopping online for home delivery, according to a 2016 report by
Mintel, and a quarter use online exclusively for that purpose. On
prime-time sports television in the UK during advertising breaks, or
via social media, consumers are slickly marketed betting services
that allow live betting on every aspect of the game as it happens.
That approach – giving consumers what they want at the push of
an app notification – is creating highly demanding consumers. If
they use services such as Spotify for music they are used to accessing
a vast library in the Cloud, and services such as Netflix, Amazon
Prime and the BBC's iPlayer have attuned viewers to getting what
they want when they want it. Live television viewing has declined
since the arrival of the internet, and the young – with alternatives
such as gaming and social media available – show no sign of picking
up the TV habit.

Why would such citizens, who are used to instant access and
speed of service, put up for long with money being the one area of

consumer activity that operates according to an old set of rules? What happens to the existing providers in banking and investment if insurgent rivals are better able to create faster and more appealing products? You only need to pose the question to see the scale of the opportunity for new companies. As the authors of the Boston Consulting Group report on digital banking published in 2016 – *Banking on Digital Simplicity* – put it: 'FinTechs are beginning to erode the profitability of traditional banks' business lines – from lending to personal finance, payments, and retail investments – often by offering faster service, less expensive products, and a better customer experience.'

The UK and the City have made a good start in this field. Indeed, on some measures London is recognised as the leading centre in FinTech development. Although California employs more people – just – London and New York benefit from their traditional hub status and opportunity to cluster people who either know or care about making money out of money. The best example can be found at Canary Wharf in the tower built by the Reichmanns, where three floors (the twenty-fourth, thirty-ninth and forty-second) are now given over to the Level39 project. The owners of Canary Wharf set out in early 2013 to make it Europe's 'largest technology accelerator space for finance, cyber-security, retail and smart-city technology companies'. It benefits from proximity to the major banks based in Docklands. Where a new Wall Street on the water was created out of the idea of von Clemm and Travelstead in the 1980s, young coders and entrepreneurs launching start-ups are attempting to reinvent finance and London all over again. Elsewhere, in the clusters of tech developments in London's East End on the edge of the Square Mile, FinTech is also a strong presence developing products for investment and retail banking.

For consumers, new ways to pay (facial recognition instead of even a contactless card) are promised, together with new online banks that will make switching accounts so easy that it takes a matter of seconds to complete. The technologists and tech giants do not always get it right, clearly. Apple made much of the launch of its payment service, in which you wave your iPhone to pay. It has not taken off as expected, and the mainstream banks have instead made a success of contactless payments using the bank-card. Apps can do more than just checking your account. If others can hook up new technology and mobile apps with fresh thinking on how to sell shares to individual investors they may even be able to revivify the notion of a share-owning democracy. Officially only 12 per cent of the market in London is estimated to be owned by small investors, although it may be somewhat higher. Why not use this as an opportunity to encourage further direct participation by small investors?

What worries the Bank of England and its Canadian Governor Mark Carney, who has spent a considerable amount of time examining FinTech and discussing it with his team, is whether or not all this highly encouraging innovation will translate into significant numbers of jobs in the next decade. The City's role since the nineteenth century as a provider of mass employment could diminish, if what FinTech produces are profitable small businesses that invent products which can be sold to existing tech giants, or if they take very little human firepower to operate. With trading increasingly automated, and overseen by a smaller staff of technologically minded experts, and retail perhaps heading that way too, what is the niche for real people? It appears to be in inventing new financial products; regulating the machines; and providing wealth management and investment advice on deals to their fellow human beings with serious money to invest and who want more than to rely purely on an app on their phone.

What no one involved in the existing financial eco-system should be in any doubt about is the speed with which the technologists can have an impact. As the experience suffered by the news business demonstrates, the transformation once it starts can be extremely rapid. Facebook was only launched in 2004, and Google in 1998, yet between them they hoover up a reported 85 per cent of online advertising revenue between them. They dwarf the legacy news companies in terms of market capitalisation, and in under two decades they have disrupted one of the hitherto most powerful of all businesses and helped destroy hundreds of long-established newspaper brands across the US.

It would be ironic if some of those thrusting international financial behemoths that were built in part out of the creative destruction of the 1980s in London, when they subsumed and then buried so many old, smaller established London firms, found now that it is their turn and they are too bureaucratic to adapt. They must spend so much time managing regulation and their own internal structures. This is what capitalism should break up, of course. It is powered by creative destruction, as it was in the City of the nineteenth century when smart immigrants outwitted those who were too slow to adapt to the spread of technology and innovative ways of thinking about finance. Or as it was by Warburg in the Aluminium War of the late 1950s, when he outplayed the City Establishment to win, or when the American banks that were successful in London from the 1970s onwards flattened their rivals.

The biggest banks and securities houses should not be written off, however, even if they face disruption and the weaker among them die. After all, when it comes to the most audacious – and fashionable – FinTech innovation of all, the banks have invested heavily. The best-known proponent of blockchain is Blythe Masters, an English former J.P. Morgan financier now based in New York. When the underground digital currency Bitcoin was launched it was built using blockchain technology. All that underpins the currency is code, a mathematical calculation, that allows the virtual currency to be produced and traded in a way both sides can see and have total trust in. No government or central bank controls it and the transaction costs, unlike in traditional banking, are zero. The insight of the firm that Masters runs was that this could be taken mainstream, so that major banks could use the underlying blockchain methodology to move dollars, pounds and euros and make trades.

The original advocates of the cryptocurrency Bitcoin see this as a revolutionary moment in which they ignore conventional currencies, trade in Bitcoin and break the banking system apart. In contrast, the biggest global banks and asset managers see it as a way to reduce their costs and empty their back offices of staff to survive. They have something which the insurgents do not have, too. For all of their crimes and misdemeanours, the existing banks are a known quantity to governments and regulators. Governments need a secure and reliable network to buy and distribute their debt, otherwise they cannot spend (which would be problematic what with them lately spending a lot more than they take in in tax revenues). The global economy is really a giant debt machine, and the global banks are conduits for that debt, funnelling it to investors and trading it and repackaging it themselves. The world's largest central banks and governments are not, any time soon, going to allow their conduit to be smashed to bits and replaced by an anarcho-group of libertarian freelance currency visionaries who from small beginnings want to challenge the supremacy of the dollar and destroy the ability of government to manipulate and devalue currencies for their own short-term electoral ends. Expect governments to leap on the first proper scandal that comes from the world of cryptocurrencies, when something goes wrong and large numbers of people notice, or terrorists are involved, and then to assure everyone that blockchain and the like is now well within the sphere of robust government regulation.

Or a central bank will use the blockchain technology and invent its own digital currency as a rival to Bitcoin. And that is just what it seems the Bank of England is doing in partnering with a team of academics from University College London who have come up with RSCoin. It is claimed to be many times faster and more reliable than Bitcoin, but the most important respect in which it differs is that it can be controlled by the central bank and the state. This appals Bitcoin advocates, who say that the point of their revolution is it constitutes a liberation, denying government control of the financial system. The Bank of England's interest is in being able to manage the money supply and help the government ensure financial stability. If the UCL scheme works, and the Bank of England reinvents the notion of the central bank as arbiter of the digital economy, it will be an echo of its innovative origins.

Assisting the government – back then to borrow – was the original purpose of the Bank of England when it was established in 1694. Eventually it became the model central bank which others copied. Now, the building which houses the Bank – which has its first foreign Governor – sits opposite Gresham's Exchange, where few City traders are to be found any longer, unless they have popped in for an espresso at the bar in the centre of the floor or a glass of something expensive to celebrate a bonus. Others may have nipped in to buy a watch or jewellery from one of the boutiques clustered around the edge of the building, because the Royal Exchange – in its third architectural incarnation since Elizabeth I opened the original building – is now a smart shopping centre. LIFFE left ages ago, and the Stock Exchange which used to be very nearby is now more distant, over in Paternoster Square next to St Paul's. These changes – evolution at the Bank, leisure at the Royal Exchange and the transformation of the Stock Exchange – are quintessentially City. For centuries its leaders and workers have been good at building something new while maintaining old facades. Adaptability and ruthless reinvention are what it is about.

It is certainly true that the range of pressures and competing demands now is daunting. Technology is reshaping the future of money. There is going to be a battle over the nature and control of digital currencies. The financial regulatory empires and blocs – of which the EU is one – may soon look very out of date. Consumer behaviour will reshape and disrupt retail banking. But of all the global financial centres facing such challenges and opportunities, nowhere else starts with more natural advantages in terms of experience, language, time zone and history than London.

The evidence of its history suggests there is little point in trying to come up with a route map into the digital future or prepare any grand scheme. Even though decisions good and bad made by countless individuals have shaped the Square Mile, the place is stubbornly resistant to too much planning. Back in the 1980s the best informed and intentioned of those who pushed through Big Bang did not get it all right, or spot what came next. In 1986, at the time of Big Bang, no one would have predicted that the euro would get going so quickly after the fall of the Berlin Wall in 1989, and that the euro, even as it struggled, would help London play such a role in global finance. There is no reason to think that the next thirty years of life after Brexit and digital disruption will be any less eventful.

All that one can say is: the City will survive, and prosper. It usually does.

SOURCES AND ACKNOWLEDGEMENTS

Crash, Bang, Wallop is not an exhaustive, complete history of the City of London and it is not meant to be. David Kynaston's peerless four volume history, covering 1815–2000, is there for those who want that and I encourage readers to buy it. In the case of this account there will no doubt be those who think that their firm or bank, or their personal story, merited inclusion or more attention. I can only apologise for any oversights or omissions.

But rather than covering everything I have attempted instead to tell the extraordinary, exciting story of the City in the 1980s, and to set it in the broader historical context in a manner that makes it, I hope, enjoyable and useful for the general reader and the City specialist. If I have succeeded in that effort even in a small way it is down to those who gave their assistance so generously.

First, I am grateful to the British Library and the staff of the oral history department for permission to access and quote from its NLSC City Lives series. The founders of that project had the foresight to interview several hundred people about their careers in the City of London. Some of the subjects are now no longer with us, and having their recollections, hearing their voices, was an invaluable resource. City Lives is more than a financial treasure trove. The contributions make for addictive reading and listening. There is fun and wisdom involved. I spent many happy hours listening to and reading the City Lives contributions, and it made me more convinced than ever that similar efforts should be made now to record the testimony of those working in contemporary finance, politics and regulation so that lessons might be learned by future generations when the next crash or financial revolution comes as it surely will.

In some cases, the City Lives transcripts and recordings were the starting point for me interviewing participants as the 30th anniversary of Big Bang approached. Many other City and political figures gave generously of their time and agreed to be interviewed. Even now there were a few participants who were more comfortable speaking off the record, perhaps fearing that even thirty years later they might find themselves shunned for saying that perhaps Big Bang let some crooks in. In the text are a smattering of off the record quotes. But others felt the urgent need to testify publicly about what it – the 1980s financial revolution – meant. Most of the quotes are drawn from those interviews by me and archive material. The British press also did a particularly good job of recording what was going on in the City in the 1980s, and where I have drawn from contemporary accounts they are credited in the text or the endnotes.

I drew too on a wealth of insights in academic papers and books, which are credited in the endnotes and bibliography.

Friends and family who had to put up with me writing my last book managed somehow to pretend that writing another one was a good idea. I am eternally grateful for the love and good humour of Jack and Margaret Martin. Pretty ace too are Alistair Martin, Carla Matassa, Ilaria and Natalia; Jim and Pamela McJannet; Guy and Sylvia Chatfield, and Sofia and Oliver Chatfield; and Douglas McJannet and Neil Oughton.

I am grateful too for the support and encouragement of Jonny Patrick, Michael Donn, Alan Cochrane, Jenny Hjul, Bruce Anderson, Edward Lucas QC, Patience Wheatcroft, Andrew Neil, Rhoda Macdonald, Alison Gray, Gerald Warner, Simon Nixon, Con Coughlin, Ben Wallace, Andy Coulson, Will Lyons, Andrew Wilson, Andrew Roberts, Adam Bruce, Richard Muschamp, Tim Montgomerie, Angus Macpherson and John Boothman. My brilliant colleagues Susan Walton, Zac Tate, Rachel Cunliffe, Olivia Archdeacon, Nicole Gray-Conchar were patient and supportive

beyond belief when I was spending time on Crash Bang Wallop.
Thank you also to J.K. Rowling, who via social media decoded some
of Margaret Thatcher's handwriting on a crucial memo from the
National Archives. Xavier Rolet, chief executive of the London
Stock Exchange, was also very generous with his time and his
insights on the future of finance.

My agent Peter Robinson is simply the business and my editor
Drummond Moir and his team at Sceptre have been terrific to work
with throughout.

Most of all, I want to thank my wife Fi and son William for their
endless patience. They both said never again after my last book, and
then they relented, despite knowing what it would entail. I am glad
they did, because it allowed me to immerse myself completely in a
fascinating period. Until writing this book I thought of 1986 and the
events of the years around it, my formative years, as being recent,
barely history. Now, as it must, it is slipping into the historical middle
distance and prejudices have hardened to the point that it seems the
1980s financial revolution can mean whatever you want it to mean,
whether that be market-driven liberation or the dawn of a new selfishness. I hope *Crash, Bang, Wallop* demonstrates that what really
happened and the complexity of what it meant is much more interesting than the myth.

BIBLIOGRAPHY

Books

Ackroyd, Peter, *London: A Biography*, Chatto & Windus, 2000.

Augar, Phillip, *The Death of Gentlemanly Capitalism: The Rise and Fall of London's Investment Banks*, Penguin, 2008.

Augar, Phillip, *Reckless: The Rise and Fall of the City*, Vintage, 2010.

Bagehot, Walter, *Lombard Street: A Description of the Money Market*, Henry S. King & Co, 1873.

Balen, Malcolm, *A Very English Deceit: The Secret History of the South Sea Bubble and the First Great Financial Scandal*, Fourth Estate, 2009.

Banner, Stuart, *Anglo-American Securities Regulation: Cultural and Political Roots, 1690–1860*, Cambridge University Press, 2002.

Barnes, Paul, *Stock Market Efficiency, Insider Dealing and Market Abuse*, Gower, 2009.

Blakey, George G., *A History of the London Stock Market: 1945–2007*, Harriman House, 2009.

Burgon, John William, *The Life and Times of Sir Thomas Gresham, Founder of The Royal Exchange: Including Notices of Many of His Contemporaries With Illustrations, Volume 2*, E. Wilson, 1839.

Burk, Kathleen and Alec Cairncross, *Goodbye, Britain: The 1976 IMF Crisis*, Yale University Press, 1992.

Burrough, Brian and Heylar, John, *Barbarians at the Gate: The Fall of RJR Nabisco*, HarperCollins, 1990.

Calomiris, Charles W., *Fragile by Design: The Political Origins of Banking Crises and Scarce Credit* (The Princeton Economic History of the Western World), Princeton University Press, 2015.

Carswell, John, *The South Sea Bubble*, Cresset Press, 1961.

Cassis, Youseff, and Cottrell, Phillip L., *Private Banking in Europe: Rise, Retreat and Resurgence,* Oxford University Press, 2015.

Coggan, Phillip, *The Money Machine: How the City Works,* Penguin, 2009.

Courtney, Cathy and Thompson, Paul, *City Lives: Changing Voices of British Finance,* Methuen Publishing Ltd, 1996.

Davenport-Hines, R. P. T., *Speculators and Patriots: Essays in Business Biography,* Frank Cass and Company Ltd, 1986.

Donoughue, Bernard, *Downing Street Diary: Volume Two, With James Callaghan in No. 10,* Pimlico, 2009.

Ferguson, Niall, *The House of Rothschild: Money's Prophets 1798–1848,* Penguin, 1999.

Ferguson, Niall, *The House of Rothschild: The World's Banker 1849–1999 Vol 2,* Viking, 1999.

Ferguson, Niall, *High Financier: The Lives and Time of Siegmund Warburg,* Penguin, 2010.

Floud, Roderick (ed), *The Cambridge Economic History of Modern Britain, Vol III, Structural Change and Growth 1939–2000,* Cambridge University Press, 2004.

Galbraith, John Kenneth, *The Great Crash 1929,* Penguin, 2009.

Gaskin, Margaret, *Blitz: The Story of December 29, 1940,* Houghton Mifflin Harcourt, 2006.

George, David Lloyd, *War Memoirs of David Lloyd George, Volume 1,* Odhams Press Ltd, 1938.

Gleeson, Janet, *Millionaire: The Philanderer, Gambler, and Duellist Who Invented Modern Finance,* Simon & Schuster, 2001.

Gresham, Perry, *The Sign of the Golden Grasshopper: A Life of Sir Thomas Gresham,* Jameson Books, 1995.

Groysberg, Boris and Paul M. Healy, *Wall Street Research: Past, Present and Future,* Stanford University Press, 2013.

Handley, S., Hayton, D.W. and Cruikshanks, E. *The History of Parliament: The House of Commons 1690–1715,* Cambridge University Press, 2002.

Harris, Robin, *The Conservatives: A History,* Bantam Press, 2011.

Hennessy, Elizabeth, *Coffee House to Cyber Market: 200 Years of the London Stock Exchange,* Ebury Press, 2001.

Hilton, Anthony, *City Within a State: Portrait of Britain's Financial World, ,* Cambridge University Press. I.B. Tauris, 1987.

Ingrassia, Catherine, *Authorship, Commerce, and Gender in Early Eighteenth-Century England*, Cambridge University Press, 1998.

Kay, John, *Other People's Money: Masters of the Universe or Servants of the People?*, Profile Books, 2015.

King, Mervyn, *The End of Alchemy: Money, Banking and the Future of the Global Economy*, Little, Brown, 2016.

Kochan, Nick and Pym, Hugh, *The Guinness Affair: Anatomy of a Scandal*, Christopher Helm Publishers Ltd, 1987.

Kynaston, David, *The City of London: A World of Its Own, 1815–90*, Pimlico, 1995.

Kynaston, David, *The City of London: Golden Years, 1890–1914*, Pimlico, 1996.

Kynaston, David, *The City of London: Illusions of Gold, 1914–4*, Chatto & Windus, 1999.

Kynaston, David, *The City of London: Club No More, 1945–2000*, Chatto & Windus, 2001.

Lawson, Nigel, *The View From No. 11: Memoirs of a Tory Radical*, Bantam Press, 1992.

Lewis, Michael, *Liar's Poker*, W. W. Norton & Company, 2010.

MacFarlane, Charles, *The Life of Sir Thomas Gresham, Founder of the Royal Exchange*, Charles Knight, 1845.

Mackay, Charles, *Extraordinary Popular Delusions and the Madness of Crowds*, Richard Bentley, 1841.

Mason, A.E.W., *The Royal Exchange; A Note on the Occasion of the Bicentenary of the Royal Exchange Assurance 1920*, Royal Exchange Assurance, 1920.

Matthews, John O., *Struggle and Survival on Wall Street: The Economics of Competition Among Securities Firms*, Oxford University Press, 1994.

Michie, Ranald, *The London Stock Exchange: A History*, Oxford University Press, 1999.

Moore, Charles, *Margaret Thatcher: The Authorised Biography, Volume One: Not For Turning*, Allen Lane, 2013.

Moore, Charles, *Margaret Thatcher: The Authorised Biography, Volume Two: Everything She Wants*, Allen Lane, 2015.

Parker, David, *The Official History of Privatisation Vol 1: The Formative Years 1970–1987*, Routledge, 2009.

Parker, David, *The Official History of Privatisation, Vol 2: Popular Capitalism, 1987–1997*, Routledge, 2012.

Plender, John, *Capitalism: Money, Morals and Markets*, Biteback Publishing, 2015.

Reid, Margaret, *All Change in the City: The Revolution in Britain's Financial Sector*, Palgrave Macmillan, 1998.

Roberts, Richard, *Take Your Partners: Orion, the Consortium Banks and the Transformation of the Euromarkets*, Palgrave Macmillan, 2001.

Rogers, James Edwin Thorold, *The Industrial and Commercial History of England (Lectures Delivered to the University of Oxford)*, G.P. Putnam's, 1892.

Sherman, Sandra, *Finance and Fictionality in the Early Eighteenth Century: Accounting for Defoe*, Cambridge University Press, 1996.

Stamp, Gavin, *Anti-Ugly: Excursions in English Architecture and Design*, Aurum Press, 2013.

Stewart, Graham, *Bang! A History of Britain in the 1980s*, Atlantic Books, 2013.

Stewart, James, *Den of Thieves*, Simon & Schuster, 1991.

Stewart, Walter, *Too Big to Fail: Olympia & York: the Story Behind the Headlines*, Beard Books, 2000.

Stow, John, *A Survey of London, Written in the Year 1598*, Whittaker and co, 1842.

Thompson, Valerie, *Mastering the Euromarkets: A Guide to International Bonds, the Instruments, the Players, and the Game*, Irwin Professional Publishing, 1996.

Thorpe, D.R., *Supermac: The Life of Harold Macmillan*, Chatto & Windus, 2010.

Vogel, Steven K., *Freer Markets, More Rules: Regulatory Reform in Advanced Industrial Countries*, Cornell University Press, 1998.

Wechsberg, Joseph, *Trifles make Perfection: The Selected Essays of Joseph Wechsberg*, David R. Godine Publishers, 1999.

Williams, Richard J., *The Anxious City: British Urbanism in the Late 20th Century*, Routledge, 2004.

Articles

Draper, Nick, 'The City of London and Slavery, Evidence from the First Dock Companies 1795–1800', *Economic History Review*, 2 May 2008.

Inikori, J E, 'Measuring the Atlantic Slave Trade: A Rejoinder', *The Journal of African History*, Cambridge University Press, October 1978.

Pardo-Guerra, Juan Pablo, 'Creating Flows of Interpersonal Bits: The Automation of the London Stock Exchange 1955–90', *Economy and Society*, Volume 39, 2010.

Geoffrey Wood, Forest Capie, Frank Sensenbrenner, 'Foreign Investment in the UK: Flows, Attitudes and Implications', *Journal of Interdisciplinary Economics*, 2005.

Andrew Leyshon and Nigel Thrift, 'The capitalization of almost everything: The future of finance and capitalism', *Theory, Culture, Society*, December 2007.

NOTES

Chapter 1

1. Gresham assisted Elizabeth by agreeing to be jailer for Lady Mary Grey, keeping one of the three Grey sisters who had a claim to the royal succession under house arrest at two of his homes in the City and then at Osterley, west of London.

2. Indeed, the construction of the Exchange from 1566 represented a vindication for the Gresham family. His father Sir Richard Gresham (knighted by Henry VIII) had been Mayor of London and had attempted to get a similar scheme implemented decades before, although at the time the conservative City Corporation had rejected the idea. Merchants were told when Sir Richard's earlier plan was rejected that they must continue to do business in the open air on Lombard Street. Now, thanks to Thomas, London got its Exchange.

3. A Note on the Occasion of the Bicentenary of the Royal Exchange Assurance. A.E.W. Mason, Royal Exchange, 1920.

4. Gresham's tomb is in St Helen's, Bishopsgate, in the shadow of the Gherkin building, surrounded by the offices of modern City firms.

5. It was not until 1833 that the London Fire Engine Establishment was founded by ten fire insurance companies. The Metropolitan Fire Brigade was formed in 1866 when the insurance companies told the government that they could no longer bear the responsibility for fighting fires.

6. Barbon's will was received by his executors on 6 February 1699, although he may have died in late 1698. Will of Nicholas Barbon of Osterley, Middlesex. (National Archives).

7. The Bank of England's creation is sometimes ascribed to the poet, statesman and Chancellor of Exchequer Charles Montagu, later Earl of Halifax. Montagu subscribed money to the scheme (he was not alone in that) and

was involved in the passage of the legislation through the Commons. But see History of Parliament for an explanation of why claims made on Montagu's behalf appear exaggerated. The plan was Paterson's. He resigned from the Bank's board of directors following a disagreement and his reputation never recovered from the failure of his subsequent scheme, in which Scotland attempted and failed to colonise part of what is now Panama.

8. Joseph Addison in *The Spectator*, 19 May 1711.

Chapter 2

1. *The South Sea Ballad/Set by a Lady*, from the Baker Business Historical Collections – Kress Collection, Harvard Business School.
2. *Women's Agency in Early Modern Britain and the American Colonies*, Rosemary O'Day, p221.
3. *A Very English Deceit*, Malcolm Balen, page 321.
4. *Anglo-American Securities Regulation: Cultural and Political Roots, 1690–1860*. Stuart Banner, p66.
5. Estimate by J.T. Inikori, from 1976 in 'Measuring the Atlantic Slave Trade: A Rejoinder', published in the *Journal of African History*, Vol. 17, No. 4 (1976), pp. 607–627. A long-running academic argument has raged in recent decades over the numbers, with some contesting Inikori's estimates.
6. Not to be confused with his son and scandal-prone heir, William Thomas Beckford, the so-called 'Fool of Fonthill', the art collector and novelist who had a scandalous affair with William 'Kitty' Courtenay, from Courtenay's boyhood. With his fortune Beckford built Fonthill Abbey, which was later destroyed. There was little of the family fortune left by the time he died in 1844.
7. Anne Murphy, of the University of Hertfordshire, undertook a study for the Bank of England of working practices in the 18th and 19th century.
8. William Tite retired from architectural practice twenty years before his death in 1873. He became a Liberal MP and in the 1850s was a leading voice in the campaign to persuade the then Prime Minister, Lord Palmerston, that the building that is now the Foreign and Commonwealth Office should not be built in the Gothic style, as the architect George Gilbert Scott suggested. Tite won that battle in the war between neo-classicists and advocates of the Gothic style. Gilbert Scott designed the building in the Italianate style. Tite Street in Chelsea is named after him.

Chapter 3

1. The London Stock Exchange, Ranald Michie, page 101.
2. *City of London, the History*, David Kynaston, page 102.
3. For a good account of the career of Harry Marks and the *Financial News*, see Dilbert Porter's essay in *Speculators and Patriots: Essays in Business Biography*. Edited by R.P.T. Davenport-Hines. See also 'The war is a capitalist war,' *The Labour Party and the World*, Volume 1. Rhiannon Vickers.
4. Elizabeth Hennessy, page 86.
5. *City of London, the History*. Kynaston. page 273.
6. Lloyd George, war memoirs. Volume 1, page 70.
7. 'The Estimation of Pre-war GNP'. Nathan S. Balle and Robert J. Gordon, *Journal of Political Economy*, 1987.
8. 'Prohibition: A cautionary tale', Thomas Fleming. *The Wall Street Journal*, 3 January, 2010.
9. See M.J. Gaskin's outstanding study of the night of 29 December 1940.
10. Gaskin, page 259–60

Chapter 4

1. *Financial Times*, 7 August 1945.
2. See Professor Peter Larkham lecture on rebuilding London after the Second World War, July 2015. See http://bitly/29WSc09.
3. Sir Kenneth Kleinwort interview, NLSC City Lives.
4. Nick Durlacher interview, NLSC City Lives.
5. Warburg interview, from *Trifles Make Perfection*, essays by Joseph Wechsberg.
6. NLSC City Lives interview.
7. The full series of *Men and Money* is available to watch on the BBC's archive website. http://www.bbc.co.uk/archive/menandmoney/
8. *Spectator* notebook, 13 December 1963.
9. Peter Spira speech on the 50th anniversary of the Eurobond.
10. Bank of England Quarterly, November 1991, page 522.
11. Japanese banks in London, Bank of England Quarterly Bulletin November 1987 http://www.bankofengland.co.uk/archive/Documents/historicpubs/qb/1987/qb87q4518524.pdf
12. Haruko Fukuda interview, NLSC City Lives.

13. 'The ladies who toppled the London Stock Exchange', *Daily Telegraph*. Interview by Harry Wallop, 25 March 2013.
14. Valerie Thompson, NLSC City Lives.

Chapter 5

1. *Margaret Thatcher, The Authorised Biography*, by Charles Moore (pages 291–2).
2. Nott to Howe, 30 May 1979, National Archives.
3. John Nott, Hansard, 23 October 1979.
4. 1979 Budget speech, 12 June 1979.
5. David Smith, Something will turn up. http://www.economicsuk.com/blog/002127.html
6. *Foreign Direct Investment in the UK: Flows, Attitudes, and Implications*. Forrest Capie and Geoffrey Wood with Frank Sensenbrenner, Cass Business School, London.
7. David Walker interview, NLSC.
8. Bank of England archives, note from David Walker 4 May 1983.

Chapter 6

1. Sir John Craven interview, NLSC City Lives
2. David Montagu interview, 1993, NLSC City Lives. It is greatly to be regretted that Montagu never got to write his memoirs. His testimony to the City Lives project is endlessly entertaining and insightful. He had been a founder of London Weekend Television and ran Rothmans.
3. NLSC City Lives. The set-piece described by Montagu is worthy of being staged in the theatre as a farce.
4. Sir John Craven, NLSC City Lives.
5. 'The day Big Bang blasted the old boys into oblivion', *The Independent*, 28 October 2006.
6. Dundas Hamilton interview, NLSC City Lives.
7. US Treasury data.
8. Davina Walter interview, NLSC City Lives.
9. 'About that urban renaissance,' *Chicago* magazine, 1 May 1980.
10. Sir John Craven, NLSC City Lives.
11. George Hayter interview, *Financial Times*, 19 October 1984.

Chapter 7

1. *Downing Street Diary*, volume 2, Bernard Donoughue, page 354.
2. Nigel Lawson, *View from Number 11*, page 758.
3. British Airways, along with other established airlines, faced the prospect of court action over attempts to put the budget airline Laker Airways out of business.
4. Addressing the Tory Reform Group at the Carlton Club on 8 November 1984, Macmillan said: 'First of all the Georgian silver goes, and then all that nice furniture that used to be in the saloon. Then the Canalettos go.'
5. *Freer Markets, More Rules: Regulatory Reform in Advanced Industrial Countries*, Steven Vogel, 1996.

Chapter 8

1. See 'Reg Ward: the man who transformed London's docklands', written by Jack Brown for CapX in January 2016. Brown is writing what will no doubt be the definitive work on the remaking of Docklands and the building of Canary Wharf.
2. Michael Heseltine, *Life in the Jungle*, Hodder and Stoughton, 2000.
3. LDDC monograph – Learning to Live and Work Together, 1998.
4. OECD international sectoral database, 2002.
5. Gavin Stamp on Lloyd's of London in *Anti-Ugly: Excursions in English Architecture and Design*.
6. 1985 Jul 31 Margaret Thatcher Speech commencing construction of Broadgate, National Archives.

Chapter 9

1. George Hayter profile, *Financial Times*, 19 October 1986.
2. *Margaret Thatcher, the Authorized Biography volume II: Everything She Wants*, Charles Moore.
3. Robin Leigh Pemberton, Bank of England annual report, February 1986.
4. Rippon was a talented lawyer who did not achieve his political ambitions, although he was given responsibility by Ted Heath in 1972-73 for the negotiations that led to the admission of the UK into the European Community.
5. 'A lament for the bank I loved', by Martin Vander-Weyer, *Independent on Sunday*, 29 November 1998.

6. Thatcher party conference speech 10 October, 1986, Thatcher archive.

7. Minutes of 14th EFFAS Congress, European Federation of Financial Analysts Societies : Florence, 15/17 October, 1986 : 'Towards an integrated European financial market'.

8. Interviewed by Juan Pablo Pardo-Guerra, for 'Creating flows of interpersonal bits: the automation of the London Stock Exchange, 1955–90'.

9. *Financial Times*, 28 October 1986

10. As Joe Moran said in the *Guardian* on the 25th anniversary: 'The inauguration of the M25 was the last major road-opening to generate real public excitement. The queues at both ends of the final section were much longer than usual because drivers were itching to be the first to complete an orbit.'

Chapter 10

1. Letter to editor, *The Times*, 30 October 1986.

2. Thatcher mansion house speech 1986, Thatcher archive.

3. Anyone who doubts how crazy the situation was pre-Wapping need only read *Full Disclosure* by Andrew Neil, then editor of the *Sunday Times*. Or read *Notes From a Small Island*, which contains Bill Bryson's account of the restrictive practices and corruption of the print unions.

4. Paul Channon obituary, *The Times, 30* January 2007.

5. *The Official History of Privatisation*, page 389. David Parker's two volume history.

6. Takeover activity in the 1980s, Bank of England Quarterly 1989.

7. Reviews from *File On Churchill*, by Linda Fitzsimmons.

Chapter 11

1. See *Supermac: The Life of Harold Macmillan*, by D.R. Thorpe.

2. Quoted in the *Financial Times*, 27 October 1986.

3. New Earnings survey, cited in Leyshon and Thrift.

4. Sporting Intelligence.com, English footballer pay 1961–2010 (2011).

5. 'Business as Usual', Mimi Kramer, *The New Yorker.* 14 December 1987.

Chapter 12

1. 'Romeo would have spied the storm'. *New Scientist*, 22 October 1987.
2. *A Brief History of the 1987 Stock Market Crash, with a Discussion of the Federal Reserve Response*, Mark Carlson, Board of Governors of the Federal Reserve, November 2006.
3. *Black Monday: The Stock Market Catastrophe of October 19, 1987* by Tim Metz, Beard Books, 2003.
4. *Wall Street Journal*, by Clare Ansberry, page 42.
5. 'Black Monday remembered, 25 years on', David Thomas, *Financial News*, October 2012.
6. Brady quoted by Daniel Burnstein, *Yen!*, New York: Simon & Schuster, 1988, p. 156.

Chapter 13

1. Michie, The Global Securities Market, OUP, 2008.
2. The Tally, *Financial News*, 26 November, 2014.
3. 'Superbomb mystery. The Herrhausen Assassination.' *Wired*, July 2008.
4. *Leading From The Front*, Gerald Ronson, Mainstream, 2009.
5. Nadir's company donated £440,000 to the Conservative party and in June 1993 it was revealed that when he was initially under investigation he had been gifted a watch by the Tory minister Sir Michael Mates, on which the MP had had engraved the following message: 'Don't let the buggers get you down.'
6. In May 1996 Walker was found guilty and fined by the Lloyd's Disciplinary Committee for conducting insurance business in a disreputable manner. His conduct had been reckless rather than deliberate, it was concluded.

Chapter 14

1. Peter Spira, NLSC City Lives interview.
2. 'Cedric Brown, fat cat in the dog house'. *Independent*, Monday, 13 March 1995.
3. 'How the City was spun'. Chris Blackhurst, *Management Today*, 1 February 2000.

4. 'That Friday feeling', *Guardian*, 27 September 1999.
5. 'Does Auntie mean business?' *Observer*, Paul Farrelly, 12 November 2000.
6. Speech by Economic Secretary to the Treasury, Ed Balls MP, at the City of London Corporation Dinner, 25 October 2006.
7. Many reports were written warning of the dire likely impact of the UK not joining the single currency. One such paper was 'Consequences of saying no: an independent report into the economic consequences of the UK saying no to the euro.' Chaired by David Begg, Imperial College Business School.
8. *Jerusalem Post*, January 2008.

Chapter 15

1. His daughter is Nigella Lawson.
2. For more information on giving in the US http://nccs.urban.org/nccs/statistics/charitable-giving-in-america-some-facts-and-figures.cfm and in the UK https://www.cafonline.org/docs/default-source/about-us-publications/caf-ukgiving2014

Afterword: The Fate of the City and the Future of Money

1. Staff numbers across all fifteen firms' investment banking divisions were as follows: BNP Paribas 2,500; Goldman Sachs 5,500; Bank of America Merrill Lynch 4,500; Nomura 2,600; UniCredit 800; Deutsche Bank 7,000; UBS 4,000; RBS 2000; Société Générale 2,800; Credit Suisse 5000; although not all of them in the investment bank division: Barclays 8,000; HSBC 5,000; Morgan Stanley 5,000; JPMorgan 8000; and Citi 7,000.

INDEX

Page numbers in *italics* refer to figures.